PRAISE FOR *LEADERSHIP-DRIVEN HR*

Leadership-Driven HR is a must-have on the bookshelf of all HR professionals. It is a 'go-to' for tools and frameworks and clearly distills concepts through practical examples. David clearly lays out how HR can unlock strategies to drive value through so many paths including culture and transformation. It is an excellent training guide for new professionals and a reference guide for HR teams.

—*Karen McKay*
Vice President, Human Resources and Learning and Development
Eli Lilly Canada Inc.

With *Leadership-Driven HR*, Dr. Weiss identifies a powerful opportunity for HR professionals to drive value for the business. He demonstrates how, by using a laser-beam approach in establishing priorities, the HR executive can play a critical role in ensuring future success by building next-generation leadership. This is an easy-to-read, practical and important book for anyone who oversees HR strategy or who manages people.

—*L. Robin Cardozo*
Chief Operating Officer
SickKids Foundation

Dr. David Weiss is a thought-leader in leadership and human resources which is clear in his latest book, *Leadership-Driven HR*. This very readable book is a compelling call-to-action for HR professionals and business executives who want to advance their business results. It is a must-read!

—*Sarah Downey*
Executive Vice President, Clinical Programs
Centre for Addiction and Mental Health

Leadership-Driven HR is a departure from the usual business literature. It is not a restating of the ideas from the recent past but rather reveals what mastery in HR leadership means. Through storytelling and the use of practical examples, Dr. Weiss provides a roadmap to enhance, focus, and nurture the indispensable leadership qualities of HR. This is dynamic reading for any HR professional or business leader looking for ways to revolutionize the delivery of value for their business.

—*Emma Pavlov*
Senior Vice President, Human Resources & Organizational Development
University Health Network

Dr. David Weiss' insights, based on strong theory combined with years of practical experience provide a compelling roadmap for the next incarnation of the HR function. I am honored to review this book as it has confirmed a number of directions we have been taking, and it has strengthened my resolve to redouble efforts on those that remain. Congratulations on the final product. It is a very meaningful contribution to the science and art of HR.

—Kevin O'Farrell, CHRP
Vice President, People & Organization
Hewitt Equipment Limited

With *Leadership-Driven HR*, Dr. David Weiss directly challenges all of us who work in human resources to get on a continual improvement path that is directly aligned with—and drives implementation of—organizational business goals. He pushes us not to be everything to everyone, but to focus our efforts like a laser on only those priorities that will enable the organization, and its people, to succeed. David's passion, ideas, and business-focused solutions have been a great guide in my own personal journey of human resource leadership.

—Kerry Pond
Assistant Deputy Minister
Centre for Leadership and Learning
Ontario Public Service

It is a great pleasure for me to recommend Dr. David Weiss' latest book, *Leadership-Driven HR*, as a major step forward and upward for understanding the newly emerging key role of HR in organization success and performance—in other words a breakthrough from conventional books in the field of HRM. Based upon Dr. Weiss' very distinguished international career in consulting and executive development, this breakthrough book provides the business case for HR to be a significant player in strategic organization performance, a practical and no-holds-barred discussion of the strategic management skills that will be required by senior HR professionals, and outstanding, highly sophisticated and effective step-by-step models for implementing cultural transformation and significant changes to achieve strategic goals, probably the most sophisticated and practical texts that one can read on these key topics. This new highly readable book is a breakthrough from regular good quality books on HRM and *Leadership-Driven HR* should be a must-read for all senior HR executives who wish to perform well in their key strategic HR responsibilities.

—Dr. Dan Ondrack
Professor Emeritus
Rotman School of Management of the University of Toronto

Leadership-Driven HR

COMPLETE LIST OF BUSINESS BOOKS
BY DR. DAVID S. WEISS

Weiss, David S. *Leadership-Driven HR: Transforming HR to Deliver Value for the Business.* Toronto: John Wiley & Sons, 2013.

Weiss, David S. and Claude P. Legrand, *Innovative Intelligence: The Art and Practice of Leading Sustainable Innovation in Your Organization.* Toronto: John Wiley & Sons, 2011.
Chinese Edition:
Weiss, David S. and Claude P. Legrand. *Innovative Intelligence: The Art and Practice of Leading Sustainable Innovation in Your Organization.* Beijing: China Citic Press, In Press.

Weiss, David S., Vince Molinaro, and Liane Davey. *Leadership Solutions: The Pathway to Bridge The Leadership Gap.* Toronto: Jossey Bass, 2007.

Weiss, David S. and Vince Molinaro. *The Leadership Gap: Building Leadership Capacity for Competitive Advantage.* Toronto: John Wiley & Sons, 2005.
Korean Edition:
Weiss, David S. and Vince Molinaro. *The Leadership Gap: Building Leadership Capacity for Competitive Advantage.* Seoul: MaeKyong Publishing Inc., 2009.

Weiss, David S. *High Performance HR: Leveraging Human Resources for Competitive Advantage.* Toronto: John Wiley & Sons. 1999, 2000.

Weiss, David S. *Beyond the Walls of Conflict: Mutual Gains Negotiating for Unions and Management.* Chicago: Irwin Professional Publishing, 1996, 2003.
French Edition:
Weiss, David S. *Franchir Le Mur Des Conflits: La négociation basée sur les intérêts des syndicats et des entreprises.* Saint-Nicolas: Les Presses de l'Université Laval, 1999.

Leadership-Driven HR

Transforming HR
to Deliver Value for the Business

David S. Weiss

JOSSEY-BASS
A Wiley Imprint
www.josseybass.com

Library and Archives Canada Cataloguing in Publication Data

Weiss, David S. (David Solomon), 1953-
  Leadership-driven HR : transforming HR to deliver value for business / David S. Weiss.

Includes index.
Issued also in electronic formats.
ISBN 978-1-118-36282-2

  1. Personnel management.   2. Strategic planning.   3. Organizational
effectiveness.   I. Title.

HF5549.W4354 2012   658.3   C2012-906761-X

ISBN 978-1-118-36430-7 (eBk); 978-1-118-36431-4 (eBk);
978-1-118-36432-1 (eBk)

Production Credits
Cover design: Adrian So
Interior text design: Mike Chan, Thomson Digital
Typesetter: Thomson Digital
Printer: Friesens

John Wiley & Sons Canada, Ltd.
6045 Freemont Blvd.
Mississauga, Ontario
L5R 4J3

Printed in Canada

1 2 3 4 5 FP 17 16 15 14 13

Contents

Tables and Figures

For Nora, my true love and best friend.

Acknowledgments

This book, *Leadership-Driven HR*, was developed over many years with many contributors who provided insights and inspiration. To all those contributors, I want to express my appreciation and gratitude.

One of the joys of executive and human resources consulting is the privilege that comes from working with ambitious, dedicated, and intelligent leaders with a genuine interest in taking their organizations to higher levels of performance. They stimulated thought by presenting intriguing challenges, by being willing to try out new ideas, and by validating the approaches presented in this book. I am grateful for their ongoing confidence, support, and friendship.

I also want to express appreciation to specific colleagues who were instrumental in the evolution of my thought process. To name a few: Hugh MacDonald for his review of *High Performance HR*, which identified the parts that are still relevant a decade later, and for his ideas about HR compliance issues explored in Chapter One; Claude Legrand for his collaboration as my co-author on *Innovative Intelligence*, in which we presented ideas about innovative intelligence and a culture of innovation; Vince Molinaro for his collaboration as co-author on *The Leadership Gap*, in which we explored leadership capacity, alignment, and engagement; Vince Molinaro and Liane Davey, my co-authors on *Leadership Solutions*, in which we further articulated our ideas on leadership capacity and measurement; Jagdish Sheth for his insights on the differences between leadership and management; and Janet Burt, Bob Harris, and Leslie Keen for their early contributions to the implementing change framework. I also want to express gratitude to a number of leading authors who have contributed to my thought development over the past 20 years through their writings: David Ulrich, Jay Galbraith, Rosabeth Moss Kanter, Daniel Goleman, Edger Schein, Margaret Wheatley, and John Kotter.

I have also had many opportunities to speak publicly at over 200 conferences globally and have written over 40 trade and journal articles about these topics. All of the conference organizations that gave me the forum to speak about these ideas are very much appreciated. In particular, I extend great appreciation to Dr. Dan Ondrack of the Rotman School of Management at the University of Toronto for providing a forum to present and explore these ideas in executive development sessions in Canada, the Cayman Islands, and in Shanghai, China. Also, thank you to Emma Pavlov for providing me with the forum to present my ideas on implementing change through the Schulich School of Business at York University. As well, I would like to thank the Canadian Society for Training and Development and the Human Resources Professionals Association for an annual conference forum to present my latest thoughts to HR and learning professionals. These academic executive development experiences and association presentations helped sharpen the insights and ideas presented in this book.

I also thank the many professionals who supported me in the production of this work. Special thanks go to the Weiss International Ltd. team, with special recognition to Susan Beckley for her continual support for all of my work, and to Michele Allan for her work on the book's graphics. Also, a very special thank you to Mary Jo Beebe for her ongoing editing support, challenging comments, attention to detail, and exceptional patience, which have helped this project become clearer and more tightly formulated. Also, thank you to Karen Milner and the John Wiley & Sons team for your confidence in this project and for our 14 years of collaborating on the publication and promotion of my books.

My final and deepest thanks go to my wife, Dr. Nora Gold, and to our son, Joseph Weissgold, who fill my life with love and meaning.

To all, my thanks and love.

Dr. David S. Weiss
Toronto, Ontario, Canada, 2012

Preface

Leadership-Driven HR is the culmination of 18 years of writing and 25 years of practice. The journey began with the publication of my first two books: *Beyond the Walls of Conflict* (1996) and *High Performance HR* (2000). These books explored the strategic work of Human Resources (HR) and Labor Relations and how HR can contribute to transforming a business. *High Performance HR* became a bestseller and was widely used by HR professionals to guide their focus and by universities as part of their business and HR curriculum.

Subsequently, I became immersed with the evolving challenge of the leadership gap and researched how to overcome that gap. It was evident that the leadership gap was a global problem and that it had important implications for human resources professionals. My third, fourth, and fifth co-authored books all explored various aspects of the leadership gap. The third book, *The Leadership Gap* (2005), explored the need for leaders to be holistic and identified what organizations need to do to build leadership capacity. The fourth book, *Leadership Solutions* (2007), explored how to measure leadership capacity to pinpoint the areas where organizations should target their development of this capacity. The fifth book, *Innovative Intelligence* (2011), focused on the challenge of the innovation gap, which can be significantly reduced by developing leaders of innovation who draw out the innovative capacity of their employees and teams so that they can gain insight and discover inventive solutions to complex issues.

Leadership-Driven HR completes the circle of my journey. It reflects my return to writing directly to HR professionals about how the HR function still needs to transform with a primary focus on being leadership-driven. This book is built on my previous writings and introduces many new, important, and practical frameworks and tools that HR can use to transform in order to deliver value for the business.

Over the past decade, the human resources function has experienced a tremendous state of flux as exemplified by the plethora of names by which the HR function is now called. Although most human resources departments are still called Human Resources (HR), new names are appearing, including Talent Management, Talent and Organizational Development, People and Organizations, and People and Organizational Capabilities. Also, the senior leaders of HR are using a wider range of titles in addition to VP of HR, including chief human resources officer, chief people officer, chief talent officer, VP talent and organizational effectiveness, and VP talent and communications. Some executives explicitly reject the label "HR," suggesting that people are not resources that can be "mined" but rather that people are individuals who need to be engaged and developed. The wide variety of names for the function and titles for its senior leaders signal that HR is still in a process of discovering what it really stands for.

Rather than entering into the debate and choosing a new name for HR, *Leadership-Driven HR* uses the traditional and still widely used name "HR" but emphasizes its new focus on being leadership-driven. This book explores the way HR drives the business to lead, examines how HR delivers value through its leaders, and describes how HR itself needs to be driven to lead for business success. It also emphasizes that HR needs to have a clear line of sight to the external customer for all of its work, and that it needs to be rigorous in prioritizing its work so that it can ensure it delivers its priorities. Many executives will welcome HR's new focus on being leadership-driven in a way that eventually benefits the external customer. Based on extensive practice and research, *Leadership-Driven HR* clearly defines how HR needs to transform to deliver value for the business and describes the strategies and practical tools necessary to transform HR's priorities and accountabilities.

A DESCRIPTION OF THIS BOOK

This section presents a description of each chapter of *Leadership-Driven HR*. Most readers will want to read the book in its entirety for a full understanding of how HR needs to transform to deliver value for the business. However, some readers may want to dip into the book and explore specific topics that meet a particular need. The following descriptions should guide the reader to determine what will address their needs most effectively.

PART ONE: TRANSFORMING HR

Chapter One: Being Leadership-Driven

The HR role in businesses has changed dramatically and will continue to change over the next decade. Currently, the ratio of HR professionals to employees has shifted from 1:100 to, in some cases, 1:500. The only way for HR to deliver value for the business with these ratios is to become leadership-driven. This chapter focuses on three ways HR must transform to become leadership-driven: (1) HR as a driver for business leadership—which includes how HR takes an "outside-in" approach to the business to deliver strategic value; (2) HR as a driver of leaders—which focuses on ensuring that all leaders become people leaders and that all employees become more self-reliant; and (3) HR being driven to lead—which describes how HR must function as a center of excellence in people capabilities and organizational capabilities as it delivers value for the business.

Chapter Two: Line of Sight to the External Customer

Many HR organizations focus on internal customers as their priority work. However, when HR is leadership-driven, they must have a line of sight to the leaders' customer, which is the external customer. This chapter describes how HR can achieve the necessary insight and knowledge of external customers' needs and perceptions as they work internally with business leaders.

Chapter Three: "Lighten Up" To Deliver Priorities

The first two chapters described the additional strategic work that HR will need to accomplish as it strives to become a leadership-driven HR function with a clear line of sight to the external customer. However, if work is added, HR will have the equal challenge to balance its priorities and "lighten up" work of a lower priority. Many HR organizations have struggled to identify priority work and to reduce their workload. HR needs to use its leadership focus and clear line of sight to the external customer as filters to determine its top-priority work so that time and effort will not be spent on work of little value. In addition, HR has to become highly effective at helping business leaders become the "first line of defense" to respond to employee issues. If HR does not lighten up its work, the HR function will never have the time to deliver the value that the business requires.

PART TWO: THE WORK OF HR

Chapter Four: The HR Triangle Chart

This chapter introduces the HR triangle chart, which provides an overview of the three capabilities of leadership-driven HR. These are:

- People capabilities: The HR outcomes that reflect the flow of people through the employment life cycle—from finding talent to developing talent to retaining talent.
- Organizational capabilities: The HR outcomes that reflect the flow of work—from work entering the business to being processed by the business to delivering value for the external customer.

- HR value proposition: The top-priority people capability or organizational capability that mitigates a critical business risk. When HR delivers its value proposition, the business will have a much greater probability that it will realize its strategic direction.

Chapter Five: People Capabilities

HR needs to guide leaders to be people leaders through the entire employment life cycle, from finding talent to developing talent, to retaining talent. This chapter describes how HR guides leaders as they fulfill their part in delivering people capabilities and how HR must be a center of excellence that delivers key aspects of people capabilities.

Chapter Six: Organizational Capabilities

A significant evolution of HR over the past decade has been the expectation that HR demonstrates excellence in organizational capabilities. HR has always been expected to excel at people capabilities; however, the expectation for HR to excel at organizational capabilities is very recent. This chapter describes how HR must be a center of excellence that delivers aspects of five essential organizational capabilities and how HR must guide leaders as they fulfill their part in delivering these organizational capabilities.

PART THREE: THE HR VALUE PROPOSITION

Chapter Seven: HR Value Proposition: An Overview

This chapter provides an overview of the next three chapters, which focus on three people and organizational capabilities that are frequently elevated to the level of the HR value proposition. The HR value proposition is the promise to deliver a top-priority HR solution targeted to mitigate a critical business risk. In all cases, the HR value proposition is one of, or a combination of the people capabilities and/or the organizational capabilities. The specific people or organizational capability that mitigates a critical business risk is elevated to the level of an HR value proposition.

Chapter Eight: Build Leadership Capacity

Many businesses develop strategies with the assumption that they have the current and future leadership capacity to deliver that strategy. The HR value proposition of "build leadership capacity" is the promise to build the required leadership capacity so that the business can deliver its strategies. This chapter describes the crucial role that leaders need to play to direct, align, and engage their employees and teams on an ongoing basis. It explores how HR develops leaders to work with their employees and teams to gain insight and discover innovative solutions to complex issues. HR becomes the center of excellence to build the business's leadership capacity and to assist leaders in fulfilling these essential roles.

Chapter Nine: Accelerate Culture Transformation

Many mergers and acquisitions fail, not because the businesses are not complementary but because the cultures do not integrate well. Similarly, when a single business restructures, cultural adaptation may not be done well. Employees may cling to the previous structure and not adapt well to the culture changes. The HR value proposition of "accelerate culture transformation" is the promise to accelerate cultural transformation with existing employees so that the business can implement its strategies rapidly and effectively. This chapter describes the levers that HR should use to accelerate culture transformation and how HR should guide leaders to do so with their employees and teams.

Chapter Ten: Implement Change

Businesses are undergoing constant change in order to survive and thrive. Too often, however, they only focus on planning the change and not on implementing it. Also, almost all changes require people and organizational capabilities. Yet executives frequently assume that the people and organizational capabilities will be taken care of somehow. They ignore the risks this oversight can have for implementing change. As a result, HR frequently chooses the HR value proposition of "implement change" as the promise to implement changes so that the business achieves its strategies. This chapter presents the eight steps for HR and for leaders to implement change. HR professionals need to establish themselves as a credible source for providing guidance on the most effective way to implement change in order to achieve the desired business outcomes. They also need to be the resident experts who can advise leaders as they implement change.

Chapter Eleven: Making Leadership-Driven HR Happen

There are many challenges for HR professionals as they proceed through the leadership-driven HR transformation process. This chapter describes the major implementation challenges and barriers that occur and how leadership-driven HR can overcome them effectively. The book concludes with a challenge to businesses, education, governments, and HR departments to recognize and respond to HR's rapidly changing role and to support its transformation over the next decade.

WHO WILL BENEFIT FROM THIS BOOK?

This book has been written for those hungry for information, ideas, and proven techniques to advance HR's role in organizations. *Leadership-Driven HR: Transforming HR to Deliver Value for the Business* is very helpful both conceptually and practically. In particular, the following groups will find the book beneficial:

- Human resources professionals interested in understanding and applying leadership-driven HR.

- Executives and business leaders seeking to understand HR's changing role, the new value that HR will provide, and how they can make this change an integral part of their business.
- Associations for HR, recruitment, training, organizational development, and strategy, as well as other groups that are concerned with people and organizational capabilities.
- Members of the academic community interested in a text to teach their students about the changing role of human resources.
- Students in business school and HR programs interested in books to support their understanding of the field.

HOW TO READ THIS BOOK

Most readers will benefit from reading this book cover to cover. However, others will find that they can dip into it for specific ideas and information. Here are some alternative ways this book can be read:

- Some readers—those responsible for the development of HR professionals—may want to use the book as a study guide for HR development. A suggested approach would be to ask the members of an HR team to each read one chapter of the book and then convene a meeting to discuss the entire book one chapter at a time.
- If the readers are primarily interested in leading-edge roles for HR, they may want to focus on reading Part Three (Chapters Seven to Ten), which describes the HR value propositions.
- Other readers may want to develop an approach to understand and communicate HR's fundamental people and organizational capabilities. These readers may want to focus on Part Two of the book (Chapters Four to Six).
- Still other readers may want to explore how to lighten up HR work and learn how it is done. This can be found in Chapters Three and Four.
- Some may want to focus on how to overcome barriers to implementing leadership-driven HR, which is described in Chapter Eleven.

- Some readers may want to read the summaries at the end of each chapter and then decide which chapters to read in their entirety.
- Finally, readers may want to study a topic of their own interest. A detailed index has been prepared for referencing specific topics. For example, topics such as "teams," "employee engagement," "HR business partners," and the "role of executives" are referred to in several chapters. The reader can combine the ideas from their chosen topic areas to form their own analysis of the material.

This book is a road map for executives, business leaders, and HR professionals who are considering how to transform HR to deliver value for their businesses. It will help create an understandable story of what HR is and how it contributes value to business leaders and the external customer. And, most importantly, it will provide HR professionals with an approach to guide them in their aspirations of becoming leadership-driven HR professionals.

About the Author

DR. DAVID S. WEISS
President and CEO of Weiss International Ltd.
Author, strategist, consultant, educator

Tel: (416) 944-9080 ext. 222; david.weiss@weissinternational.ca; www.weissinternational.ca

Dr. David Weiss is president and CEO of Weiss International Ltd. David and his team of learning and organizational consultants lead innovative projects that generate effective strategy, leadership, innovation, and HR solutions for leaders throughout Canada, the USA, and Europe. David is a highly sought-after motivational speaker, having presented at conferences throughout the world.

Some of his most recent projects include:

- Facilitating strategic planning, restructuring, and change management;
- Delivering HR and leadership motivational keynotes and sessions;
- Building leadership capacity and innovative intelligence;
- Enhancing employee engagement and organizational alignment;
- Assisting HR to deliver strategic value for the business.

Previously chief innovation officer in a multinational consulting firm, David currently teaches in three executive development programs at the Rotman School of Management at the University of Toronto; the Schulich School of Business at York University; and the University College of the Cayman Islands. His doctorate is from the University of Toronto, and he has three master's degrees in education, psychology, and philosophy. David is also an advisory board member of the Canadian Society for Training and Development, a past director on the board of the Princess Margaret Hospital Foundation, and an institute-certified director (ICD.D) with the Institute of Corporate Directors. He also is a senior HR professional (SHRP) and a certified training and development professional (CTDP). The following are some of the honors he has received internationally:

1. Distinguished Lecturer by the Government of Canada and Government of Ontario;
2. HR Leadership Award by the Asia-Pacific HR Congress;
3. HR Distinction Award by the Israel HR Association;
4. First lifetime Fellow of the Canadian Society of Training and Development;
5. Lifetime Fellow Canadian HR Professional (FCHRP) of the HRPA;
6. Lifetime Member of the Global Directory of Who's Who and a VIP Lifetime Member of the Presidential Who's Who;
7. Past president of the Industrial and Organizational Psychology Section of the Ontario Psychological Association.

David has delivered over 200 conference presentations and has written over 40 journal and trade articles including "Leadership Capacity: The New Organizational Capability," "How Leaders Can Close the Innovation Gap," and "HR Metrics that Count." David has authored or co-authored five business books: *Innovative Intelligence* (Wiley, 2011; will also be available in Chinese), *Leadership Solutions* (Jossey-Bass, 2007), *The Leadership Gap* (Wiley, 2005, also available in Korean), *High Performance HR* (Wiley, 1999), and *Beyond the Walls of Conflict* (McGraw-Hill, 1996, also available in French). His recent book, *Innovative Intelligence*, was a "top five business book for 2011," as reported by CBC News (February 17, 2012), and *High Performance HR* was the #1 business book bestseller in Canada in 1999. *Leadership-Driven HR: Transforming HR to Deliver Value for the Business* is David's sixth book. Follow David on Twitter @DrDavidWeiss, and read more than 15 of David's published articles at www.weissinternational.ca.

PART ONE

TRANSFORMING HR

CHAPTER ONE
BEING LEADERSHIP-DRIVEN

In today's highly competitive marketplace, many businesses are searching for new directions and are transforming their way of working. HR is on the same journey and is changing dramatically, too. HR professionals must find innovative ways to transform and deliver value for their businesses.

The challenge to HR is for it to unleash its own potential to gain insight and to discover new ways of delivering value. HR must go beyond simply breaking the past mold, which is useful but also a reaction to the former ways of doing things. Rather, enlightened HR leaders need to investigate the current situation in their business without constraints or assumptions and seek wise ways to transform in order to deliver value. With this kind of transformation, the business will view HR as a key asset in its formula for success.

Currently, not all businesses view HR as able to help them transform. These businesses relegate HR functions to transactional internal services with a primary focus on compliance and control. This is not entirely surprising. In the post-Enron and Sarbanes-Oxley era, HR has been inundated with new regulations and legislations—with a renewed focus on risk management. In the post-9/11 world, HR professionals are expected to have expertise in workforce management, screening and orientation of new hires, and physical and other security issues—not to mention new laws regarding violence in the workplace, bullying, and safety.

The new emphasis on compliance has affected more than just HR. Many industries have established new benchmarks for privacy, information and knowledge management, process documentation and controls, contract management, strategic alliances, and mergers and acquisition management. In addition, two other functions within business—finance and legal departments—have benefited from the new regulatory and governance controls that have increased the profile of the chief financial officer and the chief legal officer to mitigate financial and legal risks for their businesses and ensure compliance. Consistent with the finance and legal developments, HR is expected to emphasize its control and compliance accountabilities to ensure that the business is compliant with legislated, regulatory, and policy-related human resources issues.

At the same time, HR has grown substantially as a profession and as a strategic asset for many businesses. Many HR professionals are able to contribute strategically and operationally to many people and organizational capabilities including business strategy, culture, change, ROI, resource allocation, talent management, and leadership capacity development.

One might think that the two perspectives—HR as a key strategic asset and HR with a focus on compliance—would function as a continuum and that many HR organizations would fall somewhere in the middle. However, it appears that business executives tend to lean either toward one perspective or the other, and that HR (as a function) tends to be perceived as either more strategic or more compliance-oriented.

It is not a sustainable solution for businesses to limit HR's contribution to compliance and security. HR needs to deliver value in both areas: strategic growth *and* compliance. Rather than seeing compliance and growth as conflicting priorities, HR needs to embrace both. HR should demonstrate that it can manage the risk associated with potential loss and at the same time mitigate risk associated with not fulfilling the potential of its talent and organization. A business needs continuous change and consolidation to happen simultaneously in order to survive and thrive. Becoming stuck in the compliance perspective without positive change can be a source of long-term problems that will eventually result in loss of market share, shareholder value, and key talent. The HR role includes both protecting the business and fostering continuous and managed change to help the business and its leaders succeed.

Leadership-Driven HR focuses on how HR contributes to transforming the business and its leaders, as well as how HR needs to transforms itself in the context of an environment that has grown in its emphasis on compliance and control. When HR focuses on being leadership-driven, it makes a major contribution to the business.

Areas of Transformation for Leadership-Driven HR
- HR as a driver of business leadership.
- HR drives value through leaders.
- HR is driven to lead.

HR AS A DRIVER OF BUSINESS LEADERSHIP

HR's role is to champion the people and organizational capabilities that are necessary to help the business succeed in today's rapidly changing market. HR has always been expected to excel at people capabilities, which refers to the flow of people through their employment life cycle. However, the expectation to excel at organizational capabilities, which refers to the flow of work through the business, is more recent. Leadership-driven HR professionals take accountability for both people and organizational capabilities as drivers of business leadership.

For HR to be a driver of strategic business leadership, it must take an "outside-in" perspective rather than an "inside-out" perspective. An outside-in perspective means that HR focuses on the business and the value that the business creates for its external customers, and then uses those insights to determine what HR should do to deliver business value. With an inside-out perspective, HR looks at itself and decides what the business needs based upon its view of the right things to do. Leadership-driven HR emphasizes the outside-in perspective. This means that HR is driven by the external context within which the business operates and that outside perspectives determine HR's internal priorities and accountabilities.

An essential way for HR to identify the outside-in priorities of the business is to understand the business risks and then to consider their implications for the HR focus areas. Risk refers to both the business scenarios where something damaging could occur as well as areas where there is a high likelihood that the business will not fulfill its potential. HR's strategic role is to understand these areas of business risk, identify the people and organizational aspects of those risks, and take accountability for implementing solutions that mitigate those risks. The term "mitigate risks" is carefully used to mean that HR should take accountability for reducing the business-scenario risks from a damaging level to an acceptable level. In most cases HR does not need to take accountability for removing the people and organizational risks entirely; it just needs to reduce the risks to an acceptable level.

Here is an example of how HR can deliver strategic value for a business so that it is able to lead in its new direction in a public sector context:

The government health department controlled the delivery of health-care services throughout the country. They decided to transform their approach of centralized service delivery and instead to distribute the responsibility for health-care services to regional and community service providers. This resulted in a dramatic change in the nature of work for the health department whereby over half of the employees would be relocated to the various regional and community networks. The HR leader identified a major risk associated with this strategy that involved the extent to which employees and leaders would transition effectively to this new working model. The HR leader focused on leadership acceptance of the change and the effective transition of employees from the health department to the regional and community networks. She and her team then took accountability for driving the implementation of this change and led the transition teams to achieve these results in a professional and effective manner. The role that HR played as a driver of business leadership in the health department was essential to the success of this transformation.

There have been many changes in the global marketplace, within industry, and within governments that have had significant impacts on the role that HR can play in driving business leadership. These changes have also had implications for the meaning of what is "strategic" for businesses and government agencies.

In the current business climate, most executives are unwilling to take a long-term strategic investment perspective. They do not believe the world is stable enough to ensure that a long-term investment will pay off. Longer-term strategies assume a stable or predictable business and global environment. In a radically transforming public and private sector environment, the future is unknown and almost unpredictable. Therefore, executives demand a much shorter-term focus and more immediate return on their strategic investments from both a business and a people perspective.

In today's market, businesses strive for a strategy to rapidly increase revenue while decreasing expenses simultaneously. The new operative definition of strategy focuses on the following:

- *Gaining sustainable competitive advantage:* These are initiatives that differentiate a business from its competitors and that are sustainable for a meaningful time period. The length of time to sustain the advantage varies from industry to industry. For example, in the high-tech industry a two-month sustainable advantage makes an initiative strategic, while in the pharmaceutical industry the length of sustainable advantage would be much longer.
- *Achieving competitive parity:* For each business that is ahead of the competition, there are multiple businesses trying to "catch up" to the leader to neutralize their advantage. Initiatives that are based on catch-up strategies focus on achieving competitive parity, or being "on par" with the leader.

A similar definition of strategy is used in the public and not-for-profit sectors. However, instead of a focus on the competition, the focus is instead on the appropriate comparators. Comparators include best practices, standards, and organizational goals. Strategy in the public and not-for-profit sectors is defined as:

- *Gaining sustainable comparative advantage:* Initiatives that gain a comparative advantage against the defined appropriate comparators are considered strategic.

- *Achieving comparative parity:* For every leader in the public or not-for-profit sectors, there are many that need to catch up. Initiatives that focus on achieving comparative parity focus on neutralizing the comparative advantage of another jurisdiction over the performance of the local public-sector or not-for-profit-sector organization.

Traditional HR activities such as recruiting, employee relations, compensation, and training are necessary but not sufficient to help businesses thrive in the new competitive marketplace. If this is HR's only focus, executives will miss out on the greater contribution that HR can provide. HR as a driver of business leadership concentrates on providing strategic value that contributes to the business by gaining sustainable competitive/comparative advantage or parity.

HR DRIVES VALUE THROUGH LEADERS

Historically, HR has looked at its ratios of how many HR professionals it has in relation to the number of employees within the business. A typical ratio of 1:100 was the benchmark for many years. However, with the advent of centralizing HR transactional services, shared services, outsourcing, and technological deployment of various HR administrative services, HR is now able to deliver similar, and sometimes better, service with far fewer HR professionals. Some organizations report ratios of 1:500 which means that HR has had to transform radically to deliver value with so few staff.

Organizations have to transform how HR delivers value in this new reality. One major feature of the transformation is that HR's focus is no longer on direct service delivery to employees. Rather, HR drives value through leaders who take accountability for people leadership. In this way, although HR may have a 1:500 ratio of HR professionals to employees, they actually have less than a 1:100 ratio of HR to people leaders. This is similar to the former ratio of 1:100 that HR had to employees. In order for HR to deliver value with fewer staff, people leaders must be effective enough to manage the other four hundred people. At the same time, employees must maximize their self-reliance so that the people leaders' responsibility is reduced. HR then must become a center of excellence that guides the leaders to function as people leaders and maximizes employees' self-reliance. The three core elements of how HR drives value through leaders are explored in this section.

Three Core Elements of How HR Drives Value through Leaders
1. All leaders are people leaders.
2. All employees are self-reliant.
3. HR is the center of excellence in people and organizational capabilities.

---

1. All Leaders Are People Leaders

Start-up businesses have been drawing considerable attention from executives in mid-size and larger businesses. These executives like what they see in start-ups and ask, "Can we create a start-up environment in a mature organization?" There are many characteristics of start-ups that mid-size and large organizations try to emulate. For example, a start-up business usually has a clear purpose and direction. The start-up business that survives has a relentless focus on the external customers who are known to everyone. The customer is the person or organization outside the business that "pays the business's bills." Everyone focuses on delivering value to the customer. The focus on the customer also helps the start-up business decide what it will focus on and what it will view as a lower priority. The leaders and employees within start-up businesses have a passionate and determined interest in making their business successful. They foster a culture that is typified by the idea that "we do whatever it takes to get the job done." The leaders are entrepreneurial and take responsibility for the development and nurturing of their employees, who are often highly engaged and aligned with the leaders' direction.

The implications of using the start-up model for mid-size and large organizations are numerous. They are attempting to simulate the start-up model by ensuring the following:

- All leaders and employees are very focused on their purpose and direction.
- All leaders and employees are focused on the external customer and how to deliver value to them. The focus on the external customer should determine what is a higher priority and what is a lower priority.
- Leaders deliver value to the external customer while striving to be people leaders at the same time.
- Leaders and employees are passionately engaged and aligned to the business direction for the business to succeed.

In mid-size and large organizations, HR has a key role of driving value through leaders. HR professionals focus on guiding and developing leaders to help them create the inspiring environment of a best practice start-up organization. HR's new focus on the umbrella strategy of "talent management" (which includes staffing, leadership development, and succession planning) gives HR multiple options for contributing to the leaders' success as people leaders. HR needs to continually ensure that leaders at all levels can be effective in their role of delivering value for the business and in their role as people leaders.

2. All Employees Are Self-Reliant

One complaint from leaders about the new expectation of them as people leaders is that they have no time to both lead the business and be leaders of people. They miss the hand-holding that HR provided as well as the direct service delivery that HR gave employees. One important parallel development that has reduced leaders' concerns is the advent of employee self-service applications. Many of these self-service applications relieve leaders from managing employees directly. The result is that while leaders need to be people leaders, some aspects of that role have been absorbed by the employees themselves, which reduces the expectation on leaders.

The growth of employee self-service is now pervasive through portals, intranet, extranet, e-Learning, and other platforms and devices. These various employee self-serve applications have changed the way that employees access and utilize HR information and services. There are dramatic implications for return on investment, service levels, and speed of delivery, as well as an improvement in the ubiquitous delivery of service, seven days a week and 24 hours a day. Employees who are comfortable with self-serve on a personal level are often very appreciative of employee self-service options. In their personal lives, these employees book their own flights, do banking online, and play video games, so they adapt very easily to the various self-serve applications introduced to and available in businesses. Other employees who are less comfortable with technology on a personal level are often more hesitant to try self-service applications and may need more support in the process of this fundamental transition in the nature of work.

Here is an example of an organization that used employee self-reliance to help leaders function as people leaders while simultaneously improving employee engagement within the organization:

The telecommunications company was struggling with the best way to find candidates who would take on leadership of or participate in major projects. The standard method was to announce the projects and then let the senior leaders pick the person they knew could best lead the assignment. Invariably, they picked the same employees over and over again. This left them unable to find the organization's hidden talents who could lead projects as well. To meet this challenge, the HR director initiated an innovative idea. All employees were asked to put work-related information into the system, including their core competencies and the kind of projects they would like to lead or participate in. Whenever a new project required a leader or new members, the self-serve system automatically provided a list of candidates from the entire organization who had indicated that they would be interested in these kinds of projects. The self-serve system then sent a note directly to all of the identified employees to invite them to apply for the opportunity. As a result of the self-serve system, the business experienced a more egalitarian recognition of talent who could take leadership or participate in major projects.

Technology advances have also radically changed the way HR deploys its administrative services to employees, which also contributes to their ability to be more self-reliant. Shared services and outsourcing have changed HR's ability to locate its administrative roles in a more centralized location and achieve transactional support with far fewer resources. Technologies in shared services have changed payroll functions, health benefits administration, and how recruiting can be done from remote locations. In many respects, technology has been a major contributor to the restructuring of HR's role and the achievement of employee self-reliance. This technology has also enabled leaders to take on more of a role as people leaders.

Social media has also had a dramatic impact on the ability of employees to be self-reliant. It has had tremendous benefits in the area of crisis management, employee relations, policy development, employee communications, and training and development. The challenges and opportunities continue to evolve within organizations as new and innovative ideas emerge for using social media within the business setting.

HR has also been leveraging technology and social media to maximize its voice in internal communications, which helps employees know directly what is expected of them, and enhances their self-reliance and resiliency as a result. Many HR executives are writing blogs; and more employees are accessing each other (without the intermediary of HR or their leaders) to resolve problems and find opportunities on an ongoing basis. HR leverages these alternative methods of internal communications to reach employees, to ensure they know what the direction is for their business, and to engage and align them to that direction. HR also leverages the communications as a way to help employees know how they can be self-reliant, which reduces the burden on their leaders to play the people-leadership role for these administrative services.

3. HR Is the Center of Excellence in People and Organizational Capabilities

One characteristic of start-up businesses that mid-size and large organizations cannot emulate is their approach to internal organizational support departments. In a start-up business, the executives are often very reluctant to invest in the overhead costs associated with HR, since all investments are devoted to their primary risk associated with the survival of the business. The executive believes either that leaders can perform HR responsibilities themselves or that they do not have to be done at all. Because start-ups usually have fewer employees, initially it may be possible for them to get by without hiring an HR professional.

However, mid-size and large organizations have more employees, thus HR is essential. HR's role is not to be the people leaders for all employees. Rather, HR should be a center of excellence to guide leaders to be people leaders and to implement the systems that will help employees develop self-reliance.

To be a center of excellence, HR must demonstrate professional discipline and become a model of innovation for the organization. Here is an example of an HR organization that took the initiative to model how it was continuously improving its performance and services. This situation demonstrated that they were willing to put their own services to the test of a significant audit review, and this became the encouragement for other departments to do it as well.

The retail business decided to implement a new program focused on continuous improvement. One of the key elements was that departments were expected to voluntarily submit a major area of work to a third-party audit to find areas for continuous improvement. The HR leader was the champion of this initiative, which was one of her priority organizational projects. The problem was that no departments volunteered any of their services for review. The HR leader recognized that she couldn't ask others in the business to do a voluntary audit if HR was not prepared to do one. As a result she took the initiative to publicly announce that HR would undertake a third-party audit of its entire talent management process, from recruitment to development and succession management. The audit assessed the extent to which HR had a talent management strategy that followed best practices and the extent to which HR was delivering value to the organization in a way that eventually delivered value to external customers. HR learned a tremendous amount from the review about how to continuously improve what they offered in talent management. It also established HR as the center of excellence and defined it as a model for other departments in how to proceed through the audit and continuously improve. After HR published its audit report to the organization with full transparency, other departments began to seek out HR's guidance and subsequently volunteered to proceed through the audit and continuous improvement process for their departments.

In addition to being a center of excellence by modeling best practices, HR can build its credibility by seeking industry and public recognition outside of the organization. For example, HR leaders should be involved in the community and contribute value beyond their business. They should be active in their associations as a way to demonstrate that they are able to contribute to a broader level of the profession. They can also contribute to other non-competitive businesses, where appropriate.

Here is an example of how HR achieved high credibility in the broader health-care sector. The result was that HR's credibility was significantly enhanced, which positioned HR within the hospital and the health-care sector as a center of excellence in people and organizational capabilities.

A hospital that was viewed by many as a best-in-class health-care institution was engaging in a talent review of its leadership. The HR VP led the review, and one of the issues that emerged was that many of their health-care executives had left the hospital to become presidents of other hospitals in the community. Some considered these departures as regrettable losses for the hospital, and they raised this question in their talent review meeting. After some discussion, the HR VP explained that the executives' departures were unique opportunities to populate the health-care system with outstanding presidents who knew how to lead in the hospital sector. Rather than viewing the executives' exits as a loss, HR reframed it as a strategic contribution to the system that enhanced the brand of this world-class hospital. Subsequently, the HR VP was approached by one of the former executives—a new president of a community hospital. He asked if she would work one day a week to help the hospital modernize their HR function. The HR VP agreed to do this and then took on two more stints for six months each to improve the hospital's HR practices so that they would deliver value to the hospital and ultimately enhance patient care. Her leadership in the system became a source of pride for the health-care institution and the HR department was established as the center of excellence in people and organizational capabilities. It also became the model for her entire HR department and for other leaders who similarly took on roles that contributed to the system and not just their own hospital.

To become a center of excellence, HR also needs to assess whether its HR practices are really excellent and whether their HR professionals have the knowledge and expertise to solve strategic challenges. HR professionals will also need to continually learn and develop to sustain their departments as centers of excellence. They will need to learn about new approaches and practices that might help their organization and then choose and incorporate those they think will be effective in their business. Indeed, a primary purpose of this book is to explore how HR can become a center of excellence by employing leadership-driven HR approaches and practices.

HR IS DRIVEN TO LEAD

Perhaps one of the more unfortunate problems that HR has brought upon itself is the rhetoric that HR should be an "enabler" for the business. As a result, HR has moved away from viewing itself as having specific accountabilities for the delivery of outcomes. For some organizations this has further marginalized the value that HR can contribute. It has increased the chances that the organization will force various accountabilities upon HR that are associated with compliance and control, while simultaneously marginalizing the value that HR can contribute strategically through people and organizational capabilities.

HR professionals need to distance themselves from the enabler image and instead become leaders who take accountability for outcomes and the delivery of results. In fact, much of the transformation of HR is reflective of this outcome-based perspective. For example, "talent management" refers to HR's commitment and accountability to deliver the talent that the business needs in order to effectively realize its strategies. Talent management allows HR to consider the multiple options for meeting the organization's talent needs, whether by recruiting the talent that is required, developing the talent that may be necessary, enhancing engagement of employees so that they achieve more with the current resources, or identifying who should be the succession talent to protect the organization as leaders depart from the business. Talent management, then, is a concept that is outcome focused; it shifts the expectation of HR from being an "enabler" to being "accountable" for the people and organizational capabilities.

One question that is often asked is, "How can HR be accountable for the people and organizational capabilities if HR does not control all aspects of these capabilities? Wouldn't it be safer if HR just indicated that it was an enabler of the capabilities and leaders were accountable for them?" The answer is that not having control over the entire capability does not absolve HR from accountability for the capability—it just makes the accountability more difficult. HR needs to excel at engaging others to do their part so that HR can fulfill its accountability in people and organizational capabilities.

HR must be driven to lead by taking accountability for delivering the outcomes of the business's people and organizational capabilities even if HR does not deliver all the parts of the work. Just as the marketing and finance departments have accountability for work they do not fully control, HR needs to be responsible for their accountabilities as well. Taking accountability for outcomes will also help HR professionals be perceived as leaders in the organization. The focus on accountability for outcomes will also change the way HR speaks to executives. Many executives become confused when HR speaks about its processes without defining its accountabilities to deliver specific outcomes. Most executives are more concerned about delivering the business outcomes and want to know how HR will contribute directly to achieving those outcomes.

Here are some examples of how HR might have viewed processes in the past. These approaches need to be refocused on the way HR can take accountability for specific outcomes.

- The process of recruitment and leadership training becomes an outcome when HR takes accountability for ensuring the business has competent leadership to deliver its strategies, regardless of whether the talent is recruited externally or developed internally.
- The process of compensation and payroll becomes an outcome when HR takes accountability for ensuring that the business has

the proper motivators (financial and non-financial) to engage and retain employees and to make the business an attractive place for new and current employees.

- The process of employee and labor relations becomes an outcome when HR takes accountability for ensuring that there is a positive employee culture and that employees are highly engaged with achieving the business's strategic directions, whether they are represented by a union or not.

- The process of recruiting takes on an entirely new concept when HR focuses on the outcome of achieving an attractive employment brand. An "employment brand" is the impression your business makes on potential employees and the emotional connection it creates between them and the business. An employment brand packages all employment initiatives under an integrated set of symbols and key messages. HR commits to the accountability of creating a strong employment brand so that new recruits will be drawn to the business. Also, HR takes accountability to ensure that the employment brand comes alive in the workplace once employees join the organization.

Taking accountability for outcomes alone will not create the desire in HR professionals to have and accept the drive to lead. They need to have an emotional commitment and the self-confidence to know that they should be in leadership positions. HR professionals need to believe that they are able to deliver value for the business and through its leaders. Here is an example of a global business where HR learned this important lesson:

The HR department in a multinational business was undertaking a review of its global HR function. This was one of the many questions each HR leader was asked: "Who is HR's competition?" Most responded that the competition included the external outsourced HR professionals who could replace them, the leaders who were doing a poor job with their employees, and the unions who challenged them regularly. Shortly after these interviews, the business executives were interviewed. They were also asked who HR's competitors were. Their answers were radically different. They said that HR's main competitor was the value created by HR professionals in their competitors' companies. They did not view the outsourced HR service providers as competitors; rather, they viewed them as partners with HR to leverage the allocated resources available to HR. They also saw leadership as a key part of the solution for HR to achieve results in a resource-constrained environment. They even saw the relationship with the unions as an opportunity to build a more positive labor-management environment that could possibly contribute to a more positive culture. Apparently, the executives were not concerned about whether HR professionals were working within the business or as external resources. Rather, they wanted HR to surpass the value their business competitors received from their HR departments. In the executives' view, the external HR professionals were not the competitors of their internal HR professionals. Instead, they believed the internal and external HR professionals should be partners and work together to provide the business with sustainable competitive advantage and competitive parity.

HR needs to be driven to lead. It needs to get beyond its own fears of being replaced, which only limits its perspective and makes it operate defensively. Rather, HR should be in a leadership position where it focuses on delivering greater value to the business than the HR departments deliver in their competitors' businesses. The implications are as follows:

- HR needs to work with the external providers and consultants as extensions of their own teams, in a similar way that a family doctor would use a specialist doctor for specific needs as they are required.
- HR needs to become far more familiar with the value that other HR departments provide in their competitors' organizations. For example, HR can review their competitors' websites to see what their HR departments contribute to their businesses and then identify how their own HR department can develop or sustain competitive advantage or at least competitive parity. They also need to understand from a business perspective where their business compares well or is behind competitors. These insights may have people—and organizational—capability ramifications that could be part of what HR contributes to their business.
- HR should be paying attention to their own business's external customers. They should be talking to the HR representatives in their customers' businesses to get feedback and gain insight into what the

customer sees as the business's strengths and limitations. HR should then see if those strengths and limitations have implications for HR's focus in people and organizational capabilities.

All of these factors are important in order for HR to be driven to lead. HR needs to have the confidence that they can make a difference for the business and its leaders. HR must be leadership-driven by (1) contributing to the business so that HR achieves a leadership position; (2) delivering value through leaders so they become people leaders; and (3) insuring that HR is driven to lead within the organization.

CONCLUSION

Businesses need leadership-driven HR in order to succeed. The challenge to HR is to unleash its own potential in order to gain insight and discover solutions for how to deliver value for the business. HR must strive to be a key asset in the transformation of business leadership with a focus on delivering its value through leaders. Although there have been significant increases in the demands placed on HR in the areas of compliance and control, HR must be driven to lead and deliver value for the business. The next two chapters explore two additional factors that are essential to HR transformation. Chapter Two describes how HR delivers all of its work with a line of sight to the external customer. Chapter Three emphasizes that HR needs to make the difficult choices and reduce its emphasis on lower priority work so that it can focus on delivering meaningful outcomes for the business.

SUMMARY

- In today's highly competitive marketplace, many businesses are searching for new directions and are transforming their way of working. HR is on the same journey and is changing dramatically, too.
- *Leadership-Driven HR* focuses on how HR contributes to transforming the business and its leaders, as well as how HR transforms itself in the context of an environment that has enhanced its emphasis on compliance and control. When HR focuses on being leadership-driven, it makes a major contribution to the business.
- HR's role is to champion the people and organizational capabilities that are necessary to help the business succeed in today's rapidly changing market. "People capabilities" refers to the flow of people through their employment life cycle. "Organizational capabilities" refers to the flow of work through the business.
- For HR to be a driver of strategic business leadership, it must take an "outside-in" perspective rather than an "inside-out" perspective. An outside-in perspective means that HR focuses on the business and the value that the business creates for its external customers and then uses those insights to determine how HR can deliver business value.
- The three areas of transformation for leadership-driven HR are:
    1. HR as a driver of business leadership
    2. HR drives value through leaders
    3. HR is driven to lead
- Three core elements of how HR drives value through leaders are:
    1. All leaders are people leaders
    2. All employees are self-reliant
    3. HR is the center of excellence in people and organizational capabilities

  Businesses need leadership-driven HR in order to succeed. The challenge to HR is for it to unleash its own potential for gaining insight and to discover solutions for delivering value to the business.

CHAPTER TWO

LINE OF SIGHT TO
THE EXTERNAL CUSTOMER

A hotel in a large chain did not have an electronic system to track guests returning for the second time. Anticipating that there was an opportunity to meet customer needs even without technology support, the HR professional partnered with the business leader. Together, they devised a people-related solution that they implemented at the reservation desk to circumvent this deficiency and yet still meet customer needs.

The corporate executive responsible for information technology came to visit this hotel to determine how and when to implement the new electronic system. When he arrived, he walked up to reception desk. The woman behind the counter said, "Welcome back! We're delighted to see you again." Since he had not been to the hotel in two years, he asked how she knew that he was there before and then said, "I am the person responsible for implementing a system so that you can welcome me back the way you just did, and I know you don't have the system yet!" Quite anxiously, the reception person explained, "Well, we have a simple system. The porter who carried your bags asked you if you had been here before, and you must have said "yes." The porter then signaled me by pulling on his ear, and I knew it meant you had stayed here before, so I welcomed you back." In the absence of a technological solution to meet customer needs, the HR professional partnered with the business leader to devise an innovative technique. The employees put the plan in place, and it worked well enough for the hotel to deliver value to the guests.

Human Resource professionals are finding inventive ways to part-ner with business leaders to meet external customer needs. They know who the business's external customers are, they are able to anticipate customer-related challenges, and then they partner with business leaders to develop people and organizational solutions to those challenges. The HR professional in the opening scenario recognized the guest relations opportunity and developed an innovative solution with the business leader that surprised even the hotel chain's corporate executive.

HR needs to excel at partnering with business leaders to become leadership-driven HR. However, not all HR departments are ready for partnerships. They may first need to journey through a two-stage process:

- Stage 1: From control to service providers;
- Stage 2: From service providers to partnerships.

STAGE 1: FROM CONTROL TO SERVICE PROVIDERS

Most businesses need their HR departments to control their business leaders from potential people-related errors associated with legal, regulation, compliance, or labor issues, or with hiring and firing practices. In some businesses, these roles are the primary reason for HR's existence—to reduce the risk that the business may not be able to manage these kinds of issues effectively.

However, most businesses want HR to provide service to the business. For these businesses, the concept of the "internal customer" is very important. HR is measured by the extent to which it satisfies its "internal customers," which refers to the internal departments that receive HR's work. The concept of the internal customer can be helpful for HR and other organizational departments when they make the transition from a control mind-set to a service mind-set. It can enable them to respond positively to the question of whether or not HR provides added value to the business.

However, the term "internal customer" can be confusing when the demands of the internal and external customers are not aligned. Here is an example of one way a food manufacturer modified its usage of the word "customer":

A company in the business of food manufacturing recognized the confusion that could be caused by using the term "customer" to describe both internal and external groups to be served. They wanted to emphasize that the ultimate customer is the external customer and that no one else should be referred to by the term "customer." They called the internal customers (departments within the company) their "clients," the external customers (the supermarkets) their "customers," and the external customer's customer (the public who purchases their products) their "consumers."

A similar exploration of words should be done in every business. The focus should be on words that are precise so that they have value. If "customer" refers to everyone, then the word has no value. Another message in this example is that to add maximum value, the focus must be on satisfying the external customer.

Most HR departments have completed the Stage I journey from control to service providers. Although it is an accomplishment for a control HR function to become service oriented, it is not enough. HR as a service function delivers value *to* the business as their service provider. HR needs to become leadership-driven HR and deliver value *for* the business in a way that eventually achieves value for their external customers.

As a service provider, HR is still "once-removed" from the external customer and is highly vulnerable to errors associated with the following issues:

- *Concern with different customers (internal versus external) can result in HR falling out of alignment with the business:* HR can have difficulty understanding the business leader's external customer requirements when HR only focuses on providing service to internal business leaders. HR professionals need to be focused on the same goal as all of the business departments—delivering external customer value.
- *Reliance on business colleagues' views of their own needs:* This internal service provider view can create errors for HR if the business leader's requests are not the best solutions or the business leader's solutions do not align with external customer needs.

- *Difficulty in prioritizing among the many requests from internal business leaders:* HR often receives many requests from internal business leaders that far exceed its resource allocation. The result is that HR has great difficulty prioritizing among the many requests. When the external customer's needs are used as the prioritization filter, HR is better able to prioritize their work and determine what is most important to do.

STAGE 2: FROM SERVICE PROVIDERS TO PARTNERSHIPS

The current and future challenge to HR is to raise its value contribution to a higher level. This can be accomplished by expanding beyond the service provider role to deliver value in a partnership role. HR needs to partner with business leaders with the expectation that together they will deliver results that will eventually create value for the external customer.

Figure 2.1 shows the differences within HR's role when it focuses on control, service, or partnerships.

The leadership-driven HR organization will always have accountabilities in all three areas of control, service, and partnerships. HR will

Figure 2.1: The Differences in HR's Role from Control to Service to Partnerships

From Control to Service to Partnerships

	CONTROL	SERVICE PROVIDER	STRATEGIC PARTNER
Focus	• Focus on own internal policies, procedures & processes	• Focus on internal customers	• Focus on the external customers
Approach	• Enforce policies & processes	• Identify needs & solutions	• Drive organizational & business results
Expectations	• Take care of people issues	• Provide consulting services to meet needs of departments	• Help organization gain competitive advantage
Impact	• Preserve corporate resources	• Provide day-to-day value-added service	• Co-create with Business Units

always need to be accountable for control roles such as ensuring that legal, regulatory, and compliance standards are met, that proper people processes are followed, and that abusers within the business are dealt with appropriately and professionally. HR will also continue to have the responsibility to provide services that meet departmental needs. However, a substantial proportion of HR's work needs to be delivered through partnerships with business leaders. All of HR's work, whether to control, service, or partner, will need to be planned and implemented with an understanding of its implications for the business's external customers.

CLEAR LINE OF SIGHT TO THE EXTERNAL CUSTOMER

Consider the following situation:

An executive asked an HR leader how many external customers the HR department employees had seen in the past year. The HR leader indicated that HR employees did not have direct contact with external customers. To which the executive replied, "Then why would I want to hear your opinion if you don't know what our customers think?" Or, said another way, why should an executive be interested in HR's opinion about the business if HR has no idea what the customers' needs are and how they affect what the business requires from HR?

Many HR professionals argue that this expectation is challenging because HR has minimal access to the external customer. However, a core message of *Leadership-Driven HR* is that HR must take a leadership role in transforming the people and organizational capabilities of its business so that it eventually delivers value to external customers.

HR must have a clear line of sight to the external customer, which requires HR to work with executives, leaders, teams, and employees to eventually deliver value to external customers. Perhaps an image will help clarify this expectation to have a "clear line of sight to the external customer." Most people can identify the North Star and can use that star to help navigate even when they may appear to be lost. The external customer is HR's North Star. As long as HR professionals know where their North

Star is, they will know how to make local choices about what direction to follow. HR professionals need to always keep their sights on their external customer and not lose their focus because of the multiple, and sometimes conflicting, demands they receive from business leaders internally.

Here are some methods for HR professionals to gain information about the external customer to help them develop a clear line of sight and be guided by their "North Star," the external customer:

- *First-hand information:* Create opportunities to gain "first-hand" information by meeting with and listening to the external customer directly. Some ways to engage with the external customer include:
    - Visiting external customer sites.
    - Reviewing key customers' websites and literature to understand their recent developments and business needs.
    - Inviting external customers to attend HR and leadership planning meetings.
    - Engaging in dialogue with HR counterparts within the customer's business.
    - Where possible, becoming an external customer of the business by purchasing the products or using the services of the business.
- *Second-hand information:* "Second-hand" information is the information HR gains from people who have direct contact with external customers and who can describe "as a witness" the external customers' needs and concerns. This information adds a level of perspective that contributes to HR's understanding of how the business departments see customer's challenges. Ways to access second-hand information include:
    - Developing partnerships and having ongoing conversations with business leaders to understand their priorities and how they are designed to deliver value to external customers.
    - Attending meetings of business departments that have regular access to external customers (operations, marketing, sales, service, etc.) in order to learn their external customer challenges.

- *Thirdhand information:* "Thirdhand" information refers to reports collected through secondhand sources about the external customer. Ways to access thirdhand information include:
  - Studying the marketing survey reports that identify what external customers want and need. Often marketing professionals do not consider that their customer surveys have implications for HR—which is incorrect. For example, if external customers are not satisfied with the sales representatives' skills or if customers believe that it is difficult to do business with a company, these issues do have people and organizational implications that should be of concern to HR. In fact, HR professionals should study the external customer survey data before they study their own employee engagement survey data. HR's outside-in perspective will lead it to be concerned first with the external view of the business and then to consider what its implications are for employees.
  - Reading industry reports about the customers' businesses to understand industry trends and their implications for the services/products the customers receive.

To discover solutions to problems, HR should partner with business leaders and concentrate on the question, "Are the HR solutions for the business in the best interest of the external customer?" By doing this, HR is more apt to resolve the external customer's problem and also satisfy the needs of their colleagues. When HR assumes this role, it shifts from a service provider to a partnership organization focused on delivering sustainable competitive/comparative advantage for the business in the best interests of the external customer.

IMPLICATIONS FOR HR'S INTERNAL RELATIONSHIPS

It can be very challenging for HR professionals to redefine their relationships internally so that they work at a partnership skill level with a clear line of sight to the external customer. After all, many HR changes are driven by the expectation of the business leader to deliver service, cut costs, and become more efficient, and HR is required to be responsive to those expectations. Nevertheless, HR must strive to partner with business leaders to deliver value to the ultimate customer, the external customer. Consider the following scenario:

In a casual conversation with an HR professional, a business unit leader mentions a difficult problem and the action he took to solve it. The HR professional tells him that she would like to know why he took that action. With a surprised look, the unit leader replies, "What do you mean you want to know why?" The HR professional points out that she has some information that may have been helpful to the leader in making his decision. She explains that she would like to collaborate with him in the future to serve external customers. After some reflection, the business unit leader says, "All right, if you don't agree with the solution—then what should we do?" To which the HR professional responds, "We should work together to determine the best solution for the external customer."

Here are five key success factors for HR to redefine its internal relationships so that HR can partner with business leaders with a clear line of sight to the external customer:

Five Key Success Factors for HR to Redefine Its Internal Relationships
1. Be strategic thinkers.
2. Build partnerships with business leaders.
3. Function as "idea merchants."
4. Develop a unique perspective of people and organizational capabilities.
5. Demonstrate strength of character.

---

1. Be Strategic Thinkers

When an HR professional is a business leader's partner, he or she is not just wearing an "HR hat" but a "business hat" as well. He or she adds value to all issues, not just those directly related to HR. In essence, the HR professional is a strategic thinker with an HR specialty. This requires the following:

- *Broad understanding of the business:* A wide knowledge of the business helps HR to offer perspectives that transcend narrow departmental concerns. This understanding helps HR contribute value to the business's overall direction.
- *Insight:* HR should have insight into the implications of their business knowledge and its impact for people and the organization.
- *Knowledge of how all activities need to align:* With this knowledge HR can help the business maximize the success of strategic initiatives and eventually deliver value to the customer.

2. Build Partnerships with Business Leaders

HR professionals need to be able to have meaningful business-related conversations with business leaders from a customer perspective. These conversations will increase the probability of effective people and organizational outcomes that achieve competitive/comparative advantage and deliver value to their external customers. A clear signal that HR professionals are functioning as partners is when business leaders are as interested in partnering with HR as HR is in partnering with them. Often, the HR VP initiates this kind of relationship by developing a strategic partnership with the president and becoming an equal member of the executive team. In this way, he or she also will have the credibility to be a mentor for the other HR professionals in their roles as partners with business leaders.

3. Function as "Idea Merchants"

HR professionals need to be able to intrigue business leaders with ideas, suggestions, links to other experiences, and so on. In this sense, HR professionals are "idea merchants" who can stimulate conversations with their business leaders. HR integrates and assimilates information about their business and the strategies of other businesses and shares them willingly with business leaders. To be "idea merchants," HR professionals must have a large "mental database" to use in conversations to help business leaders see their problems and opportunities from different perspectives. They are then able to help the business leaders discover business solutions that make sense for the external customer, the business, and the people within it.

4. Develop a Unique Perspective Regarding People and Organizational Capabilities

This perspective gives HR professionals the opportunity to increase the potential work, guidance, and support for business leaders. HR professionals need to formulate and take accountability for people and organizational solutions wherever they may reside in the business. For example, typically, when a business hires a new employee, HR is involved in the recruitment and orientation, finance sets up the financial records, real estate ensures the employee has a place to work, information technology ensures the employee has access to the business's technology, and communications lets the organization know the new employee has joined the business. It is remarkable when all of these separate units collaborate effectively so that the first day runs smoothly for new employees. HR needs to take a leadership role for this people capability so that when they hire a new recruit, all the various units work well together. HR's unique perspective for integrating the internal services delivers value to the new hire by having him or her become acclimated to the new position quickly, and HR ultimately delivers value to the external customer because the employee is in place and able to function in a capable manner to meet customer expectations.

5. Demonstrate Strength of Character

Many executives are used to thinking of HR as an organizational service department and accustomed to telling them what to do. HR will need to achieve the credibility to be accepted by business leaders as partners and not as a relationship between an organizational supplier and an internal customer. HR professionals must also have the strength of character to respectfully oppose business leader suggestions if necessary. They must be able to question a request if it does not enhance customer value but do it in a professional manner. The HR professional might say, for example, "I need to understand the problem before we can consider the best solution to pursue." Most business leaders, if they respect an HR professional, are willing to engage in dialogue to discuss the problem and then to reconsider the preferred direction to implement.

Ultimately, every HR priority should be expanded to include a statement of how that HR priority eventually delivers value to the external customer. For example, HR may be enhancing its recruitment practices to find talent to meet the needs of the business more rapidly and effectively. HR should add to this priority that the outcome will eventually meet external customer needs because the business will have the talent available to service customers effectively. By including the added phrase, "the value to the external customer," HR will be putting its "clear line of sight to the external customer" into every HR priority.

CONCLUSION

A foundation of the HR transformation starts with including the external customer in the purview of every HR professional. With a clear line of sight to the external customer, HR will be in a position to know what is and what is not important within the business. HR professionals will be able to make astute judgments about how to deploy their services and people to deliver value for the business. Eventually, HR's work will enhance the business's ability to achieve competitive/comparative advantage or parity and to deliver enhanced value to the customer.

SUMMARY

- Human resource professionals are finding they need to change their methods of solving internal people and organizational problems. They understand that they must know who the external customer is in order to identify the correct business solutions to internal problems.

- The concept of the "internal customer" has helped HR and other organizational departments to transition from a "control" mind-set to a "service" mind-set. However, the concept of the "internal customer" is not helpful if HR wants to create partnership relationships with business leaders.

- HR needs to develop partnerships with business leaders and have a clear line of sight to creating value for the external customer.

- Here are the five key success factors for HR to redefine its internal relationships so that HR can partner with business leaders with a clear line of sight to the external customer:
  1. Be strategic thinkers.
  2. Build partnerships with business leaders.
  3. Function as "idea merchants."
  4. Develop a unique perspective of people and organizational capabilities.
  5. Demonstrate strength of character.

- Ultimately, HR needs to explain how all HR priorities eventually deliver value to external customers. Every HR priority should be expanded to include a statement of how this value will eventually be delivered.

A foundation of HR's transformation starts with including the external customer in the purview of every HR professional. With a clear line of sight to the external customer, HR will be in a position to know what is and what is not important within the business. HR professionals will be able to make astute judgments about how they will deploy their services and people to deliver value for the business.

CHAPTER THREE

"LIGHTEN UP" TO DELIVER PRIORITIES

An HR leader decides to focus HR on being leadership-driven and creating a clear line of sight to the external customer. The problem is that this approach is generating additional work for HR, and this must be done in addition to each employee's "day job." Essentially, HR has assigned additional work to employees who already have a full workload. Quite naturally, they complain. The HR leader has not recognized the necessity to lighten up at least a portion of the employees' workload to allow them to devote energy to delivering the new priorities.

The first two chapters described the additional strategic work HR will need to accomplish as it strives to become a leadership-driven HR function with a clear line of sight to the external customer. However, if work is added, HR will have the equal challenge of balancing its priorities and "lightening up" work of a lower priority.

In business, the ability to lighten up is essential to any new strategy, but it must be done in a responsible, professional, and disciplined manner, meaning that the focus is on the strategic direction and on maximizing the value to the external customer. Both human resources and businesses have to learn the discipline of balancing priorities so that they can take on new ones. Many of the books that leaders read tell them what to do, but few tell them what *not* to do. Leadership's and HR's new discipline will be the skillful removal of initiatives on an ongoing basis to make room for new strategic directions.

LIGHTEN UP TO REBALANCE WORK

The need to lighten up work is driven by an imbalance in the supply of available resources and the demands of the work. There are two possible ways to regain balance in a business. These are:

- *Increase the available resources:* An increase may be necessary when there are not enough resources to meet the demands of the work. If the demand side cannot change, then HR will either have to add more resources or utilize the existing resources more effectively to gain more productivity from them.
- *Reduce the demand for work:* Reducing the demand may need to occur when existing resources are overloaded. If the resource side cannot change, then HR will either have to (1) prioritize the demand to focus on the higher priority work; (2) distribute the demand so that others outside the business do the work; or (3) simplify the demand so that it becomes less demanding.

Figure 3.1 depicts the imbalance between the supply of resources and the demands of the work. It also lists some key questions that can be used to explore how to enhance the available supply or to reduce the existing demand in order to rebalance the work of the business.

LEADERSHIP AND THE NEED TO LIGHTEN UP

Some leaders have been successful in the lighten-up process and have thus been able to eliminate work of lower value to the external customer. However, for other leaders the investment in past success blinds them to the need for a new direction. When this occurs, the business may resort to finding new leaders who can more easily give up the old and commit to change. Of course, bringing in a new leader does not guarantee successful new directions. In some cases the new leader appears to have a new perspective, but in reality it is the perspective developed at his or her prior business. In these situations, the new leader is trying to force

Figure 3.1: The Imbalance between the Supply of Resources and the Demands of the Work

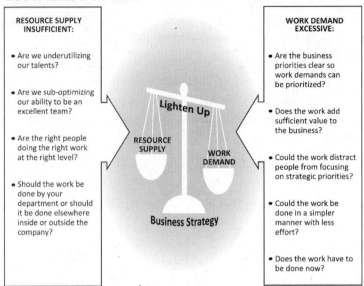

RESOURCE SUPPLY INSUFFICIENT:

- Are we underutilizing our talents?

- Are we sub-optimizing our ability to be an excellent team?

- Are the right people doing the right work at the right level?

- Should the work be done by your department or should it be done elsewhere inside or outside the company?

WORK DEMAND EXCESSIVE:

- Are the business priorities clear so work demands can be prioritized?

- Does the work add sufficient value to the business?

- Could the work distract people from focusing on strategic priorities?

- Could the work be done in a simpler manner with less effort?

- Does the work have to be done now?

Lighten Up

RESOURCE SUPPLY

WORK DEMAND

Business Strategy

an old approach to fit into the new business, which in many cases results in failure.

Here is a situation of how one group of incumbent executives proceeded to lighten up:

In one mature company, the executives realized they were having difficulty relinquishing the processes and models they had created. They were proud that the processes had brought their company success, but they realized that as their company was maturing and they would not be the ones to move it in a new direction. However, instead of stepping down, they chose a different path.

They challenged a group of seven "next-generation" executives, who were viewed as the company's future key resources, to develop the company's next strategy. The senior executives gave this group the chance to design the company they would eventually lead. They viewed this approach as an excellent leadership transfer process and as a method to ensure that the next level of management would take ownership of the future direction.

The next-generation leaders took the challenge very seriously and developed a plan for sweeping changes and strategies. To the surprise of many, the senior executives accepted all the recommendations and put the next-generation leaders in charge of the strategic object-ives they had identified. Five years after this event took place, the former senior executives have retired, and the leaders of the next-generation team are running the company and implementing most of the plans they developed five years earlier.

The easy part for leaders is developing the strategy. The hard part is letting go of the previous strategy to make room for the new. The ability to lighten up and renew has become a key success factor for leadership and is often a distinguishing factor between success and failure.

The problem, though, is that lightening up involves risk, which makes it very hard to let go of the old way of doing things. Business leaders and HR professionals tend to have a high probability of showing the following risk-taking patterns:

- *Leaders tend to avoid risk when they are exposed to gains:* There is a tendency to settle for the guaranteed amount rather than risk the gains for more. This risk pattern may limit leaders from exploring new opportunities or leveraging existing ones further.
- *Leaders tend to seek risk when they are exposed to losses:* There is a tendency to persist when leaders are losing (throwing good money after bad). Abandoning a bad situation is a guaranteed loss, so leaders often stay for the minimal chance of avoiding loss even if it results in greater loss. It is this pattern that sometimes makes it difficult for business leaders and HR to lighten up their work. To be done successfully, the lighten-up process must be disciplined, with its focus being on the strategic direction and maximizing the value to the external customer. Personal vested interests or antiquated assumptions should not be permitted to affect decisions.

The ability to lighten up to deliver priorities is a characteristic of the innovative mind.[1] To innovative thinkers, what they did yesterday

---

1. See David S. Weiss and Claude P. Legrand, *Innovative Intelligence: The Art and Practice of Leading Sustainable Innovation in Your Organization* (Toronto: John Wiley & Sons, 2011).

does not tell them how they are to behave today or tomorrow. If they are stuck in yesterday, they may never get to tomorrow. A process or project is not sacred to them but simply a means to an end. Leaders and HR professionals need to develop the ability to lighten up in a disciplined manner, especially when they are exposed to losses. They need to learn how to "fail fast" on projects, meaning that they have to let go of work before it becomes an unnecessary burden on the business.

Many businesses have engaged in a lighten-up process without calling it that. Some call it "blank sheeting" the organization; a process in which they ask, "How would we create the organization today if we were to start all over again?" This process can only be done with people who are willing to relinquish what they have done in the past. They clean their slate and consider new ideas they have not thought about before. Often it is helpful to include other people who are not involved in the past way of working because they will not be constrained by previous assumptions and processes.

The ability to lighten up is essential to add focus to the development of new strategic directions. It is a foundation piece in the creation of meaningful change. Without discarding previous work, employees will dispense with new ideas as unworkable because of the lack of time or resources to achieve both the new and old objectives simultaneously.

LIGHTEN UP BY REMOVING THE "NOISE" FROM THE SYSTEM

Businesses and HR need to be aware of the "noise" in their organizational systems. The term "noise" represents the low-level irritants that most people ignore. For example, in most office buildings, the ventilation system is constantly emitting a low-level noise. However, in some situations, the noise is so loud that it becomes intolerable.

The same occurs within organizational systems. A common area of noise in a business is the systems that perhaps were once useful but currently function as barriers to the effective implementation of change. For example, the system of "rewards and punishments" can be a source of noise because it can motivate people to do things that are against the desired strategic direction. In essence, they can be negative motivators that motivate people in the wrong direction.

Invariably, if positive motivators have to be excessive, there is some other equally strong motivator that is driving people to proceed in another direction. The alternative and recommended approach is to lighten up by targeting the strong negative motivator, reducing its impact on the system, and then implementing a gentle positive motivator. This will often be sufficient to motivate people to move in the desired direction (if the direction desired is a reasonably good idea). Here is an example of this kind of noise in the system which resulted in sales reps not being motivated to work as a team:

A pharmaceutical company recognized that it needed an integrated sales-team approach in order to meet the needs of larger customers. The executives encountered noise—resistance from employees and leaders to the new approach. Upon reflection, the HR business partner speculated that the sales reps were only rewarded for individual performance and not for team performance. She suggested that if they introduced changes to the sales reps' reward system to emphasize teamwork, the sales reps might be motivated to work in teams. To facilitate this, they removed rewards that drove the overemphasis on individualistic behavior and established rewards that encouraged teamwork. Next, they built in team measures to keep the focus on the advantages of working in teams.

Often, a low-level noise in the system is ignored or tolerated. However, in times of significant change, the noise can be the cause of problems. Once HR identifies the noise, it needs to remove it quickly so that the leaders and employees can move in the direction the business desires.

Here are some other ways HR professionals can lighten up work by identifying and removing the noise in the business:

- *Target work areas that have low engagement scores or have many complaints:* An important source of noise is related to problem leaders or employees. Too often, leaders and employees who are destructive to the work environment are tolerated for too long. The damage in this situation is to the rest of the employees. HR should target the areas that have low employee engagement scores and find out if an individual is causing the problems that are destructive to the group. Also, in unionized environments, HR should identify the work areas that are having the most grievances and investigate the situation. Rather than interpreting the excessive grievances as over-complaining, HR may find that the employees are using the grievance process to let HR know they have a dysfunctional leader. HR should target this noise and repair the damage swiftly to let the business deliver its priorities.

- *Study the business SWOT analysis (usually part of a strategic planning process) in which the internal weaknesses are identified:* In a SWOT analysis (that is, Strengths, Weaknesses, Opportunities, and Threats), the business identifies the external business opportunities and threats. Then they ask the following:
  - What are the internal strengths that will help the business capitalize on the opportunities and reduce the threats?
  - What are the internal weaknesses that will block the business from capitalizing on the opportunities and allow the threats to take effect?

  The internal weaknesses are often within the control of the business to reduce and are often the noise HR can target for elimination.

- *Determine what is negatively reinforced in the business:* What is negatively reinforced often has more power than what is rewarded. For example, most businesses have published values that reflect what the business wants people to consider important as they make decisions and do their work. If you ask employees to name the business values, sometimes they will not know the answer. However, if you ask employees what behaviors get people into trouble, they immediately have a strong opinion and response. These real or perceived negative reinforcers can become the noise in the system that will block employees' willingness to change.

- *Determine if HR has inadvertently created problems for itself while it was trying to achieve other objectives:* Here is an example where HR inadvertently created noise by its propensity to document every action of leaders and employees. Here is what they did to remove the noise that they created:

In a large manufacturing company, the HR department introduced extensive documentation of all management and employee actions. Although the HR professionals tried to convince the business leaders that the forms delivered value for the business, the leaders resisted. They viewed HR as a control function that took its greatest pride in developing another control form rather than in helping the business leaders do their jobs.

After realizing that they had inadvertently created noise in the system by requiring excessive documentation, the HR professionals engaged in an exercise to determine which of the forms were necessary. They began by collecting all electronic and paper-based forms and posting all these forms on the walls of a large training room. To their shock, they filled all the walls. They then set a target to reduce the number of forms by 50 percent. Their exercise involved evaluating each form and asking whether it reduced the risk to the external customer and, therefore, whether the business really needed it. In examining the forms, they found many that people were required to complete even though they did not know why and in spite of the fact that in some cases no one used the information. By the end of the exercise, they had discarded or simplified over 75 percent of the forms. Other important forms were simplified online for ease of use by the managers and employees. After an effective internal communication process, HR was recognized for its efforts to remove the noise that became the internal barrier to the success of the business.

THE 4DS: DELETE, DELAY, DISTRIBUTE, DIMINISH

Consider the following example of how an HR leadership team in a major financial institution proceeded to lighten up their work to ensure they could focus on their new strategic priorities. They successfully applied the 4Ds (Delete, Delay, Distribute, Diminish) to lighten up their work. Here is what they did:

An HR leadership team decided to take stock of its workload to make room for its new HR strategic initiatives. They identified that they had committed to 46 HR projects. After further analysis, the team realized it did not know why it was involved in some of the projects, how or if the projects fit together, or whether the projects delivered eventual value to the external customer.

The 12 members of the HR leadership team developed five strategic objectives for HR. They decided to engage in a lighten-up experiment to see how or if they could relinquish projects that did not contribute meaningfully to at least one of the five strategic objectives. They divided the team into six pairs of HR leaders and gave each pair a set of 46 cards, each with a name of one of the HR projects. Each pair of HR leaders sorted the project cards into the five HR strategic objectives. They also decided to lighten up those projects using the 4Ds:

- *Delete: Project could be stopped because it does not fit with the strategic objectives.*
- *Delay: Project could be delayed to a later time.*
- *Distribute: Project could be done by resources outside of HR.*
- *Diminish: Project could be simplified to place less demand on HR.*

To add drama to the event, they placed a garbage pail on the table in which they could "trash" projects that met any of these 4Ds (Delete, Delay, Distribute, Diminish). After they completed the sorting, the leaders reviewed the piles of cards under each strategic objective. They found that some of the projects appeared in more than one strategic objective category. They then reviewed the projects and developed a common understanding of what was included in each strategic objective.

Next, they emptied the garbage pail, which contained 18 project cards. After a heated discussion over the 18 projects, they finally agreed to delete three, delay six, distribute two, and diminish three. The remaining four did not align with any of the five strategic objectives, but they had to be done because of legislative and compliance requirements. The lighten-up exercise had an excellent return on investment. The HR leadership team decided how to redeploy employees to higher-priority work to advance the implementation of their strategic objectives and create greater focus for HR and the entire business.

The remainder of this chapter describes how HR professionals can lighten up work by applying the 4Ds of Delete, Delay, Distribute, and Diminish.

Delete

Delete refers to stopping work so that it is no longer done—be it by HR or by anyone else. HR often struggles to delete work that it agreed to do at an earlier point. Yet there can be major gains for HR and the business if HR stops doing work that does not add value for the business.

One area of work to delete is "rework." In one organization the entire HR team of 80 employees was asked how much of their work was rework, which included redoing work that should not have been done to begin with. The team estimated that over 30 percent of their work was rework and, if possible, should be deleted. The team then identified four areas of rework that they should delete to be able to allocate time to HR priorities. The four areas were:

- Work that was redone because it did not meet standards.
- Work that duplicated work that was developed previously.
- Work that was repeated because people did not understand the request the first time.
- Work that was never used because there was no need.

Here are other areas of work that should be targeted for deletion:

- *Work that is of lower value:* Lower-value work includes work that provides a minimal return, such as HR participating in all job interviews, or noise in the system (as described in the previous section).
- *Work that is unnecessary:* Unnecessary work includes rework as well as work on underperforming products or processes, work on underutilized metrics and reports, and work that duplicates electronic and paper-based forms and files.
- *Work that is not constructive:* For example, one company had a practice of calling customers during their dinner hour to market their products. Both the customers and the employees were very displeased with this practice. HR introduced an internal campaign called "ABC," or Stop "Annoying our Best Customers." In addition to

being humorous, the campaign stopped many activities that created customer and employee dissatisfaction.

- *HR "parenting" roles:* Parenting roles include such activities as tracking systems, reminding managers to complete employee appraisal forms, tracking attendance at training programs, focusing on the job as the unit of activity versus work, or requiring too many signatures on forms. It also may include HR practices that over-control processes and thus inadvertently limit employee self-reliance and innovation (e.g., overly rigid job descriptions, too many detailed forms to complete).

Delay

"Delay" refers to delaying activities that could be performed at a later time with minimal or no reduction in value. This tactic is the most popular method to lighten up HR work for delivering its priorities. Here is an example where HR was able to delay a significant area of work when it discovered that the process was going to proceed through a major technology overhaul in another year's time:

In one organization, the HR team thought they needed to revise their performance management system to align with the newly developed organizational values. They included this project in a list of must-do projects that would utilize a great deal of employee time and effort. In another meeting, one of the HR team members discovered that the IT department was planning to introduce a new software technology. This activity would require modification to the systems that HR deployed across the entire business, including the performance management system. The HR leadership then decided to delay the major revision until after the new software technology was in place and to make only minor modifications to reflect the new values in the existing performance management process.

Here are other areas of work that should be targeted to be delayed:

- *Work that does not have to be done immediately:* Ask the question: Does the work have to be done now? Can we do it later if the work does not require immediate attention (e.g., upgrading a system that is working well or launching a high-risk service)?

- *Non-essential revisions to HR practices:* For example, revisions to an employee survey, the performance management process, competency frameworks, or the benefit plans.

- *Work that would be adopted more readily at a later time:* Sometimes the timing of an introduction of a change may result in less resistance if it is delayed to a later time when there is less work demand on employees (e.g., introduce it midyear rather than at year-end).

Distribute

Often, most of the work HR is asked to do must be done: people have to be hired; they must be paid; and training, employee relations, and terminations still have to take place. The work will continue to be done—but not necessarily by HR. Here is an example of what one HR organization did to force the consideration of what it could distribute:

In one organization, the HR department developed a task force to explore the extent to which they could distribute HR work. The task force's challenge was to begin with the assumption that all HR work could either be outsourced or distributed internally to business leaders or employees to enhance their self-reliance through technology. HR also asked the task force to make a business case for the work that really had to be done by HR staff internally. The challenge stimulated a different kind of conversation in HR that helped them break old patterns and utilize the internal HR professionals for the more strategic roles that HR needed to adopt.

Here are other areas of work that should be targeted for distribution:

- *Work that another person/department can do equally well:* HR needs to identify whether the work can be done more efficiently by another department because it relates to work they are already doing. Also, consider consolidating overlapping work from multiple areas (e.g., consolidate planning, metrics management, and data warehousing).

- *Work that should be the accountability of business leaders:* HR can distribute some work, such as basic job descriptions and some employee relations work, to business leaders. HR does not fill the vacuum to meet the employees' needs directly. Doing that will lessen the leader's ability to lead his or her employees. As the classic "fish" maxim goes, "Feed them fish and they eat today; teach them to fish and they will eat forever." Teach the leaders to lead and distribute the responsibility to them rather than do it for them. HR can also designate an HR resource with specialized expertise in employee relations to remove this responsibility from the role of the HR business partners.

- *Work that can be outsourced to external service providers:* HR can distribute some work, such as parts of recruiting, payroll, compensation, benefits, basic training, and much of the transactional work, to external suppliers to deliver the process. At the same time, HR must be effective at managing the vendors of these activities to ensure quality performance.

- *Work that can be done as a shared service:* HR can create shared services in larger organizations that have the size and economies of scale for the work. A shared service essentially is "insourcing" transactional work that is done within the business rather than outsourcing it. When the organization is large, a shared service can be a better solution than outsourcing for several reasons:
  - It can be less expensive than outsourcing.
  - It can customize services better to the needs of the business.
  - It does not distract HR from its focus on the business's strategic needs.
  - The knowledge gained about the work performed in the shared service remains in the business.

- *Work that can be done through self-serve technology:* By allowing employees to access information electronically, HR distributes the work to the employees online and does not have to manage so many activities directly. When HR ensures that all business leaders and employees have access to the central database, many benefits can occur. For example:

- *Employees* are able to update personal information and research training information, sign up for courses, identify job and work opportunities, submit applications, identify career opportunities, change flexible benefits, manage their own flexible benefits, and find information about developments in the business.
- *Business leaders* are able to do the preceding activities as well as conduct information analysis, performance development and review, research, reports, and electronic signatures.
- *Executives* are able to do the preceding activities as well as use the database to get cost-of-labor information to help them make decisions about deploying people and allocating resources.

Diminish

This approach involves simplifying practices and processes to essentials in order to deliver value for the business. Here is an example of how HR diminished its processes, which were viewed as too cumbersome:

One HR organization recognized that they had many cumbersome processes that required multiple signatures (often three or more) on documents before approval. The multiple signatures helped control decision-making but also stifled innovation and slowed down change. They decided to simplify their processes and introduced a "Sign No More" campaign, which meant no form would have more than two signatures. If the business thought they needed more signatures, they had to make a business case to defend that level of control. The Sign No More campaign also forced important conversations among leaders about who was really accountable, and it challenged entrenched hierarchical assumptions such as: Can an employee and someone several levels higher sign documents without the middle management signature?

Here are other areas of work that should be targeted to be diminished:

- **Work that does not need to be at the "gold" standard:** Some work does not need to be perfect or at the "gold" standard. That work can be at an "acceptable" level (or "bronze" standard) and it will be good enough for the business because it does not put strategic goals at risk.

- **Work that can be streamlined:** This is work that can be streamlined through "lean" process improvements such as simplifying complex reports, tackling e-mail overload, reducing rework, and simplifying multiple hand-offs to complete the work.

- **Work that can be reduced in scope:** This work may include some complex job evaluation systems, the abundance of generic training programs, or elaborate competency-based frameworks that are not utilized.

- **Work that can be simplified through technology and social media:** Some businesses leverage their electronic methods of internal communications and social media to distribute information and update employees about developments. Employees also use the technology and social media to develop their own networks and communities of practice.

At the conclusion of a 4D lighten-up process, HR needs to develop an action plan to rapidly expedite its recommendations. HR needs to ensure that the lighten-up process does not become another major project that just adds work to an already full workload. It must quickly reduce the demands on HR's workload so that HR can refocus its efforts on delivering value for the business with a clear line of sight to the external customer. Figure 3.2 presents a Lighten-Up Action Planning Template that can be used to list the 4D recommendations, identify what needs to be done, by whom, and by when for each area of work, and to track the status of each of the areas to be lightened up.

Figure 3.2: The Lighten-Up Action Planning Template

Targeted Work	4D Strategy	*Lighten Up* Action Plans			Status
To Lighten Up Workload	Delete, Delay Distribute, or Diminish	What Will Be Done	By Whom	By When	Update Progress

HR needs to guide business leaders to lighten up and apply the same approaches to its own work within HR. By ensuring that its workload is lightened, HR will then have the available time and resources to focus on the business imperative of being leadership-driven with a clear line of sight to the external customer.

CONCLUSION

HR needs to lighten up its lower-priority work in order to deliver its higher-priority work. This involves rebalancing HR's resource supply with its work demands in order to become a leadership-driven HR function with a clear line of sight to the external customer. It requires that HR remove the noise from the organizational system that limits progress; and that HR utilizes the 4Ds (Delete, Delay, Distribute, Diminish) to reduce its overall workload so it can focus on aligning all efforts to deliver value for the business. With this focus, HR can help create an outstanding state of readiness to implement new directions quickly and repeatedly (as initiatives change) with the aim of delivering value for the business and eventually for the external customer.

The next three chapters (Part Two) explore HR's work in the areas of people capabilities and organizational capabilities. The topic of how to lighten up work is revisited in Chapter 4, which presents an overview of the areas of HR work and a process of how to identify work that can be lightened up within the people and organizational capabilities.

SUMMARY

- Both human resources and businesses have to learn how to "lighten up" and shed responsibilities so that they can take on new ones. To be done successfully, the lighten-up process must be disciplined, meaning that the focus is on the strategic direction and that the value to the external customer is paramount. The lighten-up process has become a key success factor for leadership and HR and often is a distinguishing factor between success and failure.

- The need to lighten up work is driven by an imbalance in the supply of available resources and the demands of the work. There are two possible ways to regain balance in a business: (1) increase the available resources; and (2) reduce the demand for work.

- Businesses and HR need to get rid of the "noise" in the system that blocks the business from transforming and moving forward. HR can have a major role in dismantling these barriers.

- There are four ways to lighten up work—all starting with the letter "D." The 4Ds are:
  - Delete: Project could be stopped because it does not fit with the strategic objectives.
  - Delay: Project could be delayed to a later time.
  - Distribute: Project could be done by resources outside of HR.
  - Diminish: Project could be simplified to place less demand on HR.

- The lighten-up process can help HR create a business with an outstanding state of readiness to implement new directions quickly and repeatedly (as initiatives change) for the benefit of the business.

PART TWO

THE WORK OF HR

CHAPTER FOUR

THE HR TRIANGLE CHART

Many executives do not have a clear understanding of HR's priority areas of work. They may understand that HR develops employee policies, hires people, compensates them, trains them, and so on, but they often do not have a precise idea of HR's contributions to business strategy.

HR's work has been described with a variety of models, but the HR Triangle Chart (depicted in Figure 4.1), showing HR's three areas of work, is a very effective model for communicating to executives and business leaders just what HR is about.

The three areas in the Triangle Chart can be explained as follows:

- *People capabilities:* The HR outcomes that reflect the "flow of people" through the employment life cycle from finding talent, to developing talent, to retaining/exiting talent.
- *Organizational capabilities:* The HR outcomes that reflect the "flow of work"—from work entering the business to being processed by the business to delivering value for the external customer.
- *HR value proposition:* The top-priority people capability or organizational capability that mitigates a critical business risk. When HR delivers its value proposition, the business will have a much greater probability of realizing its strategic direction.

Figure 4.1: The Triangle Chart of the Three Areas of HR Work

When HR describes these three areas of work to executives, they very often are gratified to finally understand what HR does. When they are told that HR focuses on the capabilities of people to meet the needs of the business, they begin to understand that HR's center of attention is not just on a series of required processes but rather on important outcomes for the business. When HR explains that it focuses on delivering organizational capabilities (such as culture, structure, and change) to meet business needs, executives begin to understand the value HR can provide in those areas as well. The executives also appreciate it when HR is able to articulate clearly and focus on a top HR value proposition that is designed to mitigate a critical business risk.

The Triangle Chart is also an effective way to explain HR's work to HR employees so that they understand what is expected of them. This way, they will learn about the areas that are priorities for HR and understand that they need to develop expertise in both people capabilities and organizational capabilities. They will also be able to align their efforts around a top-priority theme, which is reflected in the HR value proposition.

PEOPLE CAPABILITIES, ORGANIZATIONAL CAPABILITIES, AND HR VALUE PROPOSITIONS

Figure 4.2 on page 56 presents the three-part Triangle Chart with the list of people capabilities, organizational capabilities, and HR value propositions that are explored in detail in this book.

The people capabilities list shown on the chart will be explored in Chapter Five. The list is presented as outcomes rather than in the typical way that HR lists people processes, such as staffing, training, employee relations, and compensation.

The organizational capabilities list is explored in Chapter Six. The list presents the organization's systemic roles in which HR professionals should have expertise and should be able to contribute best practices, insights, and guidance, or at least have access to the external specialists who can contribute to these discussions. All of the organizational capabilities focus on setting the organizational context so that the business will have the readiness to implement its strategy rapidly and effectively.

Three high-probability HR value propositions are explored in greater depth in Part Three, Chapters Seven to Ten. These three HR value propositions are selected based upon experience with private, social enterprise (not-for-profit), and public sector organizations. The three that are explored in depth in Part Three are frequently selected HR value propositions for many businesses.

While it may be argued that some of the areas of HR work can be categorized differently, or even that some areas are missing or that other HR value propositions should have been selected, that is not the essential point. The message is that HR's work can be divided into these three areas of work, and it is essential to identify the top-priority HR value proposition for the business and the external customer.

Figure 4.2: The Areas of HR Work on the Triangle Chart

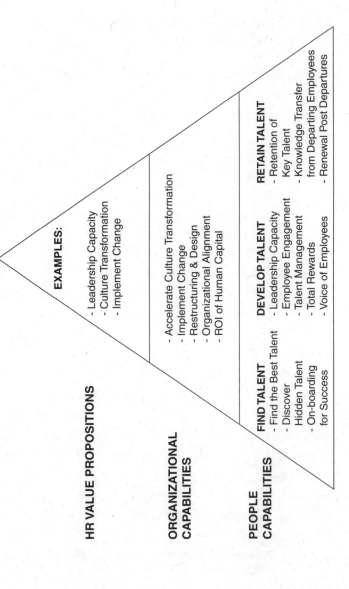

HR VALUE PROPOSITIONS

EXAMPLES:

- Leadership Capacity
- Culture Transformation
- Implement Change

ORGANIZATIONAL CAPABILITIES

- Accelerate Culture Transformation
- Implement Change
- Restructuring & Design
- Organizational Alignment
- ROI of Human Capital

PEOPLE CAPABILITIES

FIND TALENT
- Find the Best Talent
- Discover Hidden Talent
- On-boarding for Success

DEVELOP TALENT
- Leadership Capacity
- Employee Engagement
- Talent Management
- Total Rewards
- Voice of Employees

RETAIN TALENT
- Retention of Key Talent
- Knowledge Transfer from Departing Employees
- Renewal Post Departures

APPLY THE LIGHTEN-UP PROCESS TO THE HR TRIANGLE CHART

Chapter Three explained that for HR to fulfill its role of delivering value to the business, it is necessary for HR to lighten up its work. The following is a technique to engage the HR team in exploring what work it needs to lighten up, using the Triangle Chart as the basis for the discussion.

- HR needs to assess its "current situation" in terms of each team member's workload. Using the Triangle Chart for reference, each team member identifies how his or her current work time is allocated to the three areas of HR work (people capabilities, organizational capabilities, and HR value proposition).

- Next, each member does the same exercise for the "preferred future one year from now," determining how to divide his or her work time differently in order to add maximum value for external customers and advance the business's strategic direction.

- HR then aggregates the individual responses to form a group score. When this exercise is done, the overall results tend to show similar patterns. Variations are sometimes evident depending on the HR organization and how advanced it is.

The graph in Figure 4.3 on page 58 shows an example of the HR work in both the "current situation" and the "preferred future."

In this example, half of the current work is in the people capabilities area, about 35 percent is in the organizational capabilities area, and the remaining 15 percent is in the HR value proposition area. The example of the "preferred future" for HR's work shows a significant reduction of work in the people capabilities area, an increase of work in organizational capabilities, and an increase in focus on the HR value proposition.

The following are some additional points about the graph:

- The area on the right labeled "Start" is the organizational capabilities and HR value proposition work that HR needs to achieve to reach the preferred future. There may also be work to start in people

Figure 4.3: Example of the Current and the Preferred Future Work of HR

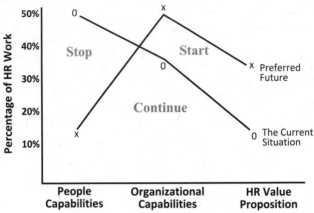

capabilities that will enhance the value HR delivers for the business. However, to simply add "Start" activities without engaging in a process to lighten up others is irresponsible.

- The area on the left of the graph labeled "Stop" reflects the people capabilities work that HR needs to lighten up to make room for the "Start" activities. There may also be work in organizational capabilities that HR should lighten up if it does not add sufficient value for the business. In many cases, HR's inability to stop what it believes it does well makes it difficult for it to discard activities. HR must be explicit about the need to lighten up as much work as it starts.
- The area marked "Continue" represents the current work that HR should continue to do.

The "start, stop, continue" chart tells the entire HR transformation story with the detail left out for later commentary. When an HR team develops the graph, they tend to be more accepting that change is necessary because most people cannot argue with their own data. The graph may indicate that HR needs to lighten up some of its current activities in order to bring new strategic initiatives into the HR repertoire (as described in the 4D process in Chapter Three). The HR professionals almost always concur that some work needs to be stopped. The next step is for HR to identify examples of what needs to be given up and what needs to be done. Of course, additional analyses must then be undertaken to identify precisely what work will be deleted, delayed, distributed, and diminished.

CONCLUSION

The HR Triangle Chart shows how HR's work can be divided into three areas: people capabilities, organizational capabilities, and the HR value proposition. Chapter Five explores the people capabilities and Chapter Six explores the organization capabilities. Following this, HR needs to identify the major HR value proposition that will mitigate a critical business risk. The HR value proposition will also elevate HR's work to a strategic business level and will ensure that HR has a meaningful voice in executive planning and decision-making processes. Chapters Seven to Ten explore three HR value propositions that are frequently chosen to mitigate critical business risks.

SUMMARY

- Many executives do not have a clear understanding of HR's priority areas of work. They may understand that HR develops employee policies, hires people, compensates them, trains them, and so on, but they often do not have a clear idea of HR's contributions to business strategy.

- HR's work has been described with a variety of models, but the Triangle Chart showing HR's three areas of work is a very effective model for communicating to executives and business leaders just what HR is about. The Triangle Chart depicts how HR allocates its work into these three areas:

  - People capabilities: The HR outcomes that reflect the "flow of people" through the employment life cycle, from finding talent, to developing talent, to retaining/exiting talent. (See Chapter Five.)

  - Organizational capabilities: The HR outcomes that reflect the "flow of work," from work entering the business, to being processed by the business, to delivering value for the external customer. (See Chapter Six.)

  - HR value proposition: The top-priority people capability or organizational capability that mitigates a critical business risk. When HR delivers their value proposition, the business will have a much greater probability of achieving its strategic direction. (See Chapters Seven to Ten.)

- HR must examine how to lighten up the workload in the area of people and organizational capabilities in order to focus on the HR value proposition. HR must be explicit about the need to lighten up as much work as they start.

- The HR value proposition elevates the work of HR to a strategic level for the business and ensures that HR will have a meaningful voice in executive planning and decision-making.

CHAPTER FIVE

PEOPLE CAPABILITIES

People Capabilities:
The HR outcomes that reflect the flow of people through the employment life cycle, from finding talent to developing talent, to retaining talent.

One of the important ways HR becomes a leadership-driven function is by excelling in the *people capabilities* roles—finding the best talent, developing the talent, and retaining the talent within the organization. HR must ensure that these people capabilities are performed in a quality manner, in a timely fashion, and at a reasonable cost. When HR delivers the people capabilities, it enhances HR's standing with business leaders in the organization and contributes to HR having a place at the table for making significant contributions to decisions that affect the achievement of the business strategies.

Often, HR is not the deliverer of all parts of the people capabilities. Some of the people capabilities will be delivered by internal resources other than HR or by external resources, while some of the people capabilities will continue to be delivered by HR. HR's focus is on ensuring that the outcomes of the people capabilities actually occur, not on delivering all of the people capabilities themselves.

For example, even in a traditional work environment, the HR people capability to find talent involves many players. These can include the business leader (who identifies the need, conducts interviews, and selects the candidate), the HR professional (who develops the approach to sourcing the candidate and participates in some interviews), the search firm (that provides candidates for positions), other employees (who may identify candidates and participate in the selection process), and internal trainers (who may not even be part of HR but who may orient the new employee to the job).

Table 5.1 presents the people capabilities—from finding talent, to developing talent, to retaining talent. As explained in Chapter One, HR needs to take accountability for the outcomes (and not just the processes). Therefore, the table presents how the people capabilities are expressed as *outcomes* versus how they might be expressed as *processes*.

Table 5.1: The Outcomes for the People Capabilities

People Capabilities	HR Outcomes	HR Processes
Find Talent	• Find the best talent • Discover hidden talent • On-boarding for success	• Selection • Orientation
Develop Talent	• Build leadership capacity • Employee engagement • Talent management • Total rewards • Voice of employees	• Training • Compensation • Employee relations • Labor relations
Retain Talent	• Retention of key talent • Knowledge transfer from departing employees • Renewal post departures	• Retention • Termination

The following sections describe each of the outcomes of the people capabilities and how HR can take accountability for delivering these outcomes.

THE *FIND* PEOPLE CAPABILITY

HR's *find* people capability (at the beginning of the employment cycle) includes delivering the outcomes of finding the best talent, discovering the hidden talent so that unknown candidates will be drawn to the business, and on-boarding new hires for success.

The Outcomes of the *Find* People Capability

- *Find the Best Talent:* Ensuring that the business finds new employees who will meet their work requirements.
- *Discover Hidden Talent:* Ensuring that the business is able to draw out the hidden talent, i.e. those individuals who may not know of the availability of the work.
- *On-Boarding for Success:* Ensuring that the new employee has become acclimated to the business, is likely to deliver the performance requirements, and is willing to remain with the business.

Find the Best Talent

Finding the best talent has always been critical to businesses. HR must have an excellent recruitment process that includes planning, attracting, assessing, hiring, and ultimately performing. In addition, many HR organizations have developed clear outcome metrics for finding the best talent, which typically include three variables: (1) time to hire; (2) cost of hire; and (3) quality of hire. For example, HR can measure the "time to hire" by tracking the time from when the internal hiring manager identifies a need for a new employee to when the employee arrives at the business. They also can measure the "costs of hire" for internal resources and external support in the process. The most challenging metric is the "quality of hire." One measure of quality is the speed with which the new employee achieves an acceptable level of performance effectiveness. HR can also enhance the quality of hire by doing the following:

- Anticipate selection needs even before there is a request for a new employee. This enables HR to forecast skills requirements based on anticipated recruitment needs.
- Teach business leaders to be more consistent in how they specify needs and how they interview, select, and orient.

- Develop a recruiting process that identifies more precise needs of the work and therefore better potential candidates.

Figure 5.1 depicts the return on investment (ROI) for the HR effort in finding the best talent. HR's role is to discover ways to reduce the time required to deliver the best possible outcomes.

Figure 5.1: The ROI of the *Finding the Best Talent* Outcome

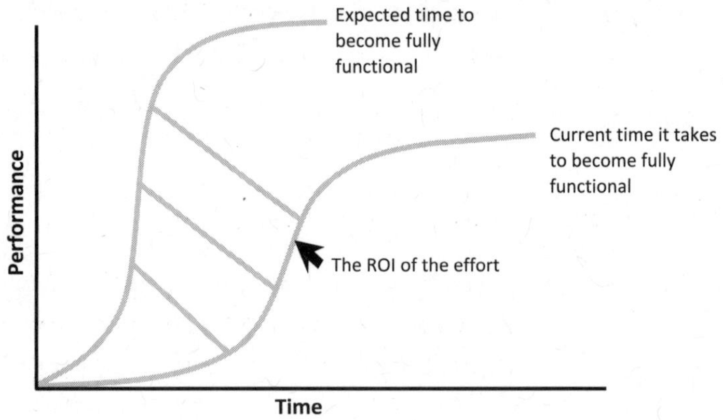

In many businesses, HR departments are discovering innovative ways to find the very best talent for their organizations. When HR achieves this outcome, the business leaders in the organization often know and appreciate HR's contribution and its leadership for the business in this people capability.

Here are some other examples of these innovations:

- An HR department in one organization has a practice of staying in contact with their second-choice candidates for jobs—those who did not get hired but who were excellent candidates. They realized that the second-choice candidate for one position may be a high-quality candidate for another position in their business and keeping in contact with them can significantly reduce the time and cost to hire.
- In one organization, HR worked with business leaders to determine exactly what the needs were for future employees. HR learned that

the organization needed employees who excelled at working in teams. They introduced innovations to meet the business needs including hiring existing teams of employees who currently worked together on projects rather than hiring one person at a time. In other situations they would hire an employee who was an effective member of an existing project team and then engage the new recruit to contact his or her former team members in their previous work situation to inform them of new work opportunities.

- Some other organizations have been effective at targeting diverse segments of the working population that are qualified but unfairly disadvantaged due to archaic biases. In one legal organization, HR noticed that there was a systemic bias against hiring visible minorities, and HR worked with the business leaders to leverage that knowledge and hire highly skilled talent to their organization. Their core values and culture of diversity allowed them to gain a sustainable competitive advantage against their legal competitors.

Discover Hidden Talent

In many business sectors, the traditional ways of finding high-performing employees are not effective enough. HR is taking the lead to leverage every possible advantage they have to find the talent they need for ongoing performance. Some are using social media to get the word out to candidates that a position may fit their talents. They are also giving candidates access to social media so that they can market their talents to their business directly.

Figure 5.2 presents the challenge for HR of discovering hidden talent. The figure compares what the organization actually did (hired or did not hire) with what the "truth" is (whether that employee should be hired or not).

Most HR organizations focus their recruitment efforts on the upper-left-hand box. They want to hire the person that should be hired and avoid hiring the candidate who should not be hired (the bottom-right-hand box). They reduce the "quality of hire" error rate associated

Figure 5.2: Discovering Hidden Talent

		In "Truth"	
		Right Hire	Wrong Hire
What you did	You hired	Congratulations! Can You Retain Them?	Choice Issue Very Costly Error
	You did not hire	Employment Branding Focus: The Missed Opportunities	Good Decision

with the top-right-hand box by assessing candidates through behaviorial interviews, references, psychological assessments, work samples, and so on. However, the greater challenge for many HR organizations is the bottom-left-hand box of "the missed opportunities," which asks: Are there available employees who would be good candidates for your organization whom you are not accessing?

Innovative HR organizations are meeting the challenge to discover the hidden talent that they often do not access through traditional recruitment processes. An effective technique to discover hidden talent is to develop an "employment brand." Essentially, HR organizations use their business's marketing approach to product and service branding for their recruitment advertising and the creation of a powerful employment brand. An "employment brand" is the labor market's perception of employment in your organization. The employment brand packages all employment initiatives under an integrated set of symbols and key messages. The messages must be clear and consistent—if not, your employment brand message may be lost.

The short supply of key talent challenges HR to expand its strategies for finding and retaining key resources. Some HR professionals focus on creative compensation models as the prime enticement of their employment brand. However, there are other compelling and exciting employment brand messages that are very attractive to potential candidates, including providing meaningful challenges, supporting personal career growth opportunities, ensuring that key resources are managed by admired leaders, and accommodating employees' needs regarding the balance between work and personal life.

HR should find ways to enlist the executive leadership's commitment to an employment brand that is appealing to current and potential employees. These ways include the following:

- Develop the employment brand with the executives based upon the business's current and anticipated future needs.
- Align the employment brand tightly with the marketing brand that is known to customers. Ensure that the employment brand reinforces the marketing brand.
- Set up cross-functional, multi-level teams to advise on the employment branding inputs and outputs and the evaluation of the branding.
- Leverage social media to create interest in high-profile locations, and market to candidates as you do to customers.

On-Boarding for Success

"On-boarding" is the final outcome in the *find* people capability. An employment position is not really filled until the business can ensure that the new employee has acclimated to the business, is likely to deliver the performance requirements, and will remain with the business.

It is preferable to place on-boarding in the *find* people capability rather than the *develop* people capability of the employment life cycle. This decision is driven by the needs of the business leader who is hiring rather than by the activities undertaken during on-boarding. When a business leader has a need for an additional employee, he or she believes that the hiring request is fulfilled when the person is selected and on board, and not simply when the person arrives on the job for the first day. HR, on the other hand, may view on-boarding as a training function because it has characteristics that are similar to training and performance development, including that it may be done in a classroom, it has a particular design, and it can be offered in a repeated fashion. HR should define this process outcome based on the perspective of the business leader who is doing the hiring.

Effective on-boarding of new employees will allow business leaders to gain more immediate value from the new hire. Employees are typically more open to instruction during the first few weeks in their new role. HR should be guiding business leaders to use that time to work closely with new employees, build relationships, and create a common language they can draw upon as the employees become more independent in their responsibilities. They also should spend time after people are hired to work with them, have conversations about work, and build their relationships.

HR also has a role in orchestrating the on-boarding process through more formal means. For example:

- One business emphasizes a new employee on-boarding process which lasts for the first three months on the job, until the completion of the employee's probation. They also build in an expectation that some new recruits will not pass probation, and they offer a small financial incentive for the employee who does not pass probation to leave the business.

- Another business has a new leader on-boarding program that includes presentations from all areas of the business and is held four to six times a year. The HR professional orients new business leaders through a one-on-one intensive session to review all elements of their new role and to begin the process of building a relationship with HR as an added-value resource. HR also participates in an assimilation process to discuss the work environment and the expectation that business leaders need to be people leaders as well.

THE *DEVELOP* PEOPLE CAPABILITY

HR's *develop* people capability (in the middle of the employment cycle) typically includes performing all HR services from the completion of the new employee orientation until the time the employee considers leaving or is about to leave the business. This capability is an important expectation of HR, since it includes the employees' full term of employment. The following are the outcomes of the *develop* people capability that are explored in this section:

The Outcomes of the *Develop* People Capability

- *Build Leadership Capacity:* Ensuring that the business has the leadership capacity it requires to continue to grow and develop.
- *Employee Engagement:* Ensuring that employees are aligned to the business direction and are engaged to give their discretionary efforts to the business.
- *Talent Management:* Ensuring that the business has the talent it requires to deliver the work.
- *Total Rewards:* Ensuring that all monetary and non-monetary rewards and recognition motivate employees to perform in the desired way.
- *Voice of Employees:* Ensuring that the business is responsive to the opinions and needs of employees and that employees can be self-reliant to meet their own needs as appropriate.

Build Leadership Capacity and Employee Engagement

Two of the outcomes of the *develop* people capability—"build leadership capacity" and "employee engagement"—are frequently chosen as value propositions that HR promises to deliver to mitigate a critical business risk. For example:

- *Build leadership capacity* is often chosen as an overall HR value proposition when the business risk is associated with not having the required leadership to help the business grow and develop.
- *Employee engagement* is chosen as an HR value proposition when the business risk is associated with a significant change (such as a merger or acquisition, change in the nature of work, or business

crisis) that may result in employees losing motivation to perform for the business.

Both of these outcomes are described in detail in Chapter Eight: *Build Leadership Capacity*. The rationale for presenting "employee engagement" as part of "build leadership capacity" is that employee engagement is one of the essential expectations of business leaders as people leaders. HR has the accountability to build the leadership capacity so that business leaders are able to effectively engage their employees and teams.

This section will therefore explore the remaining outcomes of talent management, total rewards, and being the voice of employees.

Talent Management

"Talent management" refers to the outcome of ensuring that the business has competent talent, both currently and in the future, to meet its business requirements. Figure 5.3 shows the three main areas of talent management.

Figure 5.3: The Three Main Areas of Talent Management

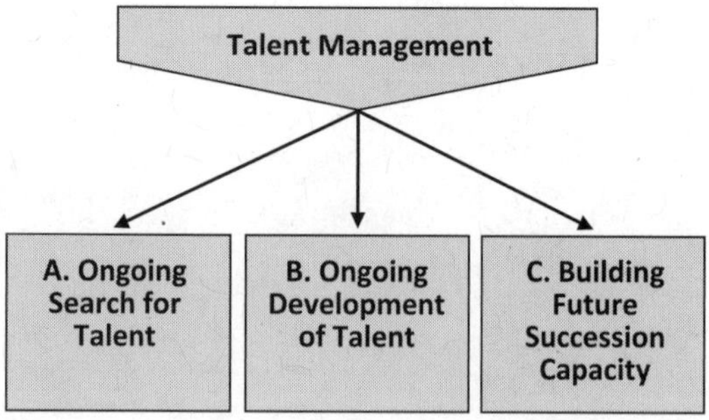

Talent management views any request for talent from the external customer perspective and asks how the needs of the external customer can be met. HR professionals are expected to consider which talent management option will ensure that the business has the talent it requires when and where it is needed. HR professionals need to find the best option to meet the request for talent, asking business leaders questions such as, "Is hiring a new employee the best solution or would it be better to develop the current cadre of employees to better meet the needs of the customer?" As a result, talent management requires HR to work collaboratively across its various specialties to deliver integrated solutions that meet business needs.

Talent management includes HR's accountability to ensure that business leaders and employees remain competent as the expectations and demands of the business change. HR does not fulfill this responsibility alone. Business leaders develop their employees, peers contribute to their learning, and employees are expected to be self-reliant and to self-learn as well. In addition, external resources are often used as experts to teach employees and managers how to perform in the desired manner.

HR should help business leaders to become people leaders by encouraging them to exercise seven essential accountabilities in the ongoing development of talent. These include the following:

1. Taking responsibility for the talent management of the employees in their units.
2. Having conversations about what is needed from leadership, employees, and teams to make the organization successful.
3. Developing backups for key talent (and for the business leader) so that the business leaders can support their employees' career development.
4. Ensuring that time is allocated for employees to receive the development they require.
5. Taking responsibility for respectful and candid feedback to employees to target development to the employees' specific needs. ·
6. Addressing problem employee performance appropriately and in a timely manner.
7. Asking for help when they are not sure what to do (i.e., the business leaders should find a mentor to talk things through—and then act).

HR also has important accountabilities in the ongoing development of talent. For example:

- Identifying the competencies needed for the work to perform at an acceptable and at a differentiating level.
- Creating the context to help employees learn continuously so that they remain competent in their work areas as they accept new responsibilities and advance in their careers.
- Designing the career development process so that employees can fulfill their potential in directions that are in the best interests of the business and the external customer.

HR's accountability is to ensure that employees have the opportunity to stay fully competent. The process outcome measure is the time, quality, and cost of the process to restore employees to full competence in their new or adjusted work responsibilities.

Consider the following scenario for a business with a traditional HR training unit:

An HR organization boasts that it has a training department with approximately 200 courses and 50 staff members to manage and deliver the programs. The HR staff believes they are doing a great service to the business. The employees who attend courses are pleased with the education and training. However, the executives see limited value and return on this significant investment. All they see is a large number of courses that look more like a school than a focused professional development process.

HR undertakes a study of the training department. Many of the courses have fewer than 10 people in attendance. Intense tracking and fee transfer efforts frustrate business leaders who send employees to the courses. The training area is viewed as an expensive school that is not focused on what the business needs to be doing and what the external customer requires.

The review includes interviews with the business's 30 executives, most of whom are new hires in newly created positions with recent experiences at other major businesses. The executives are asked how they would design a training department from scratch if they had the opportunity to start over. The overwhelming majority of

the executives, including the veterans of the business and the newcomers, recommend
the following:

- *Focus internal training and development on strategic objectives. This means that the HR training department designs and delivers internally only the programs that will give the business competitive advantage or competitive parity.*
- *Create an environment in which people will be able to be self-reliant and learn on their own.*
- *Have the HR training department broker the remainder of the courses to preferred external service providers.*
- *Have HR keep the prime contact role with business leaders to identify needs and source the appropriate suppliers.*

By focusing on planning, ongoing contact, and strategic service delivery, HR lightens up a great deal of work and energy to invest in other business outcomes. HR then proceeds to redesign the training area so that it focuses on the business requirements for the ongoing development of talent. Eventually, HR is able to run the training depart-ment with fewer people, and is able to deliver more value with its programs at a significantly lower cost.

There are five principles for HR professionals as they support the ongoing development of talent.

- *Principle 1—The primary purpose of training is to teach people how to self-learn rather than teaching them content.* Some businesses have identified lifelong learning as a critical success factor. If people are always learning and are open to learning from others, the culture will be more agile and change will be more readily accepted. Busi-ness leaders will also find that ongoing learning will help them with decision-making. Today's work environment is increasingly complex and constantly changing. Business leaders must have the opportunity to learn continuously in order to be able to deal with the ambiguity and uncertainty of making decisions. Ongoing learn-ing is also essential for all employees. Businesses should be creating opportunities for employees to upgrade continually so that their skills do not become obsolete.

HR's role must focus on teaching people how to self-learn, not on teaching content. When HR creates an environment that supports continuous learning, the nature of what people learn changes. The purpose is not to impart the content. People should be able to learn the content continuously and independently. The emphasis is on teaching people how to learn—how to stay current and up-to-date on a day-by-day basis. They no longer have to wait for a course to be presented. They are taught the learning skills so that they can access the tools online and learn by themselves.

- *Principle 2—Business leaders are accountable for creating an ongoing learning environment.* While HR can be accountable for continuous learning in the business overall, HR should guide business leaders to take responsibility for ongoing learning opportunities in their work units. Business leaders as people leaders have a major accountability for the ongoing education of employees. In addition, business leaders become sharper and more knowledgeable in their own areas of expertise when they articulate knowledge and share ideas with employees.

- *Principle 3—All employees are accountable for their own learning.* The first and second principles set the climate for employees to recognize that they are held accountable for their own learning. Employees need to have access to the appropriate sources of knowledge, and they need to take responsibility for their own continual learning—no one can do it for them. In the old working environment, knowledge was power. In the new working environment, knowledge is a shared resource. Since all knowledge is accessible, except perhaps specific strategic information, all employees have the opportunity to learn as well as to add value to discussions. It is essential for HR to respect the intellectual capacity of every employee to correctly grasp and comprehend this information in order for employees to be accountable for their own learning.

This principle also has many spin-off effects. When employees take responsibility for their own learning, they tend to share experiences readily across the business. Cross-functionality of teams is encouraged because people can contribute ideas to other areas even if they are not experts in them. HR can set the stage for this learning environment by creating group and learning settings meant for participation by all employees, not just those with the most seniority or the highest positions in the business.

- *Principle 4—Learning occurs "just in time," when and how it is needed.* "Just-in-time" learning means learning anywhere, anyhow, and any time you need it. With just-in-time learning, people are able to adapt more quickly to changes. In the optimum environment, everyone is able to access knowledge that is readily available when they have a compelling need for it. Through the use of online technology, shared knowledge can come just in time. The prerequisite is for people to be willing to share information freely and openly and to have people prepared to self-learn. The principle of teaching people how to learn rather than teaching them content is based on employees getting information when they actually need to learn and not when they are scheduled to attend a course. Here is an example of just-in-time learning in a traditional manufacturing environment:

> Consider a manufacturing plant where an inventive plant manager decides to facilitate just-in-time learning. In this work environment, stopping the workflow for a brief period of time will not put a severe dent in efficiency. He places a flip chart in each work unit and then instructs each manager to stop everyone in his or her unit from working when something goes wrong and ask them to gather around the flip chart. The manager uses the flip chart to illustrate the scenario and to facilitate a discussion about how to do it right the next time. Learning in this plant environment is designed to happen as the need to learn occurs.

- *Principle 5—The entire organization shares what has been learned.* On a much broader scale, the entire organization can share what they learn about effective and ineffective practices. If everyone knows what others know, the organization will have a wealth of knowledge. Also, the organization can lose a lot of knowledge when a person retires or leaves. It is important to discover ongoing ways to map what people know and ensure that the intellectual capital remains with the organization as much as possible.

The idea of sharing information about ineffective practices may be even more important than sharing information about what is effective. Ineffective practices are those actions that the organization needs to "unlearn." When these practices are shared with employees, it helps them avoid the pathway to the problems previously encountered. The work environment should support sharing about what to lighten up so that others know what no longer applies and should not be done. Sharing ineffective practices can help people avoid wasting time by making someone else's mistakes.

By following these five principles, HR can transform the role of training and development to an essential element of talent management that delivers value for the business. HR can also create an environment for continuous learning in which employees have the tools to adapt as changes occur and to help set the stage for the implementation of the business's strategic direction.

The talent management outcome also includes identifying successors for positions that may become vacant in the future. In particular, HR should focus on talent management solutions for critical business positions that need successor candidates. Most businesses have very few positions that could be considered critical positions. Critical positions[1] are defined as positions that have two features:

1. The position is essential to the strategic direction of the business.

2. The position has "unique characteristics" (e.g., unique stakeholder relations, highly specialized knowledge or technology, requirement for specialized experience) that need to be developed internally in order to accelerate the learning curve for the candidate.

---

1. See David S. Weiss and Vince Molinaro, "Focus on Critical Positions and Key Talent," in *The Leadership Gap* (Toronto: John Wiley & Sons, 2005), ch. 12.

Once the critical positions are identified, then the business allocates specialized funding for the targeted development of internal candidates to be the successors for these positions (especially for positions where the incumbent is likely to leave the business). Metrics are also used to track successors' development to reduce the possibility of risk to the business in those critical positions. The other non-critical senior positions still have identified candidates who are ready to replace them in the event of a sudden or planned departure. However, it is clearly understood that in most cases these candidates are interim replacements and not formal successors for the positions.

A different kind of problem appears in building future succession capacity in owner-operated businesses. The owner's emotional ties can sometimes block his or her ability to see the need to pass the leadership to the next person. Also, owners often select one of their children to be the next leader even when that child may not be the best qualified or their selection process may create family problems that carry well beyond the workplace. Succession in owner-operated businesses often operates with a model of concentric circles. The owner is in the center. The immediate family is often in the next circle outside the center. In the third circle are the trusted, long-standing colleagues (regardless of their positions in the business). The other circles are for the rest of the employees. Usually, those in the inner circles are considered for succession for senior positions before those in the outer circles. When I explained this concept to a frustrated HR VP in an owner-operated business, she began to understand why she felt excluded from the inner-circle conversations. It also clarified why her opinions as well as some other executives' ideas were ignored and some more junior directors' ideas were listened to. It shaped her understanding of the owner's desires for succession and how he would most likely want to proceed. She confirmed this impression with the owner and discovered that acceptable candidates for succession came primarily from the inner circles.

Total Rewards

The "total rewards" outcome focuses on the full suite of monetary and non-monetary rewards that can be offered to employees to motivate them to perform and stay with the business. This includes designing compensation and recognition programs to create a desirable environment and eliminating motivators that encourage people to do things that are not desirable. The question for HR and the business leaders is whether the total rewards actually drive the desired behaviors that the business requires.

It is often helpful if HR annually provides each employee with a total compensation statement to increase their knowledge of their total rewards package. HR can also lighten up some of its roles in the total rewards area. For example, HR can streamline most of the technical components of pay and benefits and outsource them to specialists in this area.

In addition, some businesses have empowered employees to adjust their mix of total compensation as well as their flexible benefits within specific guidelines. If employees need financial guidance, they could have resources available to them for advice up to a specific budgetary limit. The flexibility to adjust their compensation and benefits allows employees to allocate their financial assets to meet their individual needs (e.g., dental care for families with young children versus life insurance and pension plans for older employees). Some businesses apply this flexible total-rewards approach to executive perquisites as well. They allow each executive to select the combination of perquisites they would like (based on the funds allocated for this purpose), whether they join a health club or move some of these dollars into a retirement plan. This approach also removes HR from the transactional role of managing these perquisites for the executives.

Voice of Employees

A traditional expectation of HR is to be the voice of employees. HR can assist in a number of ways, such as:

- Creating an environment wherein employees can have direct access to voice their own opinions within the organization.

- Voicing employees' concerns and ideas if they do not receive satisfaction through their leaders.
- Helping executives know what employees think and feel.

HR has direct ways to learn about the feelings and perceptions of employees—for example, through employee surveys. Some businesses are using sampling theory to survey employees and to increase the frequency of the survey process. Here is what one HR organization did:

HR decided to use sampling theory to collect data from employees more frequently. Their usual method of gathering data was through an annual employee survey but the executives wanted data to be collected monthly. HR decided to conduct a "pulse" survey with a random sample of 10 percent of the population. The sample was large enough to give a reliable prediction of the entire workforce population. They were thus able to collect the data and have a better sense of employee attitudes and beliefs without burdening all employees to complete a survey monthly.

This approach is particularly useful for businesses undergoing rapid change. HR works as a business partner to executives, often helping them to know what the employees feel and how they are responding to the change. HR should prepare the executives to anticipate that the employee survey results will be uneven. Employees may not receive changes well, even if the changes are in the best interests of the customer and/or the business. However, if HR and the executives know that the response to changes tends to fluctuate, they will have a better chance to respond quickly to the needs of employees and the business.

HR often offers employee relations (ER) services as a one-on-one counseling support function to give voice to employees' issues. The employee relations role can be a challenge for HR professionals if they are the first point of contact for employees' concerns. Sometimes it can also be all-consuming for HR to have to respond to unplanned individual crises. HR can lighten up their work in employee relations in the following ways:

- Educate and support business leaders in fulfilling their role in employee relations. HR is then positioned as the second line of defense to address employee issues in situations where the business leader has not resolved the issue effectively.

- Designate an HR professional who is an employee relations specialist to respond to employee relations issues. This will remove the unpredictable employee relations interruptions for HR business partners.

- Position HR as the first line of defense to address employee issues in situations where it would be inappropriate for the business leader to handle them (e.g., harassment cases, human rights situations, illegal acts by employees, compliance issues, or legal cases).

- Provide employee assistance programs through external, confidential service providers for employees' personal, family, and work-related issues.

In some cases the voice of employees is represented by a collective body (not HR) such as a union or an employee association. However, HR still has an important role as the voice of employees along with these employee representatives.

Figure 5.4 presents two conflicting scenarios. The left-hand scenario suggests that when employees select a representative body (i.e., a union or employee association), those representatives become the intermediary between the employees and management. This scenario suggests that all communications proceed through the union. However, although unions

Figure 5.4: The Three-Way Relationship in a Unionized Environment

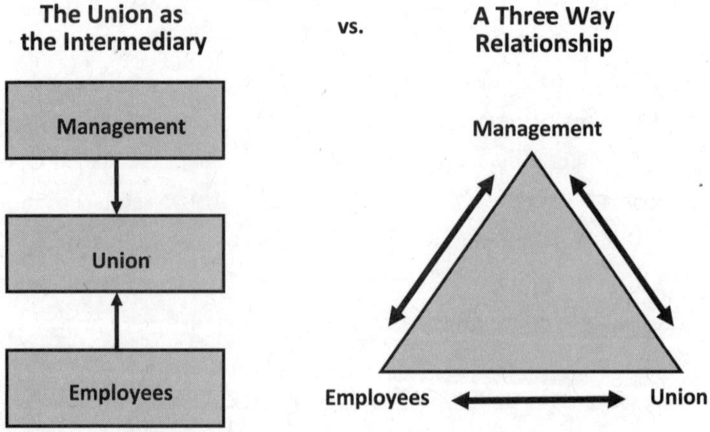

The Union as the Intermediary vs. A Three Way Relationship

may prefer the intermediary scenario, it is almost always dysfunctional for businesses. It is within business leaders' management rights to communicate directly with their employees. The scenario on the right-hand side of Figure 5.4 shows the proper way of communicating.

There are times when the union is the voice of the employees—for example, during collective bargaining and when representing employees for grievances and arbitrations. There are also specific times when management will engage in discussions and negotiations directly with the union. However, on a day-to-day basis, the managers continue to have direct contact with employees for all work assignments and for other performance-related matters. HR functions as the voice of employees in this scenario as well. HR can continue to be the voice of employees through talent management, employee surveys, and employee relations as long as HR does this consistently (and not as an influencing tactic during the identified time for bargaining a new collective agreement).

In addition, HR has recognized that the traditional adversarial way of approaching unions creates internal conflict and a dysfunctional organization. Businesses that have made sincere attempts to forge new relationships with employee associations and unions have made significant gains. My first book, *Beyond the Walls of Conflict: Mutual Gains Negotiating for Unions and Management* (1996),[2] describes how to change the nature of these relationships. Businesses and unions that have used the principles and techniques proposed in that book have been able to move from adversarial relationships to ones that are more constructive. The potential is there to elevate the relationship with employee associations and unions to a level that adds value to the business. HR has the capability to transform what may be perceived as a strategic liability into a strategic asset and to partner with business leaders in this process. When HR contributes to making that kind of change, it often has a huge impact on the business, its leaders, and its employees.

---

2. The book, written by David S. Weiss, has been reprinted and is now available under a new title: *In Search of the 18th Camel: Discovering the Mutual Gains Oasis for Unions and Management* (Kingston, ON: Queen's University IRC Press, 2003).

THE *RETAIN* PEOPLE CAPABILITY

The *retain* people capability focuses on retaining employees, or at least their knowledge, to avoid the risk associated with early departures and unwanted terminations.

Employees leave organizations for many reasons, including seeking other career opportunities, escaping from the current employment situation, being asked to leave by the organization (terminations, downsizing), and completing their fixed term of employment (retirement, contract completion). HR is accountable for ensuring that people who leave the business do so with dignity. The challenge to HR in the *retain* people capability is to increase the probability that key talent is retained in the organization and, if employees do depart, that they transfer their knowledge so that the business does not lose the key asset of the employees' intellectual capital when they leave.

Here are the essential outcomes in the *retain* people capability:

The Outcomes of the *Retain* People Capability

- *Retention of Key Talent:* Ensuring that the business does not have any unwanted departures that could compromise the enterprise's performance.
- *Knowledge Transfer from Departing Employees:* Ensuring that the business continues to have access to valuable knowledge when an employee departs.
- *Renewal Post-Departures:* Ensuring that the business is able to renew the employee commitment after other employees leave the organization (voluntarily or involuntarily).

Retention of Key Talent

HR must develop strategies for retaining key talent—especially those who are instrumental in providing competitive advantage for the business. When other businesses are raiding key talent, retention strategies take on an even higher degree of importance.

Here is an example of how an organization was able to retain their key talent:

A financial planning business had an urgent need to develop a retention plan for highly coveted financial analysts because of its competitor's aggressive recruiting practices. The competitor placed many advertisements that compared its benefits plan with the financial planning business's benefits plan (the competitor's package was considerably better) and concluded with a strong message to call the competitor. HR saw the risk and worked with the business leaders to develop a countering strategy to retain the talented financial analysts. Their strategy was to build the employment brand for their business for both external recruits and existing key talent. Some of the retention tactics that HR devised included:

- *Financial incentives such as flexibility in pay and benefits to meet employees' personal needs;*
- *Workplace environment incentives such as personalized work space and flexibility regarding work and personal life balance, including working from home options;*
- *Focus on achieving employees' full potential by providing continuous development, additional autonomy to make decisions, and specific career advancement opportunities;*
- *Developing plans with the key talent "fast trackers." This approach included letting the key talent know they were fast trackers and that they would be given the opportunity to develop new skills through work transfers or by playing leadership roles on various projects;*
- *Providing a special page on the business's intranet site: "How to Talk to Headhunters." It included a list of questions to ask recruiters so that employees could make an educated choice if they were considering an opportunity elsewhere.*

The principle in retention is to have one-on-one conversations to discover the underlying motivators that will entice employees to stay rather than leave. HR then provides a menu of choices from which employees are able to design their own retention plan that will meet their needs precisely.

For example:

One business was populated by young, highly skilled industrial designers. Many of these employees were coveted by their competitors. HR needed to develop a retention strategy. They realized that these employees did not care about some of the organization's traditional recognitions, which were very important in other parts of their business. For example, family BBQ parties and 10-year pins had little motivation for them.

This task was quite complex because what tends to keep younger employees happy is very different from what matters to older employees. Benefits and compensation were, of course, part of this retention strategy. However, they found that new ideas were required for younger employees. HR decided to develop a menu of choices with a specific budget for the indirect methods of retention. They were able to fashion a retention approach that suited the individual needs of the younger key resources.

Knowledge Transfer from Departing Employees

Some organizations lose more than talent when employees depart from the business—they lose the employees' intellectual capital. HR is then challenged to find a way to retain the intellectual capital before the person leaves the organization. HR shares this outcome with both the departing employee and his or her business leader. The accountabilities can be divided as follows:

- *Departing employee:* The departing employee should be held accountable for recording the knowledge either through interviews or by directly inputting the knowledge in a wiki system on themes and topics that employees can easily search.
- *Business leader of the departing employee:* The business leader of the departing employee should be accountable for ensuring that the employee's knowledge is not lost from the business.
- *Human resources:* HR is accountable for defining the process, ensuring that business leaders are able to fulfill this accountability, and monitoring the process to be certain that the knowledge transfer has taken place. In some cases, HR may be the content limiter to control the dissemination of the knowledge so it is used by the proper resources.

There are many challenges with knowledge transfer from departing employees. Here are some suggestions for how each challenge can be addressed:

- *How can the process be controlled so that it does not become an overwhelming challenge?* One organization decided to invest in knowledge transfer only for employees who were perceived to have specialized knowledge or experience that was not readily available in the public domain.

- *How can useful information that should be transferred be determined versus information that is not useful or is out of date?* One HR organization decided to collect information and questions from the associates of the departing employee, who clearly defined what the associates wanted to know. The departing employee was asked specific questions and the responses were documented in a central database that was searchable. This approach increased the associates' interest in the departing employee's knowledge after it was collected. Another organization asked new employees what they needed to know, and those employees met with the departing employees to collect the information. The new employees then met together to share what they had learned.

- *How can a business motivate employees who are departing to share their knowledge?* In most situations where employees depart voluntarily (e.g., retiring, transferring to another role, taking a leave of absence), the departing employees are quite honored to share what they know as a legacy for the business. One organization hired a cadre of students from the local university to collect the departing retirees' career stories. The stories were printed in a self-published internal book that became part of the business archives. Each departing employee received a copy of the book as a gift when they retired.

- *How can a business leverage knowledge from employees after their departure?* One organization decided to offer mentorship roles to employees close to retirement as a way to encourage knowledge transfer. The organization then used the retirees to be mentors post-departure. For example, one retired senior vice president with experience on the board of directors became the mentor for a new VP who was starting to get involved with the board.

Here are some innovative examples of how HR in various organizations has ensured knowledge transfer from departing employees:

Story #1: *One retiring vice president believed her experience and knowledge was not widely known in the business. She worked with HR to invest some of her training budget to hire a consultant who could help her document her experiences in her role over many years and the key insights that she believed should be shared. The report was eventually used in the on-boarding of her replacement.*

Story #2: *An HR director of training and development in a large college was retiring. He had established some innovative development programs for faculty, administration, and management. He took on the accountability to document his journey over the past 10 years in order to build the training and development programs, with particular emphasis on the compelling reasons for the programs and their unique features. He also developed an ex post facto vision and a set of strategic objectives. Although that plan had not been in place 10 years earlier, it helped in the communication of what he achieved to his eventual replacement.*

Story #3: *The CEO of a well-known center for people with disabilities was retiring after 20 years of outstanding leadership, innovation, and fundraising. HR coordinated a meeting for over 100 people, including current and former employees, key stakeholders, health-care providers, and funders. They divided the large group into eight major themes, and participants self-selected themselves into groups to answer three questions: (1) What was the situation like 20 years ago? (2) How is that situation different today as a result of the CEO? and (3) What were the major milestones that occurred in the journey from 20 years ago to today? The ideas were documented, shared with the entire group, and compiled in a book of impact stories in the eight areas of exploration.*

Renewal Post-Departures

HR's *retain* people capability includes ensuring that the business is able to renew employee commitments after a major downsizing. The challenge, though, is that downsizing and terminations can become a major time consumer for many HR professionals. It also can have a negative impact on the employees who stay with the business if the downsizing is not done properly. As a result, HR must ensure that the following best practices in downsizing guide them when employees depart the business:

- Provide early warning for employees and sufficient time for them to prepare and execute redeployment and re-employment initiatives.
- Adopt aggressive redeployment efforts to minimize the need for layoffs.
- Identify and secure alternatives to job elimination (e.g., job sharing, reduced wages, reduced work weeks).
- Provide funds and/or opportunities for employees to develop skills or retrain and facilitate access to internal and external resources (e.g., colleges and universities) for these services.
- Provide ongoing outplacement and support services up to the time of termination and, preferably, to the point of reemployment.

If staff reductions must occur, HR needs to be able to ensure that the impact of the downsizing is minimized for those who are retained. Therefore, it is advisable for HR to let an outplacement firm focus on the downsizing of staff while HR concentrates on rebuilding for the long term and motivating the retained employees. HR should concentrate on the renewal of the business, investing in human capital to enable the retained employees to rebuild the enterprise, and delivering value for the business and the external customer. Some renewal practices that HR should emphasize in partnership with business leaders include the following:

- Ensure the employees understand the compelling reasons that necessitated the downsizing and its implications for the ongoing viability of the business. Be open about information and share knowledge willingly.
- Engage retained employees in problem-solving groups to help determine the future direction for their part of the business.
- Honor the past and provide retained employees with the opportunity for social support through the transition. At the same time, look to the future evolution of the business.

- Avoid referring to the retained employees as "survivors," as if they were lucky they were not fired. The more appropriate language is to refer to the business as being in a renewal stage that will be built with the business's valued employees.

CONCLUSION

When HR is able to deliver the people capabilities of *find, develop,* and *retain,* the business leaders will be more willing to partner with HR for competitive advantage. The people capabilities must be delivered with precision, quality, and timeliness, and at the appropriate cost. However, some HR organizations make the mistake of viewing success in the people capabilities as their only focus until they "get it right." Many executives are demanding more from their HR business partners and are becoming more impatient in expecting it. Just as executives want strategic value to mean higher revenue and at the same time lower cost, they want HR to deliver the people capabilities *and at the same time* contribute to the organizational capabilities and the HR value propositions that are described in the next few chapters.

SUMMARY

- One of the important ways HR becomes a leadership-driven function is to excel in the people capabilities roles—finding the best talent, developing the talent, and retaining the talent within the organization.

- HR must ensure that the people capabilities are performed in a quality manner, in a timely fashion, and at a reasonable cost. HR is not necessarily the deliverer of the people capabilities but it must ensure that they occur effectively.

- In the *find* people capability (at the beginning of the employment cycle), the outcomes include finding the best talent, excelling at discovering hidden talent, and on-boarding new hires successfully. Innovative HR organizations are taking on the challenge to discover the hidden talent that they often would not otherwise access through innovative recruitment processes.

- In the *develop* people capability (at the middle of the employment cycle), the outcomes are to ensure there is the leadership capacity to deliver the business strategy, that employees are engaged, that HR is implementing effective talent management solutions, that total rewards for employees are motivational, and that the voices of employees are heard.

- In the *retain* people capability (at the conclusion of the employment cycle), the employee either leaves the business or attempts are made to retain the employee so that he or she does not leave. HR must develop strategies for retaining key talent—especially those who are instrumental in providing competitive or comparative advantage for the business. When other businesses are raiding key talent, retention strategies take on an even higher degree of importance. HR also must ensure that there is an effective knowledge transfer during departures and a renewal of employee commitment after others leave the business.

- Many executives are demanding more from their HR business partners and are becoming more impatient in expecting it. Just as executives want strategic value to mean higher revenue and at the same time lower cost, they want HR to deliver the people capabilities and at the same time contribute to the organizational capabilities and the HR value proposition.

CHAPTER SIX

ORGANIZATIONAL CAPABILITIES

Organizational Capabilities:

The HR outcomes that reflect the flow of work—*from work entering the business, to being processed by the business, to delivering value for the external customer.*

One of the most significant changes for HR over the past decade has been the expectation that HR should demonstrate excellence in organizational capabilities. HR has always been expected to excel at the people capabilities, which refers to the *flow of people* through their employment life cycle. However, the expectation of excelling at organizational capabilities, which refers to the *flow of work* through the business, is very recent.

A University of Michigan Business School[1] study asked an important question about HR: what essential business knowledge does HR need to have? Some might guess that HR needs to have the business acumen to understand financial balance sheets. However, that is not a differentiating expectation of HR excellence. What this research found is that HR needs to understand the integrated value chain or the *flow of work* starting from when it enters into the business, how it is processed, and eventually how it delivers value to the external customer. By understanding the flow

---

1. Wayne Brockbank, "Competencies for the New HR," University of Michigan Business School, 2002.

of work, HR has the credibility to contribute to the way work is structured, to know how to align cross-functional work, to understand how changes should be implemented, and to help create the kind of culture the organization needs to enable the achievement of its business strategy. We refer to the flow-of-work roles for HR as the *organizational capabilities*.

There are five essential organizational capabilities explored in this book. They are:

The Five Major Organizational Capabilities
- *Accelerating Cultural Transformation:* Ensuring that the organizational culture transforms rapidly enough to enable the business strategy to occur.
- *Implementing Change:* Ensuring that business changes are implemented effectively and that people adjust to and adopt the changes rapidly.
- *Restructuring and Design:* Ensuring that the formal and informal organizational structures and design of work enable the business to achieve its strategy.
- *Organizational Alignment:* Ensuring that the business works effectively across functions and does not operate with dysfunctional silos.
- *ROI of Human Capital:* Ensuring that the human capital investments deliver an acceptable level of return for the business.

CULTURAL TRANSFORMATION AND IMPLEMENTING CHANGE

The first two organizational capabilities, accelerating cultural transformation and implementing change, are described in detail in Chapters Nine and Ten respectively. Both of these organizational capabilities are frequently chosen as value propositions that HR promises to deliver to mitigate a critical business risk. Here are some reasons why:

- *Accelerating cultural transformation* is often chosen as an overall HR value proposition when the business risk is that the organization's current culture motivates employees to behave in ways that are inconsistent with the business strategy. For example, if the strategy requires risk taking but the culture is characterized by risk aversion, often the cultural characteristics block the successful implementation of the strategy. HR needs to mitigate that risk by accelerating cultural transformation through the methods described in Chapter Nine.

- *Implementing change* is often chosen as an HR value proposition when the business risk is associated with a significant change that may generate employee or stakeholder resistance. For example, if a business is trying to catch up to the leader in the industry, it may need to implement numerous changes to its business and organizational processes. The business risk is that the organization will be unable to implement the changes quickly and repeatedly. HR mitigates that risk by implementing changes through the methods described in Chapter Ten.

This chapter will explore the remaining three HR organizational capabilities of restructuring and design, cross-functional alignment, and ROI of human capital.

RESTRUCTURING AND DESIGN

When HR professionals understand the flow of work, they have the prerequisite knowledge to contribute to restructuring discussions by business leaders. Here is an example of an executive team that made many mistakes in the process of restructuring their organization. They would have benefited from the guidance of a skilled HR professional.

An executive team of a chemicals company held an emergency meeting to respond to some recent surprising events. In the two weeks preceding the meeting, three key directors were recruited to join a competitor. The executives realized that they had to do something to retain their remaining directors, so they decided that they should restructure the organization to give the directors more responsibility, which would also justify paying them more. Their approach was to write all the

directors' names on yellow sticky notes and post them on a wall. They then debated how to move the
sticky notes to form a new structure for the directors, giving each a greater scope of responsibility.

As a result of this work, the executives redesigned their company and provided their
directors with a greater scope of responsibilities and increased compensation. However,
they did not think about the impact that these structural changes would have on the business
strategy. One year later, the business was successful at retaining its directors, but the new
structure made the achievement of its strategy much more difficult. It took more time to
deliver products to customers, which reduced customer loyalty, and the new departments
did not work well together to focus on business growth.

The fundamental error in this example is that the executive team
restructured around people, rather than restructuring to deliver the strategy. Too often the organizational structure is changed to create a job for
a key talent or to compensate when an individual leaves an organization.
Had there been an HR expert in restructuring or an HR professional
who had access to expert advice, then the executives might have realized
that their approach to restructuring was flawed.

Here are seven key principles that should guide how HR professionals
contribute to the organizational capability of restructuring and design.

The Seven Key Principles in Restructuring and Design

Principle #1: Structure always follows strategy, not people.

Principle #2: At the outset, establish criteria for success and "non-
negotiables" for the restructured organization.

Principle #3: Identify the hierarchical structural options to
determine where authorities reside.

Principle #4: Address hierarchical structural limitations with
lateral processes.

Principle #5: Use the least authority for the lateral processes that
allow the hierarchical structure to work well.

Principle #6: If a business is changing frequently, then leverage
the lateral processes to enable the business to change quickly.

Principle #7: Engage in the process of people mapping after
choosing the preferred hierarchical and lateral structure.

Principle #1: Structure always follows strategy, not people.

The purpose of structure is to put together the best possible flow of work to deliver the strategy. As shown is Figure 6.1, the strategy (and not the people) should inform which structure to choose for the organization.

Figure 6.1: The Strategy (and Not the People) Informs the Structure

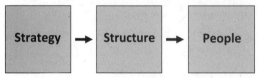

Therefore, effective businesses first develop the strategy to respond to customer needs before they consider the changes to the organizational structure that might be required. They then identify the structure that best fits the strategy. Only afterwards do they determine the gap between the talent requirements of the new structure and talent available in their organization.

Principle #2: Establish criteria for success and "non-negotiables" for the restructured organization.

At the outset of the process, ensure that the criteria for a successful structure are clearly articulated. The criteria will be used to assess the structural options to determine if the recommended structure will enable the strategy. Some typical examples of criteria include: the structure enables the strategy; customers will receive enhanced service; the structure has clear accountabilities and roles; the structure enables innovation; the structure enables career development and succession planning.

Also, determine the list of non-negotiables that must be a part of the new structure. Some typical examples include: the strategy cannot be changed by the structure; work that cannot be outsourced is specifically identified; the total number of full-time employees cannot increase.

Principle #3: Identify the hierarchical structural options to determine where authorities reside.

The hierarchical structure defines who has the authority to make the work and people decisions that will achieve the strategy. Here are three hierarchical structural options and how they can be applied to restructure an HR department:

- *Hierarchal structure by activity:* Structure around functional *activity* areas. In HR these would be recruitment, training, employee relations, compensation, and so on.
- *Hierarchal structure by outcome:* Structure around a product or service *outcome.* In HR these would be talent management, total rewards, employment brand, ROI of human capital, and so on.
- *Hierarchal structure by user:* Structure around client *user* segments. In HR these would include the roles of the HR business partners with business department leaders and/or lines of business.

Principle #4: Address hierarchical structural limitations with lateral processes.

In the best-case scenario, the preferred hierarchical option will satisfy most of the requirements of the strategy and criteria. By definition, every formal hierarchical structure has limitations. As a result, the structure will need some informal "lateral" processes, such as cross-functional teams, project teams, and group meetings, to remedy the hierarchical deficiencies. For example, if the preferred hierarchical choice is a user-based structure with business partners, then there may be compromises on the consistency and quality of approaches across various users. As a result, a lateral process could be included in the structure to enhance quality, such as an expectation that the business partners would meet monthly to review their work and ensure they work consistently.

Principle #5: Use the least authority for the lateral processes that allow the hierarchical structure to work well.

The authority vested in informal lateral processes can vary widely. For example, in the "user" model, there may be a quality control function to ensure that all independent business partners work at a similar level of quality. The level of authority for this lateral process could be anywhere on a continuum from informal (e.g., the quality control department would not have the right to direct work) to more formal (e.g., the quality control department would have the authority to direct work). The level of authority for the lateral process should be the lowest possible level that still achieves the purpose of hierarchical restructuring to deliver the strategy.

A matrix structure is defined as a structure that has equal authority vested in the hierarchical structure and in the lateral processes. The two leaders (i.e., the leader of the hierarchical structure and the leader of the lateral process) need to reach an agreement on how to proceed in the event of a dispute between them. The HR professional should encourage the two leaders to determine a method of decision-making in the event that they cannot reach an agreement. Without a clear adjudication process, the matrix structure can grind the business to a halt and create great frustration among employees as the leaders of the matrix debate their decisions.

Principle #6: If a business is changing frequently, then leverage the lateral processes to enable the business to change quickly.

Most employees believe that the hierarchical structure is a fixture of permanence; changing it is thus a wrenching experience that can cause great anxiety. The lateral processes, such as ad hoc cross-functional teams, project teams, and group meetings, are often more informal, do not generate the same level of loyalty, and therefore much less stress is created when they are dismantled. As a result, for rapidly changing competitive environments or businesses, it is advisable to retain the existing hierarchical structure as long as possible and use shorter-term lateral process solutions to meet the evolving business needs. This method allows the organization to continue to change its lateral processes as its strategic needs evolve. Once the organization settles, the hierarchical authority structure can be formally changed to reflect the new strategy.

Principle #7: Engage in the process of people mapping after choosing the preferred hierarchical structure and lateral processes.

Only after the new structure is approved does the business leader proceed to determine who will fill the positions and how the new structure will be implemented. Here are five steps in the restructuring implementation process:

1. *Define the detail-work processes and positions* for the new hierarchical and lateral structures.
2. *Select the right leaders and employees for each position.* Once the structure is in place, determine the most capable leaders to fulfill the potential of the structure. (This process provides a unique opportunity to leverage the structural change to help build an organization's leadership capacity.)
3. *Develop the change management plan.* This includes communicating the new structure in and outside of the organization. Ensure that leaders understand the explicit connection between the structure and how it expedites the business strategy and supports the organizational culture and values.
4. *Transition the current work to the new structure.* Develop the plan to change the work from the way it was done to the way it will proceed in the restructured organization. Also, revamp the metrics (i.e., goals, performance management, rewards and recognition systems) used to evaluate success to focus the organization on what needs to be achieved in the new structure.

5. *Monitor the new structure and engage in course corrections.* Build in review meetings to consider appropriate lateral processes for mitigating limitations in the structure.

Many HR professionals are invited to contribute to restructuring only when there is a need to map people to the structure and when the structure needs to be implemented. However, leadership-driven HR professionals are business partners who have expertise and process skills to contribute to the restructuring capability—from the identification of the need to restructure to the selection of the best structure and its implementation.

ORGANIZATIONAL ALIGNMENT

On the maiden voyage to the moon, the control center (NASA) decided the mission would follow a very exact course and planned the voyage with incredible precision. But even as precise as they were, the spaceship was off course for a tremendous amount of the time as it flew to the moon and back. Research to discover just how often it was off course yielded some surprising results. It was on course for only 3 percent of the time. Imagine— 97 percent of the time it was off course! The vision was very specific, but NASA had to realign their direction constantly. Once the vision was set for the course to take, NASA's job was to align, align, align.[2]

Too many leaders believe that if the business strategy is defined and the structure is in place, organizational alignment will be created automatically. They assume that the power of the design will create compliance. Unfortunately, that is not always the case in the actual implementation. As the NASA scientists found, after liftoff there is a constant challenge to align to the desired direction in order to reach

---

2. The statistic that NASA was on course for 3 percent of its maiden voyage to the moon, as well as the description of what occurred in NASA headquarters during that time, was confirmed as correct by Roger D. Launius, Ph.D., the chief historian of the NASA History Office (personal communication, August 4, 1998).

your target. Without attention to organizational alignment, a business can anticipate that there will be unaligned actions that can lead to a toxic organizational reaction. HR professionals are in a unique position to champion organizational alignment, and this section will explore how this alignment can be achieved.

Some may believe that alignment can be divided into two choices: either you are aligned or you are not. However, we can learn from microbiology that alignment should really be divided into three choices. In microbiology, alignment is not just complementary but instead should create a higher level of functioning. For example, consider an individual who is expected to take two antibiotic drugs simultaneously. Three kinds of reactions can occur:

- *A positively aligned or "synergistic" reaction:* The two antibiotics produce a higher level of functioning and a better outcome when they are combined than when either drug is used alone. This can mean that the dosage required for each drug can be reduced when the two drugs are combined, and it may produce a need for fewer antibiotics to deliver an even better outcome.
- *A neutral or "indifferent" reaction:* The two antibiotics taken in their normal dosages deliver no greater value than the more active drug taken by itself.
- *A negative or "antagonistic" reaction:* The effect of one antibiotic is either reduced by the presence of another, or it produces a toxic reaction. Often there is a need to take more drugs to deal with the side effects of the two antibiotics.

In business settings, organizational alignment has the potential to produce the same higher level of functioning as the synergistic alignment of two antibiotics. In other words, the alignment of two or more business functions results in less effort and better outcomes. It also produces greater benefit than the sum of the two business functions that are undertaken independently. HR should understand how these internal best-practice business areas are generating their synergistic alignment in order to share these approaches with others.

When there is no synergistic alignment between two or more business functions, it could have an indifferent effect, which may be acceptable. Not all functions are expected to work together synergistically. However, when multiple departments are expected to interact all the time, and when the various divisions, functions, products, and people only meet their own individual interests, the organization will not be fulfilling its potential. In these situations, HR will need to work with the various areas to ensure the areas work synergistically.

However, if there is antagonism between two or more business functions, then people and teams are working at cross-purposes and generating a toxic reaction. Wherever it occurs (whether they need alignment to be synergistic or neutral), HR should target the antagonism, identify the root causes of the dysfunction, and repair the flow of work between the two business areas to at least the neutral level of alignment.

Executive Team Alignment

In many organizations, the first need for synergistic alignment is among the executive team members. In many situations, the executive team members do not work in alignment with one another, and they therefore set in motion a pattern of disconnected business initiatives that are not linked. Executives need to have a dialogue about tough alignment questions. Consider the following example, which describes a situation in which organizational alignment is needed among executives and HR is brought in to help with achieving this.

A team of 10 senior executives holds a session to establish the company's future direction. In preparation for the meeting, they develop vision statements for their divisions. They do not share their reports, nor do they align their objectives with any of the other executives prior to this meeting.

The president and executives meet in the boardroom. As the leaders give their presentations, it is obvious they are making their presentations to the president only. It appears that the president's opinion is the only one that is important. Each executive presents detailed plans of how to make his or her vision a reality. After the first three presentations by the development, operations, and marketing departments, the president speaks out: "We sound like three different companies. Did you talk to each other before developing your presentations?" The silence in the room is deafening. Those executives who have not yet presented are doing mental somersaults to align their reports with at least one of the previous presentations.

The president continues, "Don't you understand why you each lead a division? We have one vision for the company. The company divisions must make that one vision a reality. Your charge as division leaders is to demonstrate supervision and to do your part to implement the company vision." The executives have heard the president expound on this "vision-division-supervision" idea before but have never considered it more than a cute play on words. "From now on we have only one vision for the company; all other visions are eliminated," the president says to a hushed room.

The HR vice president, who has been trying to get the other executives to collaborate and align their plans, looks around the room at her colleagues, who are obviously disturbed and fearful. The president is agitated, his face red with frustration and anger. The room remains silent for several minutes while no one moves or, as it appears, even breathes.

The HR vice president breaks the silence. "I think we should adjourn the meeting for a week. We have work to do on our plans." Some of the executives are relieved; others are surprised by the HR leader's directness. Everyone waits for the president to speak as he twirls his pen between his fingers. "Take two weeks," he says, "and make sure your presentations build the company, not your divisions." The meeting is adjourned.

The HR vice president has been waiting for this moment to champion organizational alignment with the executives. The sense of urgency for the executives to work together and align their strategies has arrived. She offers to help. "Maybe we can work together to see where the gaps and overlaps are in our presentations," she says. "We can meet to discuss our ideas and see how they align to a common company vision." After a moment of hesitation, the marketing VP agrees, and one by one the others decide it is a good idea.

The astute HR vice president is one of the few leaders who has the trust of the others. She recognizes that all the leaders are operating in good faith but are heading in different directions. Their individual visions, values, and strategies are not aligned. She is also aware of a great deal of unresolved conflict among the executives, which leads them to set up their own business to the exclusion of others, leading to a company that is splintered. The result is that when customers speak to different divisions, they complain that they are dealing with more than one company.

The HR vice president decides to mediate some of the executive disputes. To get the maximum value from her efforts, she starts with one of the more complex interpersonal conflicts. To the company's benefit, she is able to facilitate a resolution to the problem. The two disputing executives resolve some basic problems while agreeing to disagree on some matters. Once they begin to resolve their differences, they are ready to have a dialogue about how they will align their divisions. Other divisions immediately take note of the change in the leaders' relationship and begin to talk to each other.

After extensive work, the leaders meet with the president two weeks later. They affirm the importance of one company vision and one set of values. They describe the alignment process in which each division identifies its own preferred future and how it contributes to fulfilling the vision. Then they present how their divisions implement their strategic initiatives as part of the entire company.

The business president is the only person with official responsibility for aligning all strategies. He or she is the one executive who is part of only one team—the executive team. All other executive team members have the additional responsibility of leading divisional teams. The president has to bring all these strong people together and form them into one team that is aligned and synergistic. Not all presidents have the leadership skills to make this happen, and the risk that this misalignment will occur is high.

Human resource professionals are well suited to help the president and executive team ensure organizational alignment to a common direction throughout the business. Because HR professionals add value to all executives, they have a broad view of the business. In addition, they should have a deeper base of knowledge about how organizational alignment occurs and an advanced level of interpersonal excellence and trustworthiness to facilitate alignment discussions.

Cross-Functional Alignment

Many organizations suffer from what are referred to as "silos," which is a term for a part of the organization that becomes more dominant than the overall organization. A major characteristic of a silo is the unwillingness of those in the functional groups to collaborate and to share information with other groups. Members of silos are more focused on their areas of responsibility than they are on the overall business. As a result, rather than making decisions that balance the needs of their own functions and the overall needs of the business, leaders of silos prefer to make decisions in the best interest of their own silos—even if those decisions sub-optimize another silo. Sometimes the leaders of silos feel they are doing a wonderful job when their silo is successful. However, the success of one part of a business at the expense of the entire business always generates antagonism and dysfunction that should not be tolerated.

In businesses that suffer from this condition, each department is like a storage silo, only in a business context. They store their own information and objectives rather than sharing common goals and information with other departments and communicating freely with one another. The common solution to the problem is to break down the walls of the silo—not a very encouraging image for most leaders.

Assuming that HR professionals have some responsibility for the effective flow of work, the existence of silos is an HR failure to highlight and repair an antagonistic flow of work. HR professionals should take accountability for exploring ways to connect and align the silos rather than simply resorting to the restructuring option of breaking down the silos.

Perhaps part of the challenge is the image of "the silo," which by its very nature is a freestanding structure that does not connect with other silos. A more appropriate image that HR can promote is of the various units as "islands." There are many departments in a business that metaphorically live on separate islands. To become one land mass, an enterprise needs to build bridges between some of the islands (synergistic alignment), while others may only need a fast-moving boat or a ferry to travel from one island to another to connect the overall enterprise (neutral alignment). HR needs to think about all the islands within the business and determine how to connect the various parts so that the value of the total enterprise becomes greater than the sum of its individual departments. HR can also set up forums within which leaders can exchange ideas and ensure that isolation among the islands is not encouraged. This approach expands the leaders' understanding and access to other parts of the business, which can contribute to enhancing the synergy between departments.

Figure 6.2 shows where the challenge often occurs when there is a need for cross-functional alignment.

Figure 6.2: Cross-Functional Alignment and "White Space"

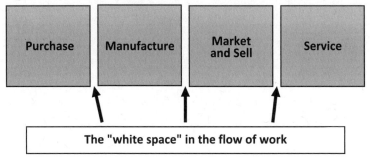

The standard hierarchical organizational chart uses boxes to represent departments and individual areas of work. In between the boxes are white spaces. The assumption is that departments and individuals need to work in alignment with each other and traverse the white space effectively. However, there is often no one who is responsible for the white space between departmental areas.

HR professionals can use the lateral processes described in the previous section to build bridges across the white space. These may include creating cross-functional teams, instituting inter-departmental meetings, planning inter-departmental social events, and so on. However, too often, HR creates these linkages when the alignment problems already exist. They should be identifying early warning signals of lack of alignment and adjusting the organization accordingly to ensure that the departments and the business leaders work together to achieve the overall business direction.

Alignment among Strategic Teams

The ability to see lack of alignment among formalized business areas is often easier than noticing the lack of alignment among strategic teams that are working in isolation. Sometimes, these special teams do not talk to each other about what they are doing and how they can collaborate. As a result, one group does not benefit from the experience of another group that is using a similar process, and sometimes they can generate disparate recommendations that work at cross-purposes with each other. Consider the following scenario, which describes how HR helped strategic teams work in alignment.

A health services business introduces seven separate cross-functional teams to implement its strategic initiatives. HR decides to ensure alignment of the strategic teams and holds a meeting with the organization's seven project leaders.

As a result of their communication in the meeting, two of the project leaders have an eye-opening experience. One tells of designing a strategy to improve health outcomes in one area of specialization. The other relates how she is designing a process to build relationships with the community health centers in local neighborhoods. After they describe their projects, the two leaders look at each other in surprise. "We should be talking to each other more," says the leader whose process is to build relationships. "I never thought of it, but in my approach to the community health centers, I should be using the strategy that we will use to improve health outcomes."

The project leaders are surprised that this is the first time they are considering leveraging the work of the health outcomes group to their benefit. "We are all too busy to find out what each other are doing," the project leader says. "We are wasting time building everything from scratch when we can work together and get it done faster with better quality and better results." They decide they have to meet on a regular basis to keep each other informed about how their projects are developing, to seek feedback from each other, and to ensure they are aligned to the business's strategic direction.

In a business in which people feel they are always reinventing the wheel, aligning strategic initiatives helps avoid duplication of effort. Many initiatives often overlap with one another. When a business misses alignment opportunities and duplicates efforts, it can incur unnecessary costs, loss of time, and employee disengagement.

Alignment with Internal Best Practices

The internal best practices in a business are another area of alignment that is often underutilized. Frequently, businesses realize they have a best practice only when an outsider points it out to them. HR can look for the practices that a business does extremely well and use them as internal best practices that all other areas of the business can emulate.

Here is an example where discovering the internal best practice was very beneficial to a business:

A business was concerned about the lack of external customer focus among its employees. The business had attempted to benchmark other organizations but did not find a model that could be translated for their unique type of work. The HR leader then suggested that they should research the departments in their own organization that had the best customer focus and potentially use their approach for the rest of the organization. They then asked HR to conduct a study of the customer service department, which had won awards for its customer focus. HR discovered that the customer service department was highly effective at three things: (1) understanding customer expectations; (2) delivering new services; and (3) evaluating service delivery through ongoing customer feedback. The business decided to implement their customer service processes in all departments. This decision was accepted widely and was a great success.

In the above example, the HR professionals explained that the rapid acceptance was due to the following alignment factors:

- *Familiarity with the systems:* Many employees were aware of the systems used with external customers. Therefore, it was easier for them to accept the processes when they were introduced to their own departments.
- *Cost savings through reuse of systems:* The business was able to realize cost savings through reusing processes that already worked within the external customer service department.
- *Alignment created:* Employees appreciated the enhanced alignment between the customer service department and the processes used by all departments.

HR Champions Organizational Alignment

HR professionals are often in a unique position to be a catalyst for change because they work with all the departmental and strategic teams. HR professionals can see the disconnects among the leaders of functional groups at an early development stage and can help business leaders work together more effectively. They can champion this kind of organizational alignment by doing the following:

- Facilitating discussions among departmental leaders and project leaders to open lines of communication about their areas of responsibility and how aligning their work with others can be beneficial to all.
- Leveraging internal best practices that already exist and are known to them through their internal database, which tracks what is being done in the business.
- Creating opportunities for alignment across geographical areas and business units to reduce duplication and achieve economies of scale that would not otherwise be realized. For example, a business's divisions located in different parts of the country or the world should use the same principles for developing systems to avoid duplications.
- Focusing on alignment to integrate new businesses with the current business and to align strategy across the business, where appropriate.
- Operating HR as a best-practice model of cross-functional alignment effectiveness to give it the credibility to contribute to the cross-functional alignment of others and to be a model that can be emulated by other parts of the business.

RETURN ON INVESTMENT IN HUMAN CAPITAL

At any phase of the growth curve, a business can enter into a struggle for survival. As this occurs, many executives focus on protecting the business. In these cases, HR may be challenged to concentrate on the bottom line and determine the return on investment in human capital. They will need to justify every dollar spent, and a return will be necessary for it to continue. Each cost in the organization has a direct impact on the business's profitability, on the bonuses paid to people, and on the strategic value the business can contribute to customers. Also, as the business transforms, information on the return on investment in human capital will be one guide to help business leaders make the wisest strategic business decisions.

In a study we conducted,[3] business leaders and senior HR professionals in England and Canada were asked about their capability to provide measurements of human capital and the anticipated level of capability required in the future. Seven percent of the organizations indicated that they could provide reports on the return on investment in human capital, and they forecasted that in the future, 70 percent would require such information. This research indicates that HR needs to have the organizational capability to analyze and provide information that determines the return on investment in human capital.

The term "return on investment in human capital" (ROIHC) refers to the following:

- *Human capital* refers to the economic value of the knowledge, skills, experiences, creativity, and innovations of people in a business that help make that business productive and give it a competitive/comparative advantage.
- *Return on investment* is the mathematical formula (return/investment) that reflects the business's current human capital return on its performance divided by the investment of money and effort it takes to cultivate that human capital.

Many HR professionals are reasonably effective at calculating the investment in human capital. They can tabulate fairly precisely the cost of hiring, development, retention programs, compensation, terminations, and so on. However, they often struggle with determining the return on performance and how to tabulate productivity measures. Part of the struggle is that measures of productivity are imprecise and often cannot be attributed to the work of HR alone. As a result, many HR professionals

---

3. David S. Weiss and Richard Finn, "HR Metrics That Count: Aligning Human Capital Management To Business Results," *Human Resources Planning* 28, no. 1 (2005): 33-38.

shy away from taking credit for productivity and performance gains and as a result are unable to determine the ROIHC for the business.

In contrast, the preferred approach is for HR to take credit for their part in the return on investment and be explicit about how they are calculating their contributions. Perhaps the best example for HR to emulate is the approach that marketing departments take when they analyze the ROI of investments into brand development. Marketing also can count the investment precisely; however, they know how to take credit for productivity and performance gains that are associated with the work on the brand even though it was not solely generated by the investment in the brand. HR should learn from marketing how to be recognized for its contribution to the return on investment in human capital.

Some HR professionals do have experience in measuring the ROI of human capital when they participate in union-management contract negotiations. To do collective bargaining negotiations successfully, HR (labor relations) determines and forecasts the costs for most aspects of labor, often predicting costs and the associated return for the subsequent three years. The analyses are sometimes so precise that HR can recommend a reduction of wages as a concession and link it to the condition that labor will recover some of its concessions through productivity gains. When no labor contract issue is involved, however, HR professionals often do not focus on the cost of labor and issues related to the investment in human capital.

HR's responsibility for the return on investment in human capital helps move it from the "softer" people side to the "harder" financial side of the business. HR finds ways to realize a better business and productivity outcome from the investment in people and their talents. Here are two actual examples of how HR contributed to business success through the organizational capability of knowing the ROI in human capital.

- *Example #1: Consider a company that is planning how it can maximize its return on a major acquisition. From the president's perspective, the opportunity associated with the cost of human capital is a compelling reason to include HR on a due-diligence team for the company about to be acquired. The HR vice president has the ability to analyze the return on investment in human capital and is therefore asked to be part of the due-diligence team. He identifies that the skills mix and know-how in both companies are equivalent and that the purchased company has the cost of human capital advantage. Therefore, he recommends that the best ROI in human capital is to redeploy specific work that has been done in the purchasing company into the acquired company. The recommendation provides the company with an almost immediate return on investment for the purchase.*

- *Example #2: In another business, the information HR collects about the ROI in human capital is treated with such priority that the only people who can access the data are the HR professional and the president. The president has a "hotline" phone directly to HR. He calls the HR professional almost daily on ROIHC issues to provide information and strategic advice about how to deploy new products and new processes in new environments. The president feels that the business finally has a major asset (human capital) that is now part of the domain of the "definable." HR sets up the people database so that they can analyze any cross section of individuals in the business. They provide data and interpret it by division, department, work unit, age group, gender, time in the business, and experience in the industry. HR is able to provide the data in almost any combination the president requests.*

Including ROI of Human Capital on the Balanced Scorecard

Many businesses use some form of a balanced scorecard[4] to monitor the performance of their businesses. Figure 6.3 presents a modified balanced scorecard that includes one area that focuses on tracking the people and organizational success that is derived from the HR people capabilities and organizational capabilities.

The "people and organizational success" area on the balanced scorecard focuses on ensuring that the human capital investments deliver an acceptable level of return throughout the business. HR should be able to provide the input data and reports to track performance on this area of the balanced scorecard.

---

4. Robert S. Kaplan and David P. Norton, *The Balanced Scorecard* (Cambridge, MA: Harvard Business School Press, 1996).

Figure 6.3: A Modified Balanced Scorecard

Figure 6.4 shows the three areas that are included in the ROIHC metric for people and organizational success.

Figure 6.4: The ROIHC Metric for People and Organizational Success

The three metric areas that contribute to people and organizational success are as follows:

Achieve business impact

This metric area focuses on the return on investment when HR mitigates a high risk or capitalizes on a major opportunity for the business. The return on the three HR value propositions described in Chapters Eight to Ten can all be included in this area. For example, if the business is merging two units, HR may be the lead on the process of implementing change. The speed with which the merged business areas deliver the desired results, the engagement of the employees and teams to the newly merged work unit, and the quality of their performance are all measures of the return on investment in the "implementing change"

HR organizational capability. Other examples of "achieve business impact" can include succession management for critical business positions, building a culture in which employees adopt innovations faster than the competition, and attracting and retaining high-performing talent. Sometimes the return cannot be easily quantified, so astute HR leaders use stories and anecdotes to describe the business impact of the investment in human capital.

Revenue generation and/or cost avoidance

This metric area deals with real financial returns. It can be divided into two parts: (1) revenue generation; and (2) cost avoidance.

- *Revenue generation:* An early study of revenue generation associated with the employee value chain claimed that an increase of 5 percent in employee engagement scores leads to a 1.3 percent improvement in customer service ratings, which then leads to a 0.5 percent increase in profits (shareholder value).[5] This analysis was replicated in the public sector to support the notion of the employee value chain. Other measures that are also associated with revenue generation include lead time measures (e.g., time to hire, time to develop full competence, etc.), impact on the business of hiring new high-performing talent, and revenue generated from new projects that result from training and development sessions.
- *Cost Avoidance:* This is probably the easiest area for HR to demonstrate return on investment. For example, the investment in better union—management relations often results in reduced legal fees for grievances and arbitrations. Also, the investment in retention programs can generate real dollar savings in the reduction of costs associated with hiring new employees. Another example is that the investment in a positive work environment can result in lower costs associated with absenteeism.

---

5. Anthony J. Rucci, Steven P. Kirn, and Richard T. Quinn, "The Employee-Customer-Profit Chain at Sears," *Harvard Business Review* (January 1998): 82-97.

Achieve industry standards

This metric area deals with comparative analyses with other businesses. HR can justify investment into the areas in which the business is not up to industry standards. They can then claim that the return is the achievement of comparative parity with other businesses. For example, a business may invest in meeting the industry standard of training hours per employee, and the return would be comparative parity with other businesses. Also, the investment in compensation analyses could yield a return that matches the compensation standards in the industry, thereby assisting the business in retaining more employees.

The three areas of measurement need to be assigned monetary values to calculate the return from those investments. This financial tally is then included in the *people and organizational success* part of the balanced scorecard for the business.

How HR Secures Investment in Human Capital through ROIHC

In some organizations, HR may find it challenging to claim credit for the return on investment in human capital, which may limit its ability to secure investments in human capital. Here are seven ways HR can secure investment in human capital by leveraging ROIHC:

1. Don't be afraid to ask for investment—put your carefully prepared proposals forward along with your anticipated ROIHC.
2. Quantify as much as possible—apply numbers to everything.
3. Always be transparent and lay out all of your assumptions for business leaders. If assumptions are challenged, use the challenger's assumptions and calculate the revised investment requirements and anticipated ROIHC.
4. Include "what if" scenarios to identify the potential losses if action is not taken—loss avoidance functions as an important executive motivator for human capital investments.

5. Identify benchmarks and best practices—many HR professionals are willing to share their best practices readily. However, ensure they are fair comparators.

6. Put forward the argument that even though multiple areas contributed to the success of the business, human capital investment was one of these areas and should be acknowledged. Understand the ROI assumptions of other departments. Are they claiming ROI in areas where HR can justifiably claim a role?

7. Always think in terms of the overall organizational benefit and not just HR—be a holistic leader who thinks about the overall business first. Combine the HR ROIHC with the return gained from other associated areas, such as communications, sales training, and process improvement, in order to build a total ROIHC of all human capital investments even beyond the specific work of the HR function.

The Implications for the Work of HR

HR needs to assume accountability for the organizational capability of identifying and measuring the ROIHC. HR professionals should be required to produce information about the investment in human capital and the productivity outputs that show the return on investments. HR needs the knowledge and ability to provide strategic advice about how to invest wisely in human capital. HR's role includes the following:

- Assist in determining the metric of human capital and its cost. With this information, HR will also be able to contribute more information to the business's annual report and strategic plans.
- Have ongoing strategic input on business and financial issues related to the return on investment in human capital as well as on how to increase the overall human capital in the business. Provide guidance regularly.
- Be part of a due-diligence process for any new acquisition to determine whether the investment in human capital in the business to be purchased is cost effective, as well as to assess cultural and leadership issues.

- Be the expert in people as an asset and in how to redeploy them so that the business can derive the best productivity and return on investment possible.
- Set the priorities with reference to people valuation. Make business recommendations about the critical issues of incentives, rewards, and recognition, and for the overall budget associated with people.

HR professionals should also be able to prepare reports for business leaders that help them run their businesses and contribute to effective decisions. These reports sometimes include specific demographic information such as numbers of employees and their educational levels. In addition, the reports include information directly related to the leader's business such as absenteeism, turnover, production downtime, lost-time accidents, and both short- and long-term disability. In the future, HR will also need to prepare dynamic reports for business leaders that will provide strategic information and will analyze the productivity of the investment in human capital. For example, with the analytical capability and the data, HR can do the following:

- *Conduct comparisons of data:* Compare the data by locations, departments, types of jobs, education, age, seniority, and so on for the individual, team, or organization to determine the best opportunities for cost-effective internal investments.
- *Produce dynamic simulations:* This includes conducting "what if" analyses and predicting what would happen if the business leaders were to invest in human capital in a different way and what the potential impact on profitability would be. HR also runs simulations to predict the best way to invest and the most cost-effective place to put work for the business based on productivity and cost of human capital.
- *Forecast the areas of best return on investment in human capital:* Identify if any opportunities have been missed or if opportunities can be discovered. For example, this forecast may include an analysis of the impact of raising salaries for specific groups and the cost of securing specific strategic employee skill sets.

Here are two examples of ROIHC analyses that HR might conduct for business leaders:

Example #1: Consider a business that defines the metric of human capital simply by the educational level of its employees. It has employees with an average of twelve years of education (high school graduates). The HR report suggests that a return on investment can be achieved if the executives decide to increase their overall metric of human capital to achieve an average educational level of 14 years. The report includes a dynamic simulation of the impact of the investment in human capital on the business's productivity and customer satisfaction measures. The dynamic report recommends that the increase in the overall metric of human capital can be achieved by targeted recruitment, turnover, and educational upgrading.

Example #2: In another business, the HR vice president uses her version of the ROIHC information to predict future required investments in human capital. She defines the metric of human capital by demographic data such as age, marital status, education, professional expertise, number of children, and gender. She combines her analysis of the investment made in human capital with the demographic and industry trends. She uses a forecasting model to do simulations to predict (within a 5 percent error rate) the anticipated number of people who will leave the business in the next five to 10 years. She then recommends the required investment in human capital to keep the metric of human capital at its desired level.

As HR's credibility in this organizational capability increases, HR professionals will be able to respond to questions about how potential business leadership decisions will affect investment in human capital. Executives will look to HR as the source of analytical information and recommendations on ROIHC.

The HR Competencies Needed to Support ROIHC Analysis

The traditional HR professional is usually not trained to do ROIHC analyses. To deliver this organizational capability, some HR departments will require the services of a labor economist or an accountant. Some of the competencies required for a person who will be accountable for ROIHC include the following:

- *The person clearly has to have a strong financial and/or labor economics background so that he or she can model this information effectively:* The individual needs to be able to generate accurate data that can be included in an overall financial report. Two sources of talent to explore for this role are individuals who are well-grounded in finance or labor economists. Another source might be industrial relations professionals in unionized environments who frequently calculate the cost of labor as part of the process of negotiating a collective agreement.
- *The person has to have the ability to handle abstract ideas:* The ability of the person to think abstractly and have a systems orientation to the business will be a critical competency for this role. Some of the financial considerations involve simple mathematics; however, some of the numbers and the dynamic analyses are probability-oriented and more abstract. The individual also needs to have the ability to convert data into information, and that information into knowledge.
- *The ability to communicate complex ideas in simple language:* Extremely clear and precise communication skills are a must for this individual. He or she needs to know the right questions to ask and be able to provide information that will help others make appropriate decisions. To be understood correctly, the individual must be able to speak in the language of the person he or she is assisting. If the person is unable to communicate clearly, then people will not understand and will not be able to derive the maximum benefit from their analyses.
- *The ability to transfer expertise:* This person cannot hoard ideas or information but must be someone with whom others are willing to collaborate. He or she must be willing and able to use the information to formulate recommendations and identify the ROIHC. The individual must also guide others to do this kind of activity independently.
- *A strong sense of ethics and confidentiality:* This person will be the holder of private and strategic information about the business and human capital. Often the only people who have direct access to this

information are the business's executives and perhaps one or two other people. A strong personal sense of ethics and confidentiality is essential for people engaged in this organizational capability.

CONCLUSION

HR professionals must enhance their competence in delivering organizational capabilities to enhance the flow of work within the business. The five organizational capabilities described in this chapter are a challenge to HR to enhance their contribution to the business and its leaders. When HR is effective at organizational capabilities in addition to people capabilities, HR moves from an important internal service to an essential partner of the business that is highly strategic and vital to the competitive and comparative success of the enterprise.

SUMMARY

- One of the most significant changes for HR over the past decade is the expectation that HR should demonstrate excellence in organizational capabilities.

- HR needs to understand the integrated value chain or the flow of work from when it enters into the business, how it is processed, and eventually how it delivers value to the external customer. By understanding the flow of work, HR has the credibility to contribute to the way work is structured, to know how to align cross-functional work, to understand how changes should be implemented, and to help create the kind of culture the organization needs to enable the achievement of the business strategy. We refer to the flow of work roles for HR as the organizational capabilities.

- There are five essential organizational capabilities:

  1. Accelerating cultural transformation: Ensuring that the organizational culture occurs rapidly enough to enable the business strategy to occur.

  2. Implementing change: Ensuring that business changes are implemented effectively and that people adjust and adopt the changes rapidly.

  3. Restructuring and design: Ensuring that the formal and informal organizational structures and design of work enable the business to achieve its strategy.

  4. Organizational alignment: Ensuring that the business works effectively across functions and does not operate with dysfunctional silos.

  5. ROI of human capital: Ensuring that the human capital investments deliver an acceptable level of return for the business.

- HR professionals must enhance their competence in delivering organizational capabilities to enhance the flow of work within the business. When HR is effective at organizational capabilities in addition to people capabilities, HR moves from an important internal service to an essential partner of the business that is highly strategic and vital to the competitive and comparative success of the enterprise.

PART THREE

THE HR VALUE PROPOSITION

CHAPTER SEVEN

HR VALUE PROPOSITION: AN OVERVIEW

An executive asks an HR leader, "What is your top priority for the year?" The HR leader hesitates and then shows a list of 15 projects that HR intends to deliver. The executive looks at the list and says, "But what is the one thing you plan to deliver that will make a real difference for our business?"

All HR leaders need to be able to answer this question. This "one thing" is the top-priority HR work that will mitigate a major business risk. As defined in Chapter One, "risk" refers to both the business scenarios in which something damaging could occur as well as those in which there is a high likelihood that the business will not fulfill its potential.

The HR value proposition is defined as follows:

An HR value proposition is the promise to deliver a top-priority HR solution targeted to mitigate a critical business risk.

While HR is accountable for more than the HR value proposition, it is the promise to deliver the value proposition that makes HR an essential part of the business's strategies. The executives are engaged because they know that the delivery of the HR value proposition is essential for their business success. It is similar to the marketing department that promises to deliver a value proposition to develop the business brand, which is essential to the business strategy. At the same time the marketing department continues to be accountable for its ongoing areas of expertise in product, price, place, and promotion.

In all cases, the HR value proposition is one of (or a combination of) the people capabilities (described in Chapter Five) and/or the organizational capabilities (described in Chapter Six) that is the ongoing work of HR. The specific people capability or organizational capability that mitigates a critical business risk is elevated to the level of an HR value proposition. It is not a different area of work for HR but rather an area of HR work that is of the highest priority to remedy a critical business risk.

For example, HR is accountable for many people and organizational capabilities. In Part Three, we explore in depth three common HR capabilities that are frequently elevated to the level of the HR value proposition:

- Build leadership capacity;
- Accelerate culture transformation;
- Implement change.

Other HR value propositions that also appear in organizations (but are not explored to the same depth) include retention of talent, succession management, organizational alignment, and HR rewards and recognition.

Consider the following example and its implications for HR work in both people and organizational capabilities, and for the choice of the HR value proposition:

Two general hospitals merge into one newly created specialist hospital. The new hospital is changing its focus to become a center of excellence in treating complex care (multiple diseases) patients using an integrated care model. Other treatment areas in the merged hospital are being distributed to local municipal hospitals or to community clinics.

The merged hospital executives realize that their health-care professionals will need to be outstanding in specialized areas to fulfill the objectives of the merger. They also identify the following major questions associated with this merger:

- *What can be done to ensure excellence in patient care during the transition?*
- *How can the hospital ensure that all health disciplines are properly represented to deliver integrated complex patient care? Historically, health-care professionals other than doctors have not had an equal voice in patient care, which needs to change in order for the newly created hospital to provide integrated care.*
- *How can everyone on the staff become engaged with the new focus for the merged hospital, especially when many staff members are still loyal to their former legacy hospitals?*

There are other specific challenges that have implications for people and organizational capabilities.

- *Leaders anticipate that the merged complex care hospital will eventually have the same total number of staff as before the merger occurred; however, the mix of talent will be different. For example, the newly created hospital will need to hire 30 percent more nurses with experience in complex care treatment than the combined total within the original two hospitals. As a result some nurses will be asked to leave the organization to avoid increasing the total number of staff.*
- *The nurses' union has responded skeptically to this major organizational restructuring, arguing that management is simply cutting costs by reducing staff. However, the new hospital leadership is hoping that nurses and their union will have a more positive attitude toward this newly merged hospital because of the focus on complex care patients, the expectation that nursing will be more involved in integrated care for patients, and the intent not to reduce the overall number of health-care staff in the combined hospital.*

HR is then asked to focus on the situation associated with hiring and firing nurses and dealing effectively with the nurses' union. However, HR convinces the executive that HR should have a broader accountability and leadership role to ensure that the newly merged hospital has the people and organizational capabilities to become a center of excellence in the treatment of complex care patients using an integrated care model. HR then proceeds to develop a broad plan that focuses on specific people capabilities, organizational capabilities, and an HR value proposition that eventually delivers great value to the merged hospital, to staff, and eventually to patient care.

The above example represents a significant challenge and opportunity for HR to deliver value to the newly created hospital. HR needs to use an outside-in approach to determine its focus in each of the three areas of HR work. The first challenge that the HR leaders must consider is what their emphasis should be in the area of people capabilities. They identify that the business needs HR to excel in each of the three areas of people capabilities:

- *Find:* Hire new talent who can work with complex care patients and ensure they are oriented to the new model of health care.
- *Develop:* Develop the current leaders to be able to work with employees and teams in the safe treatment of complex care patients. They also will need to work effectively with the unions throughout this process.
- *Retain:* Retain key talent throughout this transition. They also need to keep engagement high as they remove employees and nurses who do not have the capabilities to perform well in the new complex care hospital.

HR then explores the key organizational capabilities that are required for the business. The department realizes that the organization will encounter major challenges in several areas including the following:

- Ensuring that all employees work in alignment with the strategic directions of the merged hospital.
- Creating a newly merged hospital culture from the two legacy hospitals.

- Redesigning work so that health-care teams work in an integrated manner.
- Implementing the changes so that everyone adapts to them rapidly.

It then determines its top-priority HR value proposition that will mitigate a critical business risk for the hospital. Part of the challenge is that there are so many business risks in this situation, but nevertheless, HR must pick the priority business risk. After careful consideration, it determines that the critical business risk can be mitigated by ensuring that the two separate hospital cultures work well together as a merged complex care hospital using integrated care teams. All of the people capabilities and organizational capabilities are then aligned to support the realization of a strong positive culture for all staff.

THE SEVEN STEPS TO DEVELOP AN HR VALUE PROPOSITION

The following seven steps will enable HR to develop an HR value proposition:

Seven Steps to Develop an HR Value Proposition
1. Identify the business risks for the business and its departments.
2. Explore the implications of those business risks for people and organizational capabilities.
3. Identify the top-priority business risk associated with the people and organizational capabilities.
4. Develop the HR value proposition to mitigate the top-priority business risk.
5. Confirm with the business leaders that the HR value proposition is the right solution to mitigate the business risk.
6. Align HR's work to ensure that it delivers the HR value proposition.
7. Monitor progress on the HR value proposition regularly and report outcomes at executive strategy meetings.

A frequent question that HR leaders ask is what they should do if there are many business risks. Can they have multiple HR value propositions? In most situations, the answer is that HR needs to identify the pressing business issues and *choose the top-priority HR value proposition* to mitigate the critical business risk. Most HR leaders do not have the capability or resources to focus on more than one HR value proposition. The value proposition that HR selects will be the HR "banner" or theme, which will galvanize the HR team and the business leaders to deliver a key people capability or organizational capability outcome.

Another common question is whether HR should develop the three areas of work sequentially. For example, should HR first meet the baseline expectation of delivering the people capabilities and only move on to the organizational capabilities and the HR value proposition after that baseline is achieved? If HR adopts this approach and focuses only on its people capabilities, the other two areas will still have to be addressed. The executives may decide to meet their organizational needs independently of HR, which often results in misaligned solutions that are of uneven quality. The preferred approach is for HR to *parallel process*, which means that HR delivers the people capabilities and ensures the delivery of the organizational capabilities and the HR value proposition at the same time.

CONFIRM THAT THE HR VALUE PROPOSITION MITIGATES THE BUSINESS RISK

HR leaders need to know the major strategic business risks. Then, they can focus their HR value proposition on the single most important risk related to people and organizational capabilities that could limit the accomplishment of the business strategy. Next, HR needs to confirm with the business leaders that the HR value proposition mitigates a critical business risk and moves the business ahead. However, if the HR value proposition pushes the business too far ahead of itself or if it does not mitigate a critical business risk, there may be resistance to HR's efforts.

Here is an example of an HR vice president who selected a value proposition that did *not* remedy a critical business risk:

In a manufacturing company, the vice president of HR was very committed to trans-forming his training department into a learning organization. He positioned the learning organization as a distinct business advantage that the company should pursue. He was able to convince the company executives that his direction was the correct one.

However, as the new initiative was introduced, the reaction from the workforce was negative. The timing of the announcement was apparently off. Managers expressed concern about the lack of resources to implement the current business strategy. They were also concerned about improving the technology in the plant, enhancing quality, and delivering better results. They believed there were more important needs than a long-range investment in the creation of a learning organization.

Although this strategy is appropriate in some work environments, it apparently did not fit this one. The strategy was perceived as too far ahead of what was needed. Eventually, the approach was pursued in a very low-key fashion, and other more fundamental activities were undertaken similar to what the managers had requested.

There are three planning approaches that can help ensure the HR value proposition mitigates a critical business risk and moves the business ahead:

- *From the business strategy:* The most common approach is for the business to develop its strategy with the assumption that they have the people and organizational capabilities to deliver the strategy. HR then has its own strategy meeting to identify the priority people or organizational capability solution they will promise to deliver to mitigate the critical business risk.
- *From the people strategy:* An innovative approach to generating an HR value proposition is to conduct a *people strategy* planning session. A *people strategy* refers to a joint HR and business leader plan which articulates

the priority ways the business needs to achieve competitive advantage through its people and organizational capabilities. These planning sessions are based on the business strategy, but rather than passing the responsibility to HR to identify the HR value proposition, HR collaborates with the business leaders to identify the HR value proposition and its priorities. The participants in the people strategy planning session are often the major business leaders and the senior HR professionals (e.g., the HR VP and all of the HR directors). At the conclusion of the session, they identify the accountabilities for both the business leaders and the HR professionals to deliver the people strategy.

- *From the best assumptions about what is required:* The least effective approach occurs in organizations that have not defined their business strategy or those with a business strategy that does not clarify their assumptions about people and organizational capabilities. In these situations, HR leaders can focus attention on helping the executives develop the strategy. They often have access to strategy consultants who can facilitate such a process. They can influence the executives to spend time on developing the strategy so the business leaders can align around a common direction to gain or regain a better competitive position relative to the competition. If that does not work, then HR will need to take their best guess at identifying which people capability or organizational capability appears to be the key deliverable that the business requires. HR then tests their assumptions with the executives (if possible) to determine if they are correct.

When HR develops excellence in identifying the HR value proposition and is able to use this capability to help the business meet strategic goals, it can become a vital cog in the delivery of the business strategy. HR then has a chance to finally win its coveted seat at the executive table and to have its opinions heard and valued. Without the delivery of the HR value proposition that removes risks and/or creates opportunities,

HR will be correctly perceived as a support function that is necessary but not strategic.

HR MUST PARTNER TO DELIVER THE HR VALUE PROPOSITION

The role of a strategic business partner is essential for HR professionals when they work with executives on the HR value proposition. There are several reasons:

- Strategic business partners are part of the formulation of strategy. As a strategic partner, HR will be involved in choosing the most appropriate strategic business process on which to focus.
- Strategic business partners have the relationships to secure commitment from their executive colleagues as the business transformation proceeds. A high level of executive commitment to the strategic business processes is important to their achievement.
- Strategic business partners have ongoing access to and relationships with executive team members. This access and relationship will enable them to notice early warning signals indicating when the strategic business process is veering off course. They can make adjustments to the business transformation sooner and increase the likelihood of its successful implementation.

As strategic business partners, HR professionals need to be integrated with the business strategy. They need to have the cognitive capability to think strategically with executives and have the desire to operate at that level. They also need to think first about the business and the customer and only afterwards consider the implications for the way that HR can deliver value. They must be focusing their efforts on the external customer just like the rest of their executives.

With the right HR strategic leader and HR team in place, and with an astute understanding of the right HR value proposition on which to focus, HR can elevate itself to the strategic position it will deserve. HR will not be asking to be part of the executive team as a favor, but instead it will be welcomed as an important part of the team.

CONCLUSION

The HR value proposition is the promise to deliver a top-priority HR solution targeted to mitigate a critical business risk.

The next three chapters clarify three of the most frequently selected HR value propositions. HR leaders and the executive team work together to select the best HR value proposition. In most businesses, adopting one HR value proposition will enable the business to succeed and will be within HR's competency areas. If there is an openness to proceed with the HR value proposition, then the HR leadership will have the opportunity to provide strategic contributions and help the business gain competitive/comparative advantage.

SUMMARY

- An HR value proposition is the promise to deliver a top-priority HR solution targeted to mitigate a critical business risk.

- In all cases, the HR value proposition is one of (or a combination of) the people capabilities (described in Chapter Five) and/or the organizational capabilities (described in Chapter Six) that is the ongoing work of HR. The specific people capability or organizational capability that mitigates a critical business risk is elevated to the level of an HR value proposition. It is not a different area of work for HR but rather an area of HR work that is of the highest priority to remedy a critical business risk.

- Here are the seven steps to develop an HR value proposition:

  1. Identify the business risks for the business and its departments.

  2. Explore the implications of those business risks for people and organizational capabilities.

  3. Identify the top-priority business risk associated with the people and organizational capabilities.

  4. Develop the HR value proposition to mitigate the top-priority business risk.

  5. Confirm with the business leaders that the HR value proposition is the right solution to mitigate the business risk.

  6. Align HR's work to ensure that it delivers the HR value proposition.

  7. Monitor progress on the HR value proposition regularly and report outcomes at executive strategy meetings.

- A frequent question that HR professionals ask is what they should do if there are many business risks. Can they have multiple HR value propositions? In most situations, the answer is that HR needs to pick the top-priority HR value proposition to mitigate the critical business risk.

- Another common question is whether HR should develop the three areas of work sequentially. The preferred approach is for HR to parallel process, which means that HR delivers the people capabilities and ensures the delivery of the organizational capabilities and the HR value proposition at the same time.

- The next three chapters clarify three of the most frequently selected HR value propositions. HR leaders and the executive team will work together to select the best HR value proposition.

CHAPTER EIGHT

BUILD LEADERSHIP CAPACITY

A pharmaceuticals business forecasted that it would be able to double its revenue in the next five years. Its primary strategy was to find new businesses that were at the intersection between two related businesses. For example, one of their divisions sold over-the-counter skin-care products, and another division sold prescription pharmaceuticals. They believed they could develop a new division that would sell prescription pharmaceutical skin-care products. However, to double their revenue, they also would need to double the number of qualified senior leaders to ensure those businesses developed, grew, and flourished.

The HR VP reviewed their list of leadership talent and identified that in five years over 30 percent of their current leaders could retire, and that their younger leaders did not have the experience to lead businesses. The lack of leadership capacity was a significant threat to the overall strategy. The HR VP then proposed the HR value proposition that HR would take accountability for developing the leadership capacity required to deliver the business growth strategy. The executive team and the HR VP then co-created a five-year plan to develop the leadership capacity so that the business could dramatically expand its offerings to customers.

Leadership capacity is a major risk area for many businesses that can limit their ability to grow significantly. The opening story illustrates that without leadership, excellent strategies will have little chance of being successful. In those kinds of business situations, human resources has a very important contribution to make by focusing on the HR value proposition of building leadership capacity.

Leadership capacity refers to the gap between the current leadership talent level and the leadership talent required by the business to deliver its strategies. When there is a leadership capacity gap, the business strategy may be at risk because of a deficiency in this area.

MANAGEMENT CAPACITY VERSUS LEADERSHIP CAPACITY

The terms "management" and "leadership" have been studied and analyzed in many professional works. Dr. Jagdish Sheth of Emory University distinguishes[1] between management and leadership using financial symbols. He says that management relates to dividends and leadership to stocks. "Dividends get their value," he says, "from their past performance. Only after the company performance is known do they redistribute the earnings as dividends." In a similar way, management gets its value from past performance. If the department performs well, the manager and the team are able to reap the benefits from the dividends. "On the other hand," he says, "stocks get their value from the anticipation of the future. Once the stock performs, the anticipated growth of the stock is realized, and its value goes down." In a similar way, leadership gets its value from the anticipation of a preferred future. Leaders are able to create the hopes, the dreams, and the vision of the preferred future.

Most people with direct reports spend a great deal of time managing today's performance and very little time leading people to the preferred future. Although they can benefit from increasing the time they spend focusing on the future rather than their current performance, both are important. The issue is not an either-or question of whether one should be a manager or a leader. That debate has become somewhat dysfunctional. Rather, it's an and-also question of the proportion of time the person should spend as a manager versus as a leader, which depends on the nature of the work expectations and the strategic challenges.

---

1. Dr. Jagdish Sheth, lecture for the Telecommunications Executive Development Program, Toronto, Ontario, 1997.

People with direct reports need to have both management and leadership skills in their repertoire. However, the balance between management and leadership varies at different levels in an organization's hierarchy. For example, a typical business may have four levels of managerial hierarchy: supervisor, manager, director, and vice president, as shown in Figure 8.1.

Figure 8.1: The Proportion of Managing and Leading among Different Levels of a Hierarchy

Proportion of total time that is allocated to leading versus managing	Leading	Leading		
			Leading	Leading
	Managing			
		Managing		
			Managing	
				Managing
	By Supervisors	By Managers	By Directors	By VPs

Supervisors are responsible for a great deal of the day-to-day managerial functions of planning, delegating, evaluating, and controlling. However, they do have to be leaders as well in order to understand the overall future direction of the business and align and engage their teams to this direction. The proportion of time spent managing to that spent leading shifts at the next level of the hierarchy. Managers do less managing and more leading (because their supervisors do most of the day-to-day managing). The proportion continues to change at the director level and then at the VP level. The VP should be focused on leading but also have some managerial responsibilities.

Leaders focus their teams on the future direction and then align their employees and teams to achieve that direction. They also engage their teams in dialogue to ensure that they achieve a meaningful understanding of this future direction. When leaders are able to set direction and align and engage employees, then their employees are more likely to be confident that their independent decisions will be aligned with the overall direction.

In most cases, the required managerial capacity is not the challenge for the business. Management uses their knowledge and experience to focus on delivering today's business—a process which includes the following:

- *Plan* the work.
- *Delegate* the work among people who report to the manager.
- *Evaluate* the work performed by the employees.
- *Control* the processes so the work can be done on an ongoing basis and deliver the outcomes the manager is accountable for.

The HR value proposition of "build leadership capacity" focuses specifically on the leadership contributions at each level of the hierarchy. Leadership generates the hope of a better future. It taps into the cognitive and emotional abilities of leaders, their employees, and teams, and it enables people to see the possibility that the organization can achieve better outcomes. Leaders inspire employees and teams to new directions. They engage in conversations to share meaning about a new direction that inspires others to act.

In essence, building leadership capacity focuses on setting the future direction through applying innovative intelligence and emotional intelligence, as well as by inspiring others to act through aligning and engaging employees and teams. The four elements of leadership capacity are shown in Table 8.1.

Table 8.1: The Four Elements of Leadership Capacity

	Cognitive	Emotional
Sets Future Direction	Element 1: Applying innovative intelligence	Element 2: Applying emotional intelligence
Inspires Others to Act	Element 3: Aligning employees and teams to the future direction	Element 4: Engaging employees and teams with the future direction

The challenge for many organizations is that they lack enough leaders who can set direction by applying their innovative intelligence and emotional intelligence and who can inspire others to act by aligning and engaging their employees and teams to the desired future direction. The HR value proposition is the promise to deliver the kind of leadership capacity that is required by the business to achieve its strategy and its future direction.

ELEMENT 1: APPLYING INNOVATIVE INTELLIGENCE

What is it?

Innovative intelligence refers to the human cognitive ability to gain insight into problems or opportunities in new ways and to discover new and unforeseen implementable solutions.[2] Leaders need innovative intelligence to set the future direction, especially in uncertain times. This includes the following:

- Set future directions by leading through complexity where the issues are ambiguous, the direction is uncertain, and stakeholders disagree.
- Know when to use past knowledge and experience (also referred to as analytical intelligence) to understand an issue, but at the same time, know the limits of prior knowledge and experience for complex and ambiguous issues.
- Apply innovative thinking to gain insight and discover solutions to complex problems and opportunities.

Analysis and Implications

In 2005, I co-authored a book called *The Leadership Gap*[3] which explored the gap in leadership capacity that was widely anticipated by private and public sector organizations. The primary explanation for the leadership gap at that time was the impending retirement of the baby boomers[4] en

2. David S. Weiss and Claude P. Legrand, *Innovative Intelligence: The Art and Practice of Leading Sustainable Innovation in your Organization* (Toronto: John Wiley & Sons, 2011).
3. David S. Weiss and Vince Molinaro, *The Leadership Gap: Building Leadership Capacity for Competitive Advantage* (Toronto: John Wiley & Sons, 2005).
4. The term "baby boomers" refers to people born between 1945 and 1964, the period after World War II in which many babies were born.

masse, which would leave leadership to the next generation—a generation with limited experience as leaders. Two major things happened in the next eight years that redefined the explanation of why there is a leadership gap:

- *Baby boomers' retirement patterns did not unfold as predicted:* The economic meltdown in September 2008 and the elimination of forced retirement at age 65 in many organizations have changed the retirement patterns among baby boomers. Many have decided to continue working in order to have ongoing income, especially when they work for organizations that do not have significant pension plans. The mass retirement of baby boomers thus did not materialize. Rather, in some cases a new problem is emerging: baby boomers are not retiring, and it is creating a leadership bottleneck in some organizations.
- *The complexity of work has increased significantly:* The complexity of work has continued to increase rapidly. More and more issues that leaders encounter cannot be solved by relying on past experience and knowledge, and therefore leaders are facing issues they have never encountered before. They need to think about issues in entirely new ways to gain insight into problems and opportunities and to discover solutions in the new complex business environment.

As a result, the current understanding of why there is a leadership gap is not based on a demographic shortfall due to the lack of people to fill positions. There are more than enough people submitting applications for leadership positions. The problem is that, while many of the applicants were good managers when the kinds of issues they encountered relied on their past experience and knowledge, not enough of them have the leadership capacity associated with innovative intelligence to deal with the new complexities of the business environment.

The increase in the complexity of work is a predictable outcome of the shift to the current globalized-knowledge-based economy. Complexity is characterized by constant change and unpredictable course corrections that often have direct or indirect impact on businesses and entire industries. A fundamental premise is that the root cause of the leadership capacity gap is the shortfall of leaders with the ability to gain insight and to discover solutions to the complexity inherent in the globalized knowledge economy. The way leaders think today—relying heavily on past experience and knowledge—is the biggest obstacle to leading through complexity. Past experience and knowledge are effective for issues that are similar to what has been encountered before. However, complex issues are more ambiguous, and past experience and knowledge can actually distort a leader's view and guide him or her to poor decisions. Rather, leaders need to lead through complexity by thinking differently. HR needs to guide leaders to apply innovative thinking with their employees and teams in order to gain insight into complex issues and to work together to discover effective solutions.

Leaders also need to apply innovative intelligence in a systematic way to maximize the ability of their employees and teams to gain insight into issues and discover innovative solutions. Here is an example of how an executive made innovative intelligence process errors when working with a key talent leader on a highly complex issue. The example is useful to derive three core principles about what leaders need to do to lead through the new complexity and what HR's focus should be when they develop leaders to apply innovative intelligence.

An executive asks a key talent leader to work on a complex issue that requires innovation. The executive tells the leader that he wants "out of the box" thinking and real innovative solutions. The leader asks the question, "Do you mean that any idea is a good idea? Are there any ideas that are unacceptable?" The executive replies, "We want all of your ideas for new and innovative ways of thinking about this complex problem. There are no limits."

The leader thinks this is the career opportunity he has been waiting for, so he takes a week off to work on the project independently. His ideas are based on the executive's assurance that there are no limits on innovation. A week later, he comes to the executive meeting to present his recommendations. During the presentation, he describes many innovative ideas, including some that could be implemented immediately and others that require significant financial investment over the next three years, a restructuring of the organization to support the innovative ideas, and a significant change in the organization's technological infrastructure.

During the presentation the executives listen attentively without comment. The leader thinks, "They are really listening; they must love my ideas." As he completes his presentation, the executive who delegated the complex project slowly puts down his pen and says, "What were you thinking? Do you really believe we are going to change our overall strategy and restructure the organization for one innovation project? Do you think we are going to invest that level of resources into the ideas you are suggesting? Where is your professional judgment?"

The leader walks out of the room dejected and disengaged. He feels betrayed by the executive and believes he was treated unfairly. Within one year the organization does not implement any initiatives associated with that innovation challenge, and the key talent leader leaves the organization to join a competitor.

What went wrong in this story? As with all situations, the fault does not lie with just one individual. Everybody contributed to the problem. We can derive several core principles from the story that are essential for HR to follow in developing leaders to apply innovative intelligence in order to gain insight and discover solutions to complex issues.

Principle #1: Innovation works best within precise boundaries.

The executive who delegated the project said that he wanted "out of the box" thinking. However, when it came to the presentation, it was clear that the executive knew what the limits were in advance. The organization was not prepared to restructure, was not prepared for a three-year financial investment, and was not prepared to change its overall technological infrastructure to support the innovation.

Boundaries need to be defined precisely for innovation. In the story, the lack of precise boundaries forced the leader to guess what the boundaries were. He did the right thing when he asked if there were any limits, but the executive's answer was not truthful. There *were* limits. The executive did not want to share them, perhaps based on a false belief that any limits would constrain innovative solutions.

In the absence of precise boundaries, leaders have two options. One option is to take the executive at his or her word and present all the possible ideas. However, the outcome is often exactly as described in our story where the leader went beyond the implicit limits and as a result was seen as unprofessional. The alternative option is that leaders play it safe and ensure that they do not go beyond the implicit boundaries. This cautious approach reduces the area within which innovation can be explored, and the solutions are often inadequate. For cautious leaders, having precise boundaries actually *expands* the area within which they can discover innovative solutions.

The correct approach is for the executive to articulate the boundaries precisely. Then, within those precise boundaries, the leader should exercise unlimited creativity. In the event that the precise boundaries are not clear to anyone at the outset of the project, the leader should get confirmation from the executive of the limits of possible solutions as the project evolves.

Principle #2: Innovation works best with diverse teams.

In the story, the leader chose to develop the innovative recommendations independently. He saw this assignment as a career opportunity to show that he was an innovative leader. However, by working alone he had only his ideas to consider. He did not solicit other viewpoints to stimulate alternative ideas, and he did not collaborate with others to explore risks. Had he worked with a diverse team, they would have generated insights from their various perspectives and contributed to solutions that would have perhaps been much more acceptable. In addition, if the team had included diverse members with different perspectives, the viewpoints would have been helpful to gain insight about the issue and to define the problem more precisely. Also, the combination of ideas from the diverse team members would have been useful in the process of discovering alternative solutions and generating the best possible recommendations.

Principle #3: Sustainable innovation needs leaders of innovation rather than innovative leaders.

Many organizations focus on developing their leaders' innovative thinking abilities as the way to overcome the innovation gap. However, most leaders have spent their entire lives developing their own approach to thinking, and one training course will not change their ability to be more innovative. Perhaps they will learn several techniques, but in the stress of real work situations it's very possible that they will revert back to their normal way of thinking, which has given them success up to that point.

The alternative approach for HR is to focus the development of innovative intelligence for leaders on *becoming leaders of innovation*. This means that leaders need to excel at drawing out the innovative capacity of their employees and teams, rather than trying to lead by being the most innovative person on the team. They need to create an environment of trust and collaboration that allows all team members and employees to gain insight into issues and discover innovative solutions. Leaders can learn how to be leaders of innovation. When HR ensures that all leaders are leaders of innovation, they will have a sustainable approach to building the innovative intelligence within their organizations.

This is not to say that innovative leaders who generate a great many innovative ideas are unimportant to organizations. The opposite is true. They are great resources that HR should ensure are retained, but it is not a sustainable leadership model. When those leaders leave, it will not be easy to replace them.

HR needs to build the innovative intelligence of its leaders to make them leaders of innovation while also retaining its innovative leaders so that the business will have the capacity to deal with the new complexities it is encountering. The HR value proposition of "build leadership capacity" includes setting the future direction through the application of innovative intelligence by finding, developing, and retaining leaders with innovative intelligence to deliver this part of the promise to the business.

ELEMENT 2: APPLYING EMOTIONAL INTELLIGENCE

What is it?

Emotional intelligence is very important for leaders as they set a future direction for their business because leaders with emotional intelligence are perceptive of their own reactions and the reactions of others. They also are effective at working with others to develop the future direction collaboratively. Emotional intelligence includes the following:

- Being aware of one's own emotional reactions.
- Being socially perceptive and astute about others' emotional reactions.
- Being interpersonally mature when interacting with others.

Analysis and Implications

In the past 10 years, there has been a growing awareness that for leaders to function effectively within the changing business environment, they need to have an enhanced emotional intelligence. The need for emotional intelligence emerged in part because of the changing nature of the complexity at work. Leaders can no longer be effective by relying only on what they know and what they experience; they need to have the courage to say that they don't know the answer when a situation is complex and the results are uncertain. They require the maturity to know what they know and know what they do not know. They need the capability to ask for advice and not just tell others what they believe should be done.

Daniel Goleman[5] argues that there are many different styles of leaders; however, all successful leaders have a high level of emotional intelligence. He articulates five characteristics that are essential to emotional intelligence: self-awareness, self-regulation, motivation, empathy, and social skills. We have found that emotional intelligence can be simplified into three major areas as shown in Figure 8.2 on page 148.

---

5. Daniel Goleman, "What Makes a Leader?" *Harvard Business Review*, January (2004): 1–10.

Figure 8.2: The Three Aspects of Emotional Intelligence

Self-Aware:
Aware of your own
emotional state,
reactions & impulses

Socially-Perceptive:
Astute about the other
person's emotional state
& reactions

Interpersonally Mature:
Utilizes self-awareness and social perceptiveness in their
interactions and ongoing relationships with others

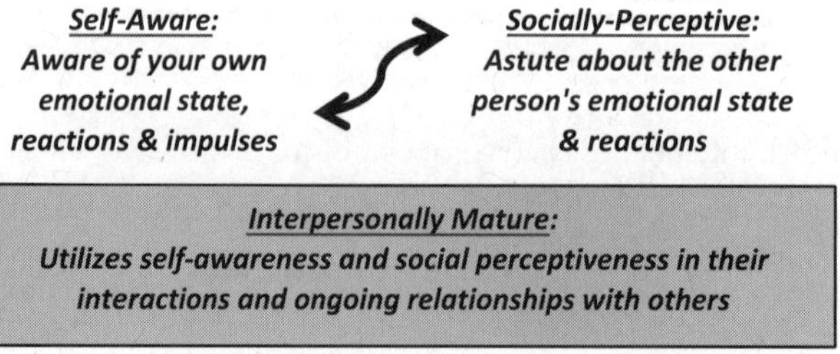

HR professionals need to build leadership capacity so that leaders have emotional intelligence in each of the three aspects.

Self-aware

Leaders need to be aware of their own emotional state and reactions to situations. This includes what Goleman[6] refers to as self-awareness, self-regulation, and motivation. Their awareness of themselves allows leaders to know what they know and what they don't know. It also enables them to have the courage to say that they need others to contribute ideas to more complex situations. At the same time, these leaders need to be sufficiently aware of their emotional responses so that they can manage their impulse control.

One characteristic that differentiates successful leaders from ineffective ones is the ability to know when to communicate an idea. One president articulated this very clearly when he said, "I imagine I have 16 arrows, and every time I shoot an arrow, I lose it forever." This leader realizes that he needs to be very thoughtful about the timing of each of his business moves so that each move has the maximum impact and employee acceptance. Impulse control is also important for leaders when encountering stressful situations. Leaders need to control their impulses during times of stress and think before they say something they will regret later.

HR needs to guide leaders to enhance their self-awareness and to demonstrate impulse control in order to have that great sense of timing.

---

6. Ibid.

The ideas developed by great leaders and average leaders may be equally good, but the difference is often the timing with which they launch their ideas, which relates directly to self-awareness and impulse control.

Socially perceptive

Effective leaders need to be perceptive of the emotional state of other individuals and groups and then know how to respond accordingly. Leaders who are able to perceive what employees, teams, stakeholders, and customers are feeling will have a greater chance of making effective decisions in response to those emotional reactions. Rather than trying to change other people's emotional reactions, effective leaders understand, respect, and validate those emotional reactions. HR thus needs to guide leaders to be perceptive of the emotional reactions of others in order to understand and validate those reactions, rather than to try to change them.

Interpersonally mature

Effective leaders utilize their self-awareness and social perceptiveness in their interactions and ongoing relationships with others. Interpersonal maturity emphasizes a leader's ability to communicate in a way that is understanding of others' emotional reactions. At the same time, interpersonal maturity reflects a leader's ability to manage his or her own emotional response. In particular, leaders need to demonstrate interpersonal maturity in times of high stress. At those times many people revert back to old emotional responses that may be less effective. Leaders who are interpersonally mature stay calm under high stress and keep the stress from having a negative impact on their self-awareness, social perceptiveness, and interpersonal maturity. These kinds of leaders are often viewed as highly effective leaders who can set a future direction while demonstrating emotional intelligence. HR has an important role to play in providing development for leaders to help them become more self-aware, socially perceptive, and interpersonally mature, and how to practice these goals effectively.

Here is an example of a team of directors who reported to a VP of marketing who they believed lacked emotional intelligence, and how this shaped the way the directors participated in setting the direction for their part of the business.

The VP of marketing was very concerned about the lack of openness and candor of his team of directors. They were working on setting a new direction for marketing and the VP tried to solicit ideas. All the directors seemed to agree with everything he said and did not contribute any alternative opinions. The VP could not believe there were no alternative views about the new direction.

He decided to engage a consultant to conduct confidential interviews with his team of directors. The consultant found that the team was frightened of the VP and believed that if they contradicted him, he would lose control, and that this could put their jobs at risk—so they decided to remain silent and not offer any contradictory opinions. After some further exploration, it became evident that most of the directors were referring to one event that had occurred three years before when the VP responded to a suggestion by raising his voice, pounding his fists on the table, and losing emotional control. Within six months the director who suggested the idea left the company.

When the consultant shared the aggregate information with the VP, the VP was stunned. He never saw himself as someone who loses control of his emotions or as someone others would fear, yet that was what was happening. Upon reflection, he did remember that outburst, and he said that he had been very upset that day because he had learned that his mother had been diagnosed with inoperative cancer. He lost control of his emotions with his team because he was out of control emotionally on a personal level. Also, he did speak to the director afterwards and apologized. When the director left the business six months later, the VP was under the impression that he was offered a better job elsewhere and that it had nothing to do with that incident.

The story has two important implications for leaders:

1. Leaders often do not know when they are perceived to lack emotional intelligence. Emotional intelligence needs to be viewed from the eyes of the beholder. In the story, this would mean that the assessment of the directors indicates the level of the VP's emotional intelligence more than the VP's self-assessment.

2. Leaders often underestimate the power of one indiscretion that demonstrates a lack of emotional intelligence. These leaders fall out of trust with their employees and teams, and as one leader said, "Trust takes forever to build and a moment to destroy, and mistrust takes forever to destroy and a moment to build." In the above story, one lapse in emotional intelligence by the leader resulted in the leader falling out of trust with the directors for the next three years.

HR professionals should emphasize the leader's need for emotional intelligence when they find, develop, and grow the business's leadership capacity. This includes:

- Ensuring that new leaders who are recruited are able to apply emotional intelligence.
- Developing leaders already in the organization on the three aspects of emotional intelligence: being self-aware, socially perceptive, and interpersonally mature.
- Finding opportunities to provide 360° feedback to leaders about their level of emotional intelligence. Sometimes leaders who lack emotional intelligence also lack the ability to accurately self-assess the extent to which they have emotional intelligence.
- Reacting swiftly when leaders do not demonstrate emotional intelligence, even if they are perceived to be high achievers.

HR should also measure the leader's leadership capacity through leadership assessments and 360° feedback surveys from employees and teams. For example, there are standardized aptitude tests to assess a leader's emotional intelligence. However, leaders should also receive feedback from others—including peers, employees, and supervisors—to learn how they are perceived. Some leaders may over-inflate their self-perception in emotional intelligence, which may be contradicted by others who see a different level of capacity. Both the leader's self-assessments and the feedback from others need to be taken into account when the plans are developed to enhance leadership capacity.

By developing emotionally intelligent leaders, HR will successfully meet the commitment to deliver another aspect of the leadership capacity that the business requires for future success. The HR value proposition of "build leadership capacity" includes setting the future direction through applying emotional intelligence by finding, developing, and retaining leaders with emotional intelligence to deliver this part of the promise to the business.

ELEMENT 3: ALIGNING EMPLOYEES AND TEAMS TO THE FUTURE DIRECTION

What is it?

Leaders inspire others to act by aligning their employees and teams to the future direction. Employees need to see the business's bigger picture and understand how their role fits into that bigger picture. The leader's role in this area includes the following:

- Aligning employees and teams to the business's holistic direction as well as horizontally across functions, and aligning employees within teams to ensure they focus on achieving the desired business outcome.
- Making ongoing adjustments as events shift the direction of the business in order to ensure that employees and teams are inspired to align to the business's future direction.

Analysis and Implications

Chapter Six described organizational alignment and how HR can contribute to ensuring that the organizational capability of alignment will occur. HR also has an important role in ensuring that leaders focus on the alignment of their employees and teams to the future business direction by doing the following:

- *Leaders need to think holistically to align employees and teams:* Leaders should have a holistic perspective and understand the macro context within which new complexities are arising. Then they need to lead the process to make sure they, their employees, and their teams maximize the value of their collective knowledge and innovative intelligence. In order for leaders to do this, HR needs to ensure that leaders are exposed to the overall business challenges, competitive issues, stakeholder interests, customer dynamics, regulatory requirements, and interdivisional issues.

- *Leaders need to have a horizontal view to align employees and teams:* Leaders should be able to work with diverse teams to gain insight and discover solutions to the new complex problems. They therefore need to excel at working horizontally across departments to bring in those diverse viewpoints and ideas. HR should provide the support needed to help leaders do this effectively. For example, HR could advise leaders to bring representatives from other departments (or key stakeholders and customers) into their teams to participate in innovative problem solving.

- *Leaders need to align employees within their teams to a common direction:* Leaders should use good management practices (proper planning, delegating, evaluation, and controlling) to align employees on their teams to the overall direction. In addition, HR needs to develop leaders who can align the team to the aspirational future of the business. When this occurs, leaders are able to trust that their employees will do the right thing on behalf of the business even when the leader is not there to oversee their work.

It is possible for leaders to be effective at inspiring others to act through alignment and achieve high performance and yet to do so in an unsustainable manner, which would be a deficiency in their leadership capacity. This can occur when a leader forces the alignment on others. Here is an example where this situation occurred:

The leader was always known as a tough leader, but many thought he was fair. Then everything seemed to change. Unbeknownst to the team, the leader was chastised by his boss for his team's performance. It seemed the team was more concerned about itself than about the company. The leader then arrived at his next team meeting and demanded that the team members do a better job of working together, collaborate more effectively with the other departments, and achieve better performance. His aggressiveness did the trick—it scared the team into compliance, they started acting more in alignment with each other and with the organization, and their performance improved. However, they were doing it out of fear. One by one, each of the team members either left the organization or transferred to another department. Although the performance improved initially out of fear, it was not a sustainable way of achieving alignment and inspiring others to act.

HR needs to ensure that leaders are aligning their teams in a way that achieves sustainable performance rather than short-lived performance based on fear, as described in the previous story. HR needs to guide leaders to constructively focus on holistic, horizontal, and within-team alignment as part of the fulfillment of the HR value proposition of "leadership capacity."

HR should also assess leaders' capacity to inspire others to act through alignment. At present, organizations rarely assess alignment. HR professionals should measure alignment to give feedback to leaders about their capacity in this area. One way to assess alignment is to focus on team alignment. In this team assessment, the team members and its leader all assess the extent to which the collective team is aligned with customer needs, the business direction, cross-functionally, and within the team. The questions focus on team alignment and not on individual employee alignment. An employee may believe that he or she is very much aligned with the business direction but that the collective team is not aligned. By focusing on team alignment, HR's assessment will have results that are less influenced by the leader's self-perception, and it will provide more feedback to team leaders about how effective they are at aligning their teams. Also, it will introduce a measure of team effectiveness that is woefully absent in many organizations, even though most organizations espouse the importance of teams to their future success.

ELEMENT 4: ENGAGING EMPLOYEES AND TEAMS WITH THE FUTURE DIRECTION

What is it?

Leaders inspire others to act through an emotional connection and through dialogue with employees and teams. They tap into what motivates employees so that they are willing to give their discretionary effort to the team and the organization. Leaders who engage others are excellent listeners, are able to draw out the deeper meaning of what is transpiring, and to inspire others to act. Engagement includes the following:

- Inspiring moderately engaged employees and teams so that, emotionally, they will give their discretionary effort toward achieving the desired future direction.
- Knowing how to reinforce those who are highly engaged with the organization so they can sustain that level of discretionary effort.
- Being effective at managing the disengaged employees and ensuring that they do not negatively influence the engagement of other employees and teams.

Analysis and Implications

In *The Leadership Gap*[7] we introduced the six factors that contribute to the engagement of employees and teams. These are:

I. *Being part of a winning organization:* Employees and teams can become highly engaged with a winning team, but this does not necessarily mean they will be disengaged if the team is not winning.

---

7. David S. Weiss and Vince Molinaro, *The Leadership Gap: Building Leadership Capacity for Competitive Advantage* (Toronto: John Wiley & Sons, 2005).

2. *Working for admired leaders:* This factor was assessed as the number one non-monetary motivator for employees.[8] Employees are more likely to stay in an organization if their leader is someone they admire, even if they are offered more pay elsewhere. Also, if employees are working for a leader they do not admire, it can become the primary reason why they leave an organization.

3. *Having positive working relationships:* Employees are more engaged when they have positive working relationships with colleagues. This applies to virtual organizations as well—which means that leaders need to find ways to have employees develop positive working relationships, even if the employees do not work together in the same location or rarely have opportunities to meet each other.

4. *Doing meaningful work:* Sometimes it is obvious to employees that they are doing meaningful work, but this is not always the case. HR needs to ensure that leaders know how to have a dialogue with employees and teams so that they understand the deeper meaning of what they are doing.

5. *Recognition and appreciation:* Recognition and appreciation for work is an important engager for many employees. HR needs to encourage leaders to show recognition and appreciation. For example, one leader followed HR's advice and tried to give employees at least two positive recognitions for each instance of negative feedback. The response was positive. Employees were more open to feedback and reported more satisfaction in their work.

6. *Living a balanced life:* Employees need to determine what their own balance needs are between work and personal life. HR should encourage leaders to respect their employees' balance needs as long as they can be accommodated and do not interfere with work performance. Some ways to be sensitive are rather simple. For example, avoid scheduling an offsite meeting in the morning on the first day of the week if it means that some employees have to travel to the meeting

---

8. Corporate Leadership Council, *Crafting a "Compelling Offer": Overview of Results From Primary Research Into The Career Decisions Of High Value Employees* (Washington DC: Corporate Executive Board, 1998).

location the night before. The meeting could be done just as easily in the afternoon of the same day.

Perhaps one of the most effective ways leaders can engage employees and teams and inspire them to act is through dialogue about the meaning of their work. Participants in effective dialogue discussions do the following:

- Articulate that which is almost subliminal and make the implicit explicit;
- Mutually share their interests (attitudes and concerns) and their intent;
- Emerge with a common understanding of the meaning of the situation.

Leaders use dialogue to be transparent and open with employees about the potential directions that the business might take and to explore the complexities in their work environment together. Dialogue engages employees with new directions and inspires them to give their discretionary effort to issues. Dialogue taps into two of the six engagement factors: doing meaningful work and working for admired leaders. It helps employees to see the significance of their work because the implicit meaning of the work is made explicit. The result is employees who have a common understanding of that meaning. Dialogue also establishes an opportunity for leaders to listen to and be transparent with their employees, which are factors in leaders being admired and trusted.

Dialogue is more easily said than done. Many leaders struggle to engage in dialogue with their employees and teams. The challenge for leaders is often that a prerequisite for dialogue is to show a high level of transparency and openness to the ideas of others. HR needs to guide leaders to be self-aware, socially perceptive, and interpersonally mature so that they can engage in meaningful dialogue with their employees and teams.

Here is an example of how a leader and an HR business partner used dialogue discussions to engage a team:

A leader was unable to break down the communication impasse among team members who were working on a strategic initiative. The team members were in the habit of shooting down a speaker before he or she had the opportunity to complete his or her thoughts. They were operating in a dysfunctional manner—not communicating with each other but at each other. The overall engagement of the members of the team was very low. People regularly opted out of meetings, which further reduced the team's effectiveness.

The HR business partner introduced the idea of a team dialogue to explore what was really going on and to determine the barriers to team effectiveness. They first developed some ground rules for the dialogue:

- *Listen to each other rather than thinking about what you want to say next.*
- *Suspend judgment and explore differences to achieve understanding.*
- *Make the ideas and beliefs that you feel are implicit, explicit. You may be surprised that what you feel is obvious is not so obvious for everybody else.*
- *Surface the underlying assumptions, issues, and concerns that are causing the miscommunication.*
- *Say what is in your hearts and not just what is in your heads.*
- *Discover a way to work together, and then move forward together.*

The leader then engaged the group in a dialogue to uncover the team's "meaningful shared goals." Usually, a dialogue session would involve all the team members openly talking with each other. In this situation, however, the HR business partner suggested a modified approach to dialogue based on the "fishbowl" technique whereby five members of the team sat in an inner circle to talk about the overlaps in their work that could be meaningful shared goals. The other five people in the team sat in an outer circle and observed the inner group's dialogue. Each person in the outer circle was asked to focus on one person in the inner circle. At any time they could tap the inner-circle person on the shoulder if they believed that person was not actively contributing to the dialogue. The outer-circle person was to explain why he or she was calling for the switch and then move into the inner circle to continue the dialogue with the other inner-circle participants.

At first, the five people in the inner circle were reluctant to participate actively, even after some prompting from the team leader. Then one of the outer-circle members tapped the shoulder of an inner-circle person and called for a switch. When the outer person moved to the inner dialogue, she opened up the conversation by saying, "Before we can talk about meaningful shared goals, we need to talk about why no one is willing to talk." Once the silence was broken, the others started participating as well. They discussed some

of the communication barriers the team experienced that related to trust and collabora-
tion issues. After some dialogue, they eventually moved on to discuss some meaningful
shared goals. After thirty minutes of dialogue and two switches, the team identified three
meaningful shared goals. They also discussed how to expand the latitude for employees to
act independently as long as they were acting in support of the meaningful shared goals.

The HR business partner then facilitated a team debrief of the process, and the team
indicated they had never spoken so openly with each other about their issues and their shared
goals. They decided that as new projects were introduced, the leader should hold dialogue
discussions about how the new projects supported the shared goals. They also decided to use
the outcomes of the dialogue discussions to engage all employees to act on new initiatives as
priorities shifted. As a result the team members became much more engaged with the team,
and they were able to deliver improved performance as the business continually evolved.

Engaging in dialogue in a nonjudgmental way demonstrates professional understanding and communication. It is similar to a due-diligence process on the thoughts and feelings of each person. The thoughts and feelings need to be fully understood so that each person truly comprehends what the other one believes. Dialogue enhances the chances of mutual understanding and shared meaning, and it improves overall engagement.

HR should guide leaders to use dialogue to enhance engagement in the following situations:

- *When they are struggling with ambiguous issues and unclear directions:* Leaders can use dialogue to build trust as team members struggle with ambiguity and discover new directions, as described in the previous story.
- *When they take ownership of people and organizational responsibilities:* When leaders need to welcome new people to the team, integrate them, and derive benefit from their new and diverse talent, it is very important to dialogue effectively.
- *When they need to enhance their ability to mentor and coach employees:* Leaders use the same dialogue approach they use in groups for their one-on-one conversations with employees.

- *When they engage in performance development discussions with their employees or teams and when they receive feedback on their own performance:* For example, when leaders receive 360° feedback on their performance from their employees and others, they debrief the feedback using dialogue discussions. Leaders create shared meaning through dialogue, and they gain a better appreciation of the underlying issues that need to be changed for them to be more effective in their role.

When leaders engage in dialogue, especially about their own performance, employees respond in predictable ways. Initially, they are surprised that the leader is willing to be open about the feedback he or she has received. After the dialogue, the employees invariably say that they respect the leader for his or her courage to engage in this kind of conversation. They suggest that the process enhanced their respect for the leader, and they feel the respect was reciprocated in the dialogue. Of course, the true test will be if the leader actually modifies his or her behavior as a result of the feedback and dialogue. If the leader does this, then trust will be enhanced among the team members and the level of engagement will improve.

HR professionals should actively promote dialogue so that leaders will use this approach to enhance the engagement of their employees and teams. In this regard, HR should do the following:

- *Champion this approach to leadership:* HR should expect leaders to have dialogues with employees and teams on an ongoing basis.
- *Coach leaders on how to have dialogues:* HR should coach leaders on how to take *apparent* consensus and deepen it through dialogue so that people will understand differences and reach more meaningful resolutions to dilemmas.
- *Teach employees how to participate in dialogue:* Leaders will have difficulty facilitating dialogue if their employees do not know how to participate. HR needs to develop employees so that they are better able to self-manage their contributions to the team's dialogue discussions and develop their skills as leaders and followers.

- *Facilitate dialogue on sensitive issues that require shared meaning:* HR professionals should facilitate dialogue on sensitive issues. For example, in one situation an HR professional facilitated dialogue with a team that was upset about their team leader who had recently been terminated because of some inappropriate behaviors.

HR should assess the capacity of leaders to inspire others to act through engagement. Organizations often use engagement surveys to give leaders feedback on their team members and to compare that feedback with that from the rest of the organization and with standardized benchmarks. It would also be useful to have team members assess the extent to which they believe the collective team works together in an engaged manner. For example, does the team give discretionary effort to achieve its collective goals? Do the team members believe they are focused on meaningful work? Do the team members believe collectively that they are working for an admired leader?

The individual and team engagement surveys work very closely together, but they provide different insights about employee and team engagement and the level of leadership capacity demonstrated by the leader. For example, if a team is comprised of 10 people and one person is not engaged, the team could be rated as highly engaged because nine out 10 employees are highly engaged. However, when the team members assess the collective team, that one disengaged person could be dragging down the overall team engagement. As a result the team members may assess the team as not being highly engaged or aligned (even though nine out of 10 people are individually engaged and aligned).

INTEGRATING THE FOUR ELEMENTS OF LEADERSHIP CAPACITY

The four elements of leadership capacity—innovative intelligence, emotional intelligence, alignment, and engagement—are presented in this chapter as discrete elements, but in reality they are very interdependent. All four are needed for a leader to have the leadership capacity that the business requires. Table 8.2 on the opposite page shows how a lack in any one of the leadership capacity elements affects a leader's capacity in the other three.

Table 8.2: How a Deficiency in One Element of Leadership Capacity Affects the Others

If a leader is lacking in one of the leadership capacity elements …	…then the implications for the other three elements are as follows:
Lacking innovative intelligence: These leaders will have limited ability to gain insight and discover solutions to complex issues independently or with their teams.	These leaders will have a difficult time aligning their team members if they do not have a clear direction. They also will miss the opportunity to use innovative problem-solving as a way to engage their employees and teams.
Lacking emotional intelligence: These leaders will not be self-aware, socially perceptive, or interpersonally mature as they explore future directions and work with their employees and teams.	These leaders may respond poorly to uncertainty in the business environment and may panic under some stressful conditions, which can inhibit innovative thinking. Also, they will likely not be perceptive of the emotional sensitivities of employees and teams, so engagement may be reduced.
Lacking the ability to align employees and teams: These leaders will have teams that are not working well together and not doing their work with a focus on how it adds to the business direction and to delivering customer value.	These leaders will likely have difficulty applying innovative thinking with diverse teams if employees and teams do not collaborate effectively, both horizontally and cross-functionally. Also, they will likely have employees who are not as engaged because when employees are aligned to a common direction, their engagement with the team is enhanced.
Lacking the ability to engage employees and teams: These leaders will have teams that are not giving their discretionary effort, and the overall performance will thus be mediocre. Also, some stronger employees may leave to find other employment where they can be more engaged.	These leaders will have difficulty engaging employees in innovative thinking to resolve complex issues because the employees may not give the extra effort required for that process. Also, it is likely that a leader who does not engage his or her employees and teams is deficient in emotional intelligence and therefore may not even know that the employees and the team are not engaged.

HR must align and engage the executive team with the HR value proposition of building leadership capacity. Here are some of the ways they can do this:

- Position leadership capacity as a strategic priority for the business and gain executive commitment to the HR value proposition.
- Engage the executive team to define the precise focus for the HR value proposition of building leadership capacity so that it mitigates the associated business risk.
- Focus on all four elements of leadership capacity as HR delivers its HR value proposition. Executives need to view the four elements as interdependent and integrated so that they are able to fulfill the leadership capacity required for the business.
- Use measurements of the leaders, employees, and teams to provide feedback to leaders regarding the extent to which they have the required leadership capacity and to determine how leaders can build this capacity.

HR can also sustain the executive team focus on the HR value proposition of leadership capacity by ensuring that the following three things occur:

- The executive team works collaboratively, applying innovative intelligence and emotional intelligence to set the future direction. They regularly discuss ways to inspire others to act through aligning and engaging employees and teams.
- The senior HR leader conducts leadership talent reviews with the executive team to track the organization's leadership capacity and to identify areas that need further investment of time and resources.
- The executives personally continue to develop their leadership capacity and accept their role as models of the required leadership capacity. They also make leadership capacity development a priority for their direct reports.

CONCLUSION

HR professionals identify leadership capacity as an HR value proposition when the business strategy could be at risk because of a deficiency in this area. Leadership capacity focuses on how leaders need to set the future direction through applying innovative intelligence and emotional intelligence and how they need to inspire others to act by aligning and engaging employees and teams. HR needs to view the four elements of leadership capacity as integrated and interdependent in order to deliver the HR value proposition of leadership capacity. The next two chapters explore two other HR value propositions that are often chosen to mitigate potentially damaging risks to business strategy: culture transformation and change implementation.

SUMMARY

- Leadership capacity refers to the gap between the current leadership talent level and the leadership talent required by the business to deliver its strategies.
- The four elements of leadership capacity are as follows:
  1. Element 1: Innovative intelligence refers to the human cognitive ability to gain insight into problems or opportunities in new ways and to discover new and unforeseen implementable solutions. Leaders need innovative intelligence to set the future direction, especially in uncertain times. The three principles of leading with innovative intelligence are as follows:
     - Principle #1: Innovation works best within precise boundaries.
     - Principle #2: Innovation works best with diverse teams.
     - Principle #3: Sustainable innovation needs leaders of innovation rather than innovative leaders.
  2. Element 2: Emotional intelligence is very important for leaders as they set a future direction because leaders with emotional intelligence are perceptive of their own reactions and the reactions of others as they choose where to direct their business. They are also effective at working with others to develop their future direction collaboratively.
  3. Element 3: Aligning employees and teams to the future direction. Leaders inspire others to act by aligning their employees and teams to the future direction. Employees need to see the business's bigger picture and understand how what they do fits into that bigger picture.

4. Element 4: Engaging employees and teams with the future direction. Leaders inspire others to act through an emotional connection and through dialogue with employees and teams. They tap into what motivates employees so that they are willing to give their discretionary efforts to the team and the organization. Leaders who engage others are excellent listeners and are able to draw out the deeper meaning of what is transpiring and inspire others to act.

- There is a need to view the four elements as interdependent and integrated so that the leader is able to fulfill the leadership capacity required for the business. Also, HR should use measurements of the leaders, employees, and teams to provide feedback to leaders regarding the extent to which they have the required leadership capacity and how they can build that capacity.

- HR also must align and engage the executive team with the HR value proposition of building leadership capacity. HR needs to position leadership capacity as a strategic priority for the business and gain executive commitment to the HR value proposition. HR also needs to engage the executive team to define the precise focus for the HR value proposition of building leadership capacity so that it mitigates the associated business risk.

CHAPTER NINE

ACCELERATE CULTURE TRANSFORMATION

A company acquired a competitor with the idea that a merger would be very beneficial to their organization. Before the acquisition the executives were very focused on the upcoming merger. However, they did not consider the cultural differences between the two businesses. They decided to set up a mid-level management team headed by a director to champion the takeover process. The team encountered intense resistance from both the purchasing company and the acquired business.

A major reason for this resistance was culture clash. The acquiring company was results-oriented and not very sensitive to employee needs. The purchased company was people-focused and interested in employee input and needs. The executives were not prepared for the cultural differences and so they did not deal with the culture clash effectively. The benefits of the acquisition looked good on paper but did not come to fruition. Eventually, after most of the acquired company's executives were laid off and portions of that company were sold, the remaining departments were reorganized into the existing company. The customers, shareholders, and employees voiced their displeasure with the way the company handled the merger. In the privacy of their boardroom, the executives deemed the acquisition a failure because they did not mitigate the risk of the culture differences between the two companies.

Studies have found that many mergers and acquisitions fail not because the businesses are not complementary, but because the cultures do not integrate well. Similarly, when a single business restructures, cultural adaption may not be done well. Employees may cling to the previous structure and not adapt well to the culture changes.

There is an advantage for businesses in which mergers, acquisitions, and restructuring occur because there is a visible, explicit change in the business which makes it obvious that some cultural changes may be required. However, when there are no visible signs of the need for culture change, it is sometimes an even greater challenge to transform culture. For example, a change of business direction or a new president who is hired into the business could result in a new direction and need for cultural transformation. The employment agreement that existed in the past and enabled the business to reach its former success may no longer be applicable to achieve the business's future success. The business may need to change, and that often involves the need for cultural transformation.

Human resources professionals need to closely study the business changes that occur in mergers, acquisitions, and restructuring, as well as business changes in overall direction and executive leadership. They need to explore the implications of those changes for the people and organizational capabilities and develop the appropriate HR value proposition. In these situations, the risks associated with culture are often great, and HR needs to mitigate the risks by accelerating the cultural transformation to help the strategy and new direction occur rapidly and effectively.

WHY IS ACCELERATING CULTURE TRANSFORMATION SO CHALLENGING?

Executives are often told that cultural transformation requires five to seven years before it can be realized. However, few executives have that much time. There is a critical need to accelerate cultural transformation to mitigate the cultural risks associated with a new business direction.

What we have found[1] is that very little is actually being done to help existing employees adopt a new culture. The culture changes occur during that five- to seven-year period because attrition and turnover bring new people into the organization who are more willing to support

---

1. See David S. Weiss and Claude Legrand, *Innovative Intelligence: The Art and Practice of Leading Sustainable Innovation in your Organization* (Toronto: John Wiley & Sons, 2011), ch. 12.

the new culture. In general, if attrition and turnover in an organization affect 5 to 10 percent of employees annually, then approximately 30 to 50 percent are likely to leave within a five-year time frame. If organizations are effective at selecting new employees who operate according to the desired culture, then within five to seven years there will be a critical mass of new employees who will support the new culture. Rather than waiting for attrition to achieve that outcome, businesses need to accelerate cultural transformation by finding the levers to work with the *existing employees* to help them adopt the new culture.

WHAT IS CULTURE?

The way culture functions for groups is similar to the way personality functions for individuals. Personality helps individuals define who they are, and it helps achieve personal stability. To protect one's personality, an individual often develops self-defenses to resist attempts to change his or her own personality. In a similar way, groups develop a group personality, which is referred to as "culture." The culture defines who the group is and helps the group achieve stability and predictability within the culture. The group then develops protective mechanisms so that it can defend itself against those who want to change the culture. If there are attempts to change the group's culture, the group will collectively resist, thereby protecting their stability. In other words, the definition of "culture" is group personality.[2]

A culture can form in groups of any size—for example, in a project team, in an intact work team, or in the entire business—but it always occurs in groups. It functions as a group of implicit assumptions about the way the group does things. One senior executive said it well when he defined culture in very straightforward terms: "culture is what people do and say when no one is looking."[3] Culture is not a demand placed

---

2. Edgar H. Schein, *Organizational Culture and Leadership* (San Francisco: John Wiley & Sons, 2004).

3. This definition of culture was articulated by John Helou, General Manager Specialty Care Products, of Pfizer Canada Inc. It is quoted with his written permission.

upon the group by the business. Instead, it is the group's self-directed and self-motivated assumptions and methods of behaving.

The only time that a group is willing to transform its culture is when the group understands that the compelling need for the change is worth it. If employees believe that an organization has decided to introduce a new culture for the sake of cultural transformation and not for meaningful business outcomes, it is very likely that they will resist those attempts at cultural transformation. If an organization deems it important to create a new culture, it needs to have meaningful and compelling business needs to justify the groups' willingness to endure the instability of cultural transformation.

Here is an example of an HR group that identified the risks to the business strategy that were associated with culture. They adopted an HR value proposition to accelerate culture transformation that would sustain the business during very difficult times. The HR professionals were able to achieve the cultural transformation because the urgency for a culture transformation from a business perspective far exceeded the employees' anxiety over the required culture transformation. Here is the story:

For years, a printing company had been successfully producing high-quality products for its many multinational customers. The organizational culture was characterized by high-quality activity by all employees, and they were very careful at all times to ensure that level of quality was maintained. There was a collegial environment where people were very supportive of each other, but quality was clearly paramount for everybody.

Several major competitors introduced technological advancements that made some of the company's major product lines obsolete. The company's profits started to erode rapidly, and there was great concern by all that the company might not be able to stay in business if it could not compete against the new competitive technologies.

The executives recognized that they needed to modernize their technologies in order to stay competitive. They developed a strategy of business acquisitions and modernization that they believed would address the problem. However, the HR VP revealed that their current cultural patterns were inconsistent with the culture that would be required to achieve the business strategy. She proposed an HR value proposition that would help the business transform its culture. She explained that the new culture would be essential for the business to implement the new strategy and compete in the new environment. The new culture needed to focus on groups being far more innovative and willing to take risks in order for the business to survive.

The HR VP guided the executives through the process of how to engage employees with the need for this kind of cultural transformation. They decided to conduct group sessions with employees to share the financial trends of the overall business. They also showed all employees examples of the competitors' technological advances and brought in a customer panel that reinforced the need for those advances. Although the customers were loyal to the company, they preferred the competitors' new technologies. These presentations and discussions were very compelling for employees, helping them to understand that something radical needed to happen.

The HR VP helped the executives realize that they needed a shift to a culture of innovation that would augment the focus on quality. HR then coordinated a targeted approach to reinforce the focus on quality while introducing an emphasis on innovative thinking. Through this effort the company was successful at implementing its strategy. They were able to redesign their product offering, invest heavily into new technology, and acquire several smaller technology companies that they integrated into their business to modernize their offering to their customers and sustain their business. The executives also recognized that the key to the success of the strategy was the HR value proposition to accelerate culture transformation to achieve a culture of innovation.[4]

THE *LASER-BEAM* APPROACH TO CULTURAL TRANSFORMATION

Any significant change within an organization needs a plan in order for it to be implemented effectively. A transformation in culture needs to be thoughtfully planned as well. The approach to accelerating cultural transformation described in this chapter is a targeted approach to modifying the culture so that risk to the business is reduced. It emphasizes a *laser-beam* focus on reinforcing a few cultural aspects and modifying several other aspects, rather than attempting to change the entire culture.

---

4. See Chapter Twelve of *Innovative Intelligence: The Art and Practice of Leading Sustainable Innovation in your Organization* by David S. Weiss and Claude P. Legrand (Toronto: John Wiley & Sons, 2011) for a more extensive discussion of how to create a culture of innovation.

Figure 9.1 shows the six steps in the *laser-beam* approach for cultural transformation:

Figure 9.1: The Six Steps in the *Laser-Beam* Approach to Cultural Transformation

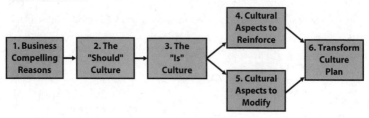

The six steps can be summarized as follows:

The Six Steps in the *Laser-Beam* Approach to Cultural Transformation

1. Identify the compelling business reasons for cultural transformation.
2. Articulate what the desired culture "should" be.
3. Describe what the current culture "is."
4. Target aspects of the current culture to retain.
5. Target aspects of the current culture to modify.
6. Develop the culture transformation implementation plan.

The next sections explore how HR professionals implement the six steps in the *laser-beam* approach to cultural transformation.

Step 1: Identify the Compelling Business Reasons for Cultural Transformation

What is Done in this Step?

- Understand the compelling business strategy and the risks to that strategy that relate to culture.

- Confirm that accelerating culture transformation should be the HR value proposition for the business to help it achieve its strategy.

The Merger Case Example

The following story about a business merger will be used throughout the remainder of this chapter to illustrate how to apply the *laser-beam* approach to cultural transformation. First, a brief overview is given that describes the compelling business issues and why accelerating cultural transformation was chosen as the HR value proposition. The merger case example is then revisited at the conclusion of each *laser-beam* step to describe how the step was applied to accelerate culture transformation.

A company has just acquired a major competitor and is in the process of merging the two businesses. The business benefits of the acquisition are clear: the merged business will have the size to compete for much larger contracts, and the removal of a major competitor will pave the way to reach many more customers and increase profitability. The HR VP indicates that the strategy has a major risk associated with the effective merger of the cultures of the two businesses. She highlights the business risks associated with culture change and takes accountability to accelerate the cultural transformation. This offer from HR gives the executives confidence that the HR value proposition will be addressed with expertise and as a priority. The executives agree that HR should take accountability for the HR value proposition of accelerating cultural transformation to mitigate the cultural risks associated with the merger.

Step 2: Articulate What the Desired Culture "Should" Be

What is Done in this Step?
- Develop a clear description of the *desired culture* and why it is essential for the achievement of the business strategy.
- Include in the desired culture the expected values, required behaviors (dos and don'ts), and desired cultural assumptions.
- Initiate a dialogue with employees about the business's urgency for the desired culture and what the expected employee behaviors are in the new culture.

How is this Step Applied to the Merger Case Example?
Here is how the HR VP orchestrates the development of the "should"
state for the desired culture of the merged businesses:

*The HR VP proposes a plan to develop the "should" state for the culture of the two busi-
nesses. She recommends that they form a cultural integration team consisting of the 12
most talented people from both companies, six from each company. The HR VP selects the
12 key people for the cultural integration team carefully but with a sense of urgency. The
"Group of 12" (referred to as G-12) are guaranteed a role in the integrated business and
are released from the responsibilities of their regular jobs for the next month. The 12 key
resources who are selected are both honored (because of the cultural integration team's strategic
importance) and relieved (because of the increased job security) to be selected for the cultural
integration team. One of the 12, a high-potential HR director who understands the laser-
beam approach to cultural transformation, is asked to chair the cultural integration team.*

*The G-12 bond well as a team. Their first meeting focuses on learning the six
laser-beam steps to accelerate cultural transformation. They understand the compelling
business reasons for a focus on cultural transformation (Step 1) and then they focus
on articulating what "should" be the culture for the integrated business (Step 2). They
decide to engage in the process of developing the new culture by exploring the values and
behaviors the business requires. They approach the task by asking, "What business culture
must the business have to succeed and how does that compare with our personal values?"
Business-driven values that overlap with personal values are easier to live by. The team
identifies the values that are to the business's benefit, such as a passion for customer focus,
multidisciplinary teamwork, and innovation with quality. They then identify their personal
values that gravitate to issues of respect for every individual, excellence in everything they
do, and openness and honesty. (Figure 9.2 on the next page illustrates the overlap between
business and personal values.)*

*They choose a short list of values to which they all feel they can commit: a passion for
customer focus, respect for every individual, multidisciplinary teamwork, and excellence
in everything they do. They believe they will have no difficulty being accountable for these
values in the new merged company. They record the agreed-upon values, definitions, and
associated behaviors, and then sign the document.*

*The HR chair observes that the cultural integration team feels so good about the values
they developed that it would be useful to engage all employees in this process to enhance*

Figure 9.2: Identify the Overlap of Values

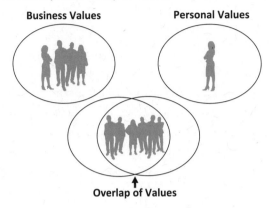

their commitment and ownership as well. They decide to bring the signed values document and their employee engagement recommendation to an executive meeting to describe the culture they believe is needed for the merged business and their suggestion for the next step.

The executives review the list of values and how it advances their objective to develop one culture; however, not all of the key elements that are needed in the new culture are reflected in the values. A major cultural requirement that is absent is the need for a culture that is adaptable and scalable to the changing business environment. The executives believe that their newly merged business will change significantly over the next few years. Leaders and employees will need to be able to learn new skills and adapt to new roles, responsibilities, and work teams relatively frequently. Also, the business will likely be affected by rapid shifts in the competitive and consumer marketplace, so the business will need to be able to scale up to a larger size or scale down to a smaller size rapidly, efficiently, and effectively. As a result, they add "adaptability" to the list of values that will shape the new culture of the business. The executives then support the recommendation of the cultural integration team.

Step 3: Describe What the Current Culture "Is"

What is Done in this Step?

- Describe the current culture with a focus on its values, its group behaviors (dos and don'ts), and the cultural assumptions that have sustained those values and behaviors.

- Compare the current culture (what "is") to the desired culture (what "should" be) identified in Step 2.

HR professionals need to lead the process of understanding the current culture in order to determine which parts of the culture should be retained and which should be modified. One way to understand the current culture is to talk to newly hired people about the group's current culture. People who are new to an organization are often able to contrast the way the group operates, makes decisions, and resolves conflicts with the way that other groups they have been associated with have acted and behaved. HR should take advantage of the observations of the newest group members and ask them to describe the behavioral aspects of the group in comparison with groups in their previous work experiences.

Another way to describe the current culture is for HR to ask the group to describe its patterns of behavior, either through a survey process or in group discussions. The behaviors that the newest employees or the overall group identify can be obvious and tangible (such as dress, office space, furniture, technology, or locks on doors). They also can be more subtle and intangible (such as how the group utilizes meetings, how they make decisions, whether they defer to hierarchy, what the gender relations are like, how they respond to conflict, or whether they are open to diversity). Next, the group formulates assumptions—explicit or implicit—that they accept as valid. The group then adopts these collective assumptions as the way it works together and solves problems, and these assumptions begin to function as the "group's personality."

How is this Step Applied to the Merger Case Example?

The G-12 proceed with a series of large group employee sessions, both face-to-face and virtual. In these sessions the HR director and the cultural integration team explain the purpose of the integration of the two businesses and its implications for the new culture. They then present the values and behaviors they identified and that were supported by the executives. They then engage all employees in a dialogue process to refine the new values required for the business and to compare them with the current culture of each of the two legacy businesses. Here is the process they use:

- *They emphasize the need for one set of values that all employees will adopt to drive the new integrated business. They then present the priority values that the business should adopt as the foundation of its new culture.*
- *The employees are asked to identify the current values of their organizations and to compare them to the desired values for the new integrated business.*
- *They then explore the "yellow line," or the line below which people begin to yell. The current behaviors below the yellow line are those that are just beyond the tolerable level in the new desired culture. The participants explore the "yellow line" with intensity. Some of the comments include the following:*
    - *"If we value respect for every individual, does that mean we do not refer to people by their legacy company anymore?"*
    - *"Does excellence in everything we do mean we don't sacrifice quality for timeliness?"*
    - *"Does multidisciplinary teamwork mean that we don't have silos anymore?"*

The feelings are deep, and the dialogue starts to create shared meaning. Through the vehicle of the "yellow line," the employees reveal their assumptions and concerns about the way work is done and how it compares to what the new business requires. When the final values list is complete, an all-employees virtual meeting is held. There, the multilevel, cross-functional team unveils to all employees the final list of values that are needed in the new culture and how it compares with the way each legacy company functions currently. The understanding of the need for transformation appears to be widespread.

Step 4: Target Aspects of the Current Culture to Retain

What is Done in this Step?
- Identify key assumptions of the current culture that need to be reinforced because they are *consistent* with the desired culture.
- Generate a top-priority list and develop the tactics to reinforce those cultural aspects.

Steps 4 and 5 of the *laser-beam* approach to cultural transformation focus on how to transform culture from the "is" culture state (Step 3) to the "should" culture state (Step 2). It is important to understand how culture develops in order to figure out how to change it. The process of creating culture in organizations often happens in a haphazard way. Here is the way groups often develop culture in organizations:[5]

1. *The group experiences an urgent problem or opportunity:* The problem or opportunity may be how to work either externally or internally, and it must be compelling and urgent.

2. *The group collectively discovers a solution that works well enough to be considered valid:* Working together to develop insight about the problem or opportunity, the group will discover some possible solutions. A top priority will be to determine which of the solutions will be most effective. The solution that is considered most effective will be the valid solution.

3. *The group formulates explicit or implicit assumptions:* The group formulates assumptions—explicit or implicit—that they accept as valid methods of responding to similar and future problems and opportunities. The group then adopts these collective assumptions as the way they solve problems, and these assumptions begin to define the group's personality. Culture only adheres when the group accepts the assumptions as the way they collectively perceive, think, feel, and do things, even without an external authority telling them to behave that way.

4. *The group teaches the assumptions to new members of the group:* The group then teaches the explicit or implicit assumptions to new members as the correct way to think, feel, and perceive when they work on current and future problems and opportunities. In order to belong to the group, the new members adopt these assumptions as the valid way to respond, sometimes without fully understanding how the assumptions developed originally.

---

5. See Edgar Schein, *Organizational Culture and Leadership* (San Francisco: John Wiley & Sons, 2004), where he defines culture as "A pattern of shared basic assumptions that was learned by a group as it solved its problems of external adaptation and internal integration, that has worked well enough to be considered valid and, therefore, to be taught to new members as the correct way to perceive, think, and feel in relation to those problems."

Rather than letting organizational culture occur haphazardly, orchestrating the events to create culture using the *laser-beam* approach will accelerate cultural transformation. For example, some leaders think they should respond to a challenging issue or crisis independently to protect their employees from the issue. In some cases, that may be the right decision. However, it is a lost opportunity in terms of building the culture of the group. If the leader wants to resolve the problem and at the same time build a common culture, the leader would be wise to engage the group with the problem and have them work together to discover solutions. This process has two positive outcomes:

- The group will likely input diverse insights and solutions that may be better than what the leader might have generated independently.
- The process of the group engaging with the problem and generating solutions can build a common culture for the group so that they will be able to resolve these kinds of issues independently in the future.

Once a culture is embedded in a group, an essential part of accelerating cultural transformation is focusing on current cultural behaviors and assumptions that can be retained and reinforced in the new culture. This process has several benefits. First, it reduces the anxiety of the cultural transformation if employees feel that some aspects of their current culture will be retained and validated. Second, it builds trust that will allow the organization to request that other behaviors and assumptions should be modified. HR professionals need to discover the current assumptions that need to be retained, reinforced, and even celebrated.

Using Step 4 in the *laser-beam* approach, we can target aspects of the current culture to retain. Here is the method to reinforce the cultural behaviors and assumptions that are *consistent* with the desired culture:

1. Identify observable aspects that distinguish the work environment. Ask if these aspects have any importance for the new culture that needs to be created. If they are important, then there must be some assumption that explains why people are motivated to behave that way.

2. Discuss the extent to which the behavioral aspects are *consistent* with the desired culture and identify the top behaviors to reinforce.
3. Identify the assumptions for the behavioral aspects that are *consistent* with the desired culture.
4. Devise ways to retain, reinforce, and celebrate the assumptions that are *consistent* with the desired culture.

How is this Step Applied to the Merger Case Example?

Let's return to the merger case example and see how they apply this step of the cultural transformation acceleration process:

The collaborative work of the G-12 and the involvement of employees in the development of the new values launch the emphasis on one culture. This contributes to creating team environments throughout the integrated business where employees feel they can contribute ideas with greater safety. The teams are also more open to diverse opinions and to generating new ideas. These are aspects of the emerging culture that are desired in the new culture. They then explore the assumptions of employees and learn that in each legacy company there was a team focus that contributed to the rapid adoption of the employee-involvement process in the development of the businesses' values.

However, the new business needs to go beyond the existing values and augment them with a culture that will ensure that employees and teams are adaptable to changing business requirements and that the organization is scalable to respond to changing competitive and customer dynamics. The organization needs to expand or contract when such business needs arise. It also needs to be able to revert back to its original structure when the tension is released. The HR chairperson leads a dialogue discussion with the G-12 to explore the cultural challenges associated with deploying various organizational tactics including the following:

- *Develop preferred supplier relationships for specialized work: The new team in this business will consist of full-time employees and external preferred suppliers who assist them on specialized work. When the external resources are asked to be part of the team, the team needs to expand to include them and treat them as team members.*
- *Form time-limited, multidisciplinary, and cross-functional teams: The executives plan to form multidisciplinary teams (similar to the G-12 design team) that*

work on strategic projects for a period of time and then split up to return to their daily work. The temporary nature of the teams creates the opportunity for individuals who can add the most value to an initiative to join the multidisciplinary team when their skills are needed. These multidisciplinary teams often have either "sunset clauses" that identify when they will conclude their responsibility or decision points to determine whether they will continue on the team.

- **Ensure effective communications throughout the levels of the hierarchy:** *The organization will need to move rapidly when the competitive and customer dynamics change. As a result, all employees need to understand the changing business dynamics and their implications for the need for adaptability and scalability. Leaders need to send transparent and consistent messages throughout the organization and from the top of the hierarchy to the front-line employees.*

The HR chairperson leads the process whereby the G-12 decide to reinforce the two cultural assumptions that are consistent with the desired culture: joint problem-solving between teams and the openness to generating new ideas. They plan to use the values and the two assumptions as a way to lay the foundation for the need to be adaptable and scalable. Here are some specific strategies they use to reinforce the cultural assumptions they want to retain:

- **Executive role modeling:** *The executives find opportunities to role model the desired culture so that employees see that the executive team believes in a multidisciplinary team-based approach and that they are open to diverse opinions.*
- **Build in reinforcers:** *They retain and actually embellish upon the importance of multidisciplinary team discussions to generate new ideas and the importance of openness to diverse viewpoints. For example, they celebrate success stories of groups that work well as teams and that are able to leverage team dialogue discussions to find new ideas and solutions.*
- **Allocate resources to the team-based culture:** *They allocate time and resources to the work of multidisciplinary teams that are exhibiting the desired behaviors. Also, they allocate funds to bring people together from across the business to attend group meetings that will reinforce the multidisciplinary team-based culture and the openness to new ideas.*

These three mechanisms of role modeling, reinforcers, and resources reduce employee anxiety as other cultural transformations are introduced. These mechanisms also build employee trust to modify or eliminate aspects of the current culture that are inconsistent with the desired culture needed to drive the new business outcomes.

Step 5: Target Aspects of the Current Culture to Modify

What is Done in this Step?

- Identify the aspects of the current culture that need to be modified or eliminated because they are *inconsistent* with the desired culture.
- Generate a top-priority list and develop the tactics to modify the inconsistent cultural assumptions in the least anxiety-provoking way.

It is important to focus on the critical few cultural behaviors and assumptions (no more than five) that need to be modified or eliminated in the new culture. This process has several benefits. First, it targets the top-priority cultural assumptions to be modified so the expected changes will not be overwhelming. Second, the process of cultural transformation generates anxiety, and by highlighting a few assumptions to modify or eliminate, the cultural transformation may meet with less resistance. HR professionals need to discover the critical few cultural assumptions that need to be modified or eliminated and develop a targeted approach to modifying those cultural assumptions.

The processes in this step to identify the behaviors and assumptions are similar to those used to identify the cultural behaviors and assumptions that are *consistent* with the desired culture. The only difference is that the focus is on what is *inconsistent* with the desired culture. Again, the newest person to be hired or join a group is the best person to describe the group's current culture. Alternatively, HR can ask the group to describe its patterns of behavior and explore which cultural behaviors and assumptions are inconsistent with the desired culture.

Here is the process to modify cultural assumptions that are *inconsistent* with the desired culture.

I.   Explore the observable aspects of the work environment. Identify if they have importance for the new culture. If they are important, there must be some assumption that explains why people are motivated to behave that way.

2. Discuss the extent to which the behavioral aspects are *inconsistent* with the desired culture and identify the top behaviors to modify.

3. Identify the assumptions for the behavioral aspects that are *inconsistent* with the desired culture.

4. Devise ways to modify and eliminate the assumptions that are *inconsistent* with the desired culture.

There are three ways that one can respond to cultural assumptions that are inconsistent with the desired culture and thus need to be modified.

- *Rechanneling:* *Rechanneling* is the process of redirecting the current cultural assumptions to achieve an outcome consistent with what the desired culture requires. It is the least anxiety-provoking method of transformation because it validates aspects of what the group currently does, and it shifts the group's current cultural assumptions to the assumptions of the preferred culture. Rechanneling is similar to the technique used in karate when blocking a punch, whereby the defender diverts the punch to the side rather than stopping it so that the punch does not cause direct damage.

For example, in one organization, the leaders were highly facilitative and rarely took personal accountability for their results. This cultural pattern was based on the assumption that leaders who took personal accountability were not working as team players. The HR professional rechanneled this cultural assumption by building on the leaders' role as facilitators of effective discussions to a rechanneled role of being the final authority in determining direction. The HR professional also worked as a coach for the leaders in some group meetings to encourage them to make the decision by the end of the meeting so that they would be able to proceed and to take accountability for their decisions. This process used the leaders' facilitative approach in a very non-threatening way to propel the leaders to start taking personal accountability in their decision-making.

- *Counterbalancing:* This approach focuses on identifying areas that can be the model of the new culture and giving them recognition to counter-balance the old cultural approach. This is often the primary technique that leaders use when they successfully transform culture after five to seven years. They eventually succeed at culture transformation through employee attrition and turnover (as described earlier in this chapter). The counterbalancing technique is more anxiety-provoking for groups than the rechanneling technique. Hiring and promoting employees and leaders who bring in new ideas and operate with the new cultural assumptions may directly conflict with employees and leaders who are operating with the old cultural assumptions.

For example, one organization had an assumption that all cross-functional meetings had to have representatives from all areas. This assumption let to a dysfunctional pattern of meetings with over 20 participants, and often nothing was accomplished. To counterbalance this assumption, the HR professional recommended that they set a limit of 10 people for any new cross-functional team that was formed and to gradually phase out the existing cross-functional teams that had over 20 members. They celebrated the successes and the speed of decision-making that these new, smaller teams were able to achieve. The HR professionals also encouraged some of the facilitators of the larger teams to observe the new cross-functional teams. This showed the other facilitators that the smaller cross-functional teams could generate high-quality discussions and represent all areas even though only 10 people attended the meetings.

- *Confronting:* Confronting is the most anxiety-provoking method of modifying cultural assumptions that are inconsistent with the desired culture. Some leaders resort to confrontation out of frustration with the lack of speed of their employees' cultural transformation.

For example, leaders may terminate the employment of key people as a signal to the organization that the cultural transformation is serious, or they may engage in a major restructuring of the organization to force people to work in another way, or they may unilaterally introduce radical changes to compensation and rewards. Although confronting can be effective in a crisis situation, in most situations it is a high-risk approach that is often unsustainable. Confronting may generate a fearful response from employees and teams, and they may become immobilized or leave the organization because of a perception that the culture is toxic. HR professionals should guide leaders to use the confrontational approach only after they have explored other means such as reinforcing the desired cultural aspects and rechanneling or counterbalancing the undesirable culture aspects.

How is this Step Applied to the Merger Case Example?

Let's return to our merger case example to see how they apply this step to accelerate cultural transformation:

To reduce the risk to an adaptable and scalable culture, HR professionals uncover the cultural assumptions that are sustaining the current way of operating. The HR professionals identify three cultural assumptions that need to be modified so that the newly integrated business can have an adaptable and scalable culture. Here are the key assumptions that were inconsistent with the desired culture and how they were modified:

- *Inconsistent assumption #1—Leaders believe they should be more committed to hierarchy than to adaptability: Leaders in the organization believe that to get ahead they need to work within a strictly defined hierarchy. The leaders need to modify this assumption and be mature enough to recognize that they will be more successful if they operate flexibly rather than with an approach that is based on a rigid hierarchical control. The HR professionals use the counterbalancing technique to reinforce the leaders who demonstrate adaptability. For example, one leader meets regularly with employees in "skip-level" meetings (one level of the hierarchy speaking to employees two or more levels below them). HR uses this example in an all-employees meeting to recognize and reward this leader for that approach. HR also uses the rechanneling technique to encourage leaders to show how they value openness and honesty with employees (something employees are comfortable with) by extending it to have leaders speak regularly with employees two or more levels below them in the hierarchy (the new cultural aspect).*

- *Inconsistent assumption #2—Leaders believe that the way to succeed is to build their departmental silo: The prevailing leadership belief is that employees and teams should "keep their heads down" and work within their area or department. Some leaders and employees believe that building strong departments, even at the expense of other departments, is the right way to succeed. The HR professionals set up quarterly leadership forums. These are half-day meetings to create an environment where leaders can get to know each other and share experiences cross-functionally. They reframe the notion of departments as silos that can never connect, to departments as islands that need to build bridges to succeed. They also use the counterbalancing technique with the leadership forum members to highlight that the G-12 was so successful because they demonstrated excellence as a multi-disciplinary team in the integration of the two businesses. The G-12 group becomes the model of how leaders should work as a multidisciplinary team. HR also uses the counterbalancing technique to measure, reward, and recognize the work of specific cross-functional teams that are working well. They also include a measure of cross-functional effectiveness into the bonus plan and confront the departments that do not work well cross-functionally by reducing their bonus payout if they are not collaborative.*

- *Inconsistent assumption #3—Employees believe that rigid definitions of jobs are the best way to get work done: Job descriptions do create structure for employees, but they also can limit adaptability. The new organization needs to move away from tight job descriptions to allow people to be adaptable to work in different ways and in different contexts. The HR professionals use the rechanneling technique and develop job descriptions (something employees are comfortable with) for cross-departmental positions and for multi-skilled jobs (the new cultural aspect). Rather than removing the job descriptions, they use them to achieve the more adaptable multidisciplinary work outcome. They also use the counterbalancing technique to reinforce and celebrate employees who are working collaboratively to achieve team targets (even if it is outside their job descriptions).*

Step 6: Develop the Culture Transformation Implementation Plan

What is Done in this Step?

- Develop a plan of action to implement the culture transformation plan in a targeted manner (what will be done, by when, by whom, and with what resources).
- Include ways to measure and track the cultural transformation to ensure that it directly affects the business outcome that it was designed to achieve in an accelerated manner.

How is this Step Applied to the Merger Case Example?

Let us return to the merger case example one last time:

The HR professionals guide the cultural integration team to document the gap between the "should" (preferred) culture and the "is" (current) culture. The integration team then identifies the specific cultural recommendations, outlining the current cultural aspects that are targeted to be reinforced and the current cultural aspects that are targeted to be modified or eliminated. The team also develops the metrics to track the effectiveness of the cultural transformation plan. The report also includes an implementation plan that identifies what should be done, by whom, by when, and with what resource requirements. The implementation plan also includes specific recommendations for the executive team about how to model the desired culture. The report is presented and discussed with the executive team, and it is then approved. The cultural transformation plan is then implemented in the organization as one of the business's top priorities with a target to implement the new culture within the next 18 months.

FINAL OBSERVATIONS ABOUT CULTURE TRANSFORMATION

Cultural transformation will not occur unless the urgency for the cultural transformation exceeds the group's resistance to it. The business leadership needs to clearly articulate the compelling business reasons for the cultural transformation in order for employees to feel it is worth their time and energy to participate in it.

Why was the cultural transformation in the merger case so successful? There are several reasons that are important to highlight.

Leverage Group Problem-Solving to Develop Culture

As described earlier, organizations often allow culture to develop haphazardly. Most often, a group encounters a problem or opportunity and then determines a way to resolve the issue in an adequate manner. In that process they develop assumptions about how to resolve problems and approach opportunities in the future. They then teach new employees how to respond to those issues "without even thinking," as a way they do business in that group on an ongoing basis. However, in this case, HR orchestrated the sequence of events for culture development to the organization's advantage. The G-12 was faced with an urgent problem. They needed to find solutions that would work well enough to be considered valid. They were then given the responsibility to implement the solutions as new leaders. This required them to teach the solutions and the new cultural directions to other employees. As a result the G-12 became a subculture that was able to propel the acceleration of the cultural transformation.

HR professionals should set up a process for all groups in the organization to use the shared values as criteria to select their preferred decisions. This process will reinforce the desired culture by utilizing the values in daily problem-solving and decision-making. Groups will also need to be adept at applying the values as criteria, especially when a potential decision meets one value at the expense of another. For example, in the merger case, there may be a situation where a department wants to make a decision to independently meet a customer's needs (which is consistent with "passion for customer focus" and "adaptability") that inadvertently undermines another department (which is inconsistent with "multidisciplinary teamwork" and "respect for every individual"). Groups need to be skilled at knowing how to make the appropriate trade-offs and the best decisions that will bring their values, behavior, and culture to life on a daily basis.

Build the Leadership Culture to Accelerate Cultural Transformation

The fastest route to the cultural transformation of an entire organization is to first change the leadership culture. Just like any group in an organization, a group of leaders can be formed that has its own culture. As a cross-functional group, they can formulate assumptions of how work needs to be done and how they can be successful. Since they are often the most admired group in an organization, they can have great influence because of their role in the organization as well as through their role modeling. As a result, HR professionals should ensure that the key leaders support the cultural transformation and that they can play a leadership role in enlisting employees to support the transformation. The HR professionals in the case example used this technique by engaging the executives in the culture change process, by working through the G-12 group of leaders, and by setting up the quarterly leadership forum meetings. Once leaders are enthusiastic in promoting a cultural transformation, the chances that the employees will follow are greatly improved.

Develop an Engaging Retention Strategy for Key Talent

In the case example, the HR VP recommended that they form a cultural integration team made up of 12 high-potential leaders who were key talents from both businesses. Many search firms knew about the acquisition, and they saw this as an opportunity to recruit the high-potential leaders to other companies. However, when members of the G-12 were contacted, they declined to meet with the search firms because they were excited to take part in creating the new integrated business culture. Also, the key talents who reported to the G-12 members were given acting leadership roles in the G-12's vacated positions. They were also enthusiastic about the potential of the new integrated business, so they also declined recruitment offers from search firms. As a result, no key talent left the business during the merger.

Engage the Expertise of HR

The business leveraged the expertise of the HR professionals to take accountability for the HR value proposition to develop the business's new culture. The confidence and credibility of HR continued to increase as HR delivered successful outcomes on the HR value proposition. Here are some additional ways that HR can drive cultural transformation:

- *Redesign the rewards and recognition process:* HR can redesign the rewards and recognition process outcomes to reinforce the new culture, values, and behaviors. For example, HR professionals can include the new values in the performance agreements between management and employees, in performance reviews, and in employee and team surveys. Also, they can identify team behavioral commitments based on these values.

- *Use team problem-solving to develop and reinforce the desired culture:* HR professionals should encourage leaders to leverage the problems and opportunities they encounter as ways to forge a new culture within their groups. In particular, HR professionals can advise leaders to do the following:
    - If the group is newly formed through a merger or reorganization, the leader should present the group with meaningful problems and opportunities that require them to work together to gain insight into problems and discover solutions. Working together in this way will help the group develop their new culture and give them confidence that they can collaborate to resolve important issues.
    - If the organization is changing direction with the same employees, then it is even more important to engage the group to understand the purpose of the new direction and to

generate workable solutions that resolve the issues associated with the new direction.

- *Use the shared values and behaviors to make it easier for employees to transfer to other areas:* Employees are able to adjust faster when they know the cultural assumptions about how to behave based on the shared values. Overall, when values are developed and adopted throughout the organization, the orientation of members to new teams is accelerated.

- *Commit to reflecting the values and behaviors in each HR initiative that is introduced:* The people capabilities and organizational capabilities should be designed to align with the new values and behaviors. For example, when an employee faces a personal crisis and the business's values are "respect for every individual" and "excellence in everything we do," HR should design policies to ensure that the business will help that individual through that difficult time without compromising on the need to deliver excellent work for the customer. HR ensures that these values and behaviors are exhibited whether the work is done by HR professionals themselves, by others in the business, or by an external service provider.

CONCLUSION

Accelerating culture transformation is a very important HR value proposition at which HR professionals need to excel. It is important for HR to demonstrate expertise in the *laser-beam* approach to cultural transformation in order to accelerate the process of cultural transformation. HR must ensure that the culture is clearly defined and that it is directly linked with the organization's priority business outcome. The organization also needs to celebrate aspects of the current culture that need to be retained and reinforced. The organization needs to find ways to modify specific aspects of the existing culture in the least anxiety-provoking way in order to reduce resistance to transformation and still achieve the business outcome desired. The entire process needs to be followed conscientiously and in an accelerated manner to make sure it mitigates the associated business risk.

SUMMARY

- Human resources professionals need to closely study the business changes that occur in mergers, acquisitions, and restructuring, as well as business changes in overall direction and executive leadership. They need to explore the implications of those changes for the people and organizational capabilities and develop the appropriate HR value proposition. Often in these situations, the risks associated with culture are great and HR needs to mitigate these risks by accelerating the cultural transformation to help the strategy and new direction occur rapidly and effectively.

- A culture can form in groups of any size—whether it is a project team, an intact work team, or the entire enterprise—but it always occurs in groups. It functions as the implicit assumptions of the way the group does things.

- The only way that a group will be willing to change its culture is if the compelling need for the cultural transformation makes it worth it. There needs to be a very strong business reason for groups to transform their culture. The leadership in an organization needs to clearly articulate the compelling business reasons for the cultural transformation in order to make it worth it for employees to participate in cultural transformation.

- A critical aspect of accelerating culture transformation is to make sure that the only parts that are changed are the ones that must be changed. HR professionals need to discover the current assumptions that need to be retained and the current assumptions that need to be modified or eliminated.

- A transformation in culture needs to be planned thoughtfully. The approach to accelerating cultural transformation described in this chapter is a targeted approach to how the culture needs to be modified to mitigate risks for the business.

It emphasizes a laser-beam focus on reinforcing a few cultural aspects and modifying several other aspects, rather than attempting to change the entire culture. The six-step laser-beam approach to cultural transformation is as follows:

1. Identify the compelling business reasons for cultural transformation.
2. Articulate what the desired culture "should" be.
3. Describe what the current culture "is."
4. Target aspects of the current culture to retain.
5. Target aspects of the current culture to modify.
6. Develop the cultural transformation implementation plan.

CHAPTER TEN

IMPLEMENT CHANGE

A business has had great success in their industry for over 10 years but now finds its market share slipping. The organization's leaders develop a business strategy to infuse new ideas and energy into their processes and appoint a leader to implement the change that will be required. The executives then proceed to plan the next major project. Several months after delegating the initiative to the leader, the executives find out that little change has been accomplished. The employees perceive the strategy as another example of how the business loses focus as it tries to implement change. At an executive meeting, the HR vice president suggests that the leaders and employees need a strong message to convince them that the business is committed to carrying good ideas to implementation. The executive team agrees.

The president takes the initiative, and in her annual employee address she begins her remarks with a surprising opening comment: "Our vision is only as good as what it makes us do today." Later she explains, "This year we will not have any new major change initiatives. We are overloaded with good initiatives that still need to be achieved." She then proceeds to articulate what becomes known in the business as the "year of the tissue paper strategy." "I can fit a tissue paper between our strategy and our competition's," she says. "We all read the same books, listen to the same gurus, and target the same markets. The only difference between the winners and the losers is who will implement the strategy successfully." The president backs up her words with action. She and the executive team make certain that the business focuses on implementing the chosen changes successfully.

Businesses are undergoing constant change in order to survive and thrive. Too often, though, they only focus on planning the change and not on implementing it. Also, although almost all changes require people and organizational capabilities, executives frequently assume that the people and organizational capabilities will be taken care of somehow. They ignore the risks this oversight can have for implementing change. As a result, HR must assume a critical role as the experts on change implementation. They need to establish themselves as a credible source for providing guidance on the most effective way to implement change in order to achieve the desired business outcomes. HR professionals also need to be the resident experts who can advise leaders as they implement change.

HR may select implementing change as its HR value proposition in the following kinds of situations:

- *Where the business is undergoing a major change that requires leaders, teams, and employees to make significant changes in the way they work:* HR professionals need to guide leaders of change so that they are able to build an effective change team, engage stakeholders, ensure that employees adopt the changes rapidly and effectively, and learn the lessons from each change process.
- *When many small business changes are occurring throughout the organization, rather than one major one:* Here is an example of where that occurred:

    An HR organization conducted interviews with each of the senior leaders of the divisions in its company. The interviews focused on four questions:

    1. *What are your major business challenges for the upcoming year?*
    2. *What are the priority people implications of those challenges?*
    3. *What are the priority organizational implications of those challenges?*
    4. *What is the one thing you must get from HR in order to believe that they have added value for your business?*

    The HR team then presented their findings to each other. What they identified was that each of the divisional leaders had major changes that they planned to introduce within the upcoming year. It became evident that HR needed to galvanize all its resources to deliver excellence in implementing change for all of the various divisions. By focusing on that HR value proposition, they were able to help implement multiple divisional changes effectively.

When HR chooses the HR value proposition of implementing change, they can mitigate a major risk associated with business strategies not being implemented effectively. Indeed, implementing change was one of the first organizational capabilities identified as part of the HR areas of work. In *Human Resources Champions,*[1] change management was one of the four quadrants that were identified as part of HR work. That challenge of implementing change continues to be a significant area of accountability for HR to deliver value for the business.

Some businesses are fortunate to have leaders who are able to focus on implementing change. Others are not so fortunate. Leaders must select the changes that are in alignment with their business's strategic direction. At the same time, they must ensure that the changes actually occur. HR professionals assist leaders by taking a far greater role in advocating and facilitating the effective implementation of change.

CHANGE AND TRANSITION

To implement change successfully, a balance must be achieved between attaining excellence in the process and focusing on the outcomes that are expected from the process. Change and transition represent distinctly different parts of the change implementation process:

- *Change* refers to the *business* steps required when planning and implementing change. The business steps include understanding the urgency for the change; identifying the change concept; developing a detailed implementation plan; and making the change happen.

---

1. David Ulrich, *Human Resources Champions* (Cambridge, MA: Harvard Business Books, 1996).

- *Transition* refers to the *human* steps that are important in change. The human steps include selecting the right change leaders and change team; engaging key stakeholders; communicating, training, and helping people adjust; and ensuring that there are lessons learned from the change implementation process.

Leaders sometimes implement changes but do not give equal attention to the human transition steps that help people understand and commit to the changes. In other cases, external changes are imposed that require the leadership and employees to adjust quickly to the new reality. These are situations in which HR professionals can have a great impact. They can facilitate or assist leaders to facilitate the human transition factors that help people adjust, accept, and participate in change. Also, leaders may not balance their focus between change and transition, which will make it less likely that the business will implement the change successfully. HR plays an important role in ensuring that there is an effective balance of both change and transition.

EIGHT-STEP IMPLEMENTING CHANGE PROCESS

Many organizational thinkers have developed models of how change can be defined and implemented. Most of the processes (called by various names, such as organizational change and change management) have common features. However, too many approaches and models confuse employees and can become a barrier to successful implementation. Figure 10.1 shows the eight-step change implementation process, which is based on our research in this area.

The eight steps in the process provide the structure for this chapter and define HR's role to help the change occur successfully. Four of the steps (1, 3, 5, and 7) are the *business change* aspects of implementing change. The other four steps (2, 4, 6, and 8) are the *human transition* aspects. Often, the human transition steps require the change leaders to influence and educate people so that they will be open to the changes that will occur and will also commit to them.

Figure 10.1: The Implementing Change Process

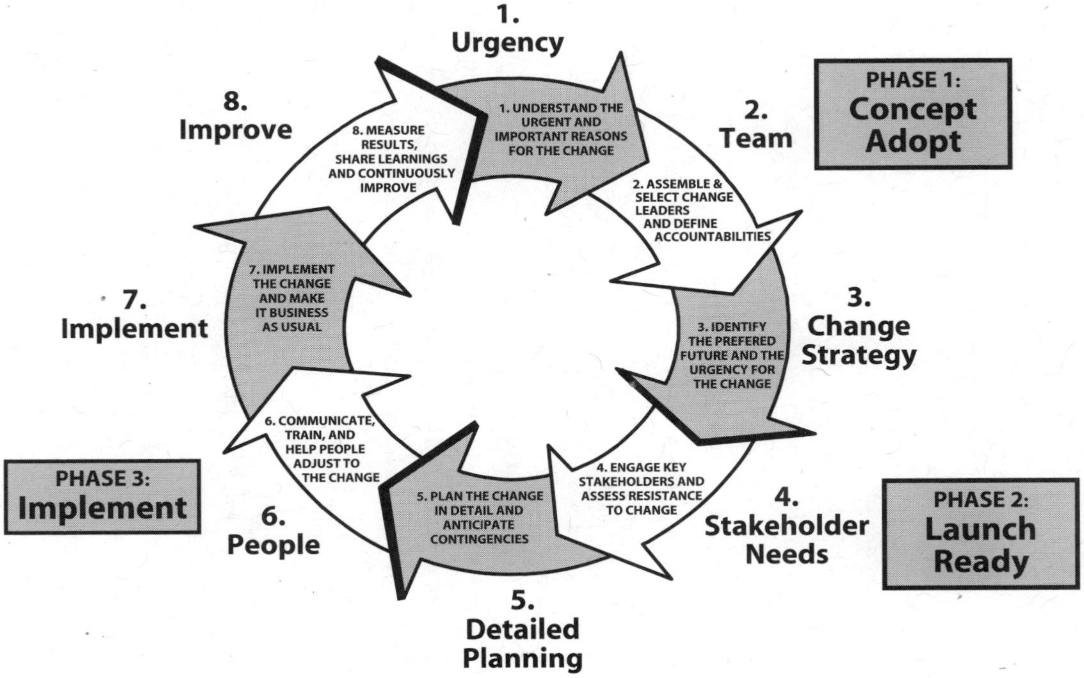

PHASE 1:
Concept
Adopt

PHASE 2:
Launch
Ready

PHASE 3:
Implement

1.
Urgency

2.
Team

3.
Change
Strategy

4.
Stakeholder
Needs

5.
Detailed
Planning

6.
People

7.
Implement

8.
Improve

1. UNDERSTAND THE URGENT AND IMPORTANT REASONS FOR THE CHANGE

2. ASSEMBLE & SELECT CHANGE LEADERS AND DEFINE ACCOUNTABILITIES

3. IDENTIFY THE PREFERED FUTURE AND THE URGENCY FOR THE CHANGE

4. ENGAGE KEY STAKEHOLDERS AND ASSESS RESISTANCE TO CHANGE

5. PLAN THE CHANGE IN DETAIL AND ANTICIPATE CONTINGENCIES

6. COMMUNICATE, TRAIN, AND HELP PEOPLE ADJUST TO THE CHANGE

7. IMPLEMENT THE CHANGE AND MAKE IT BUSINESS AS USUAL

8. MEASURE RESULTS, SHARE LEARNINGS AND CONTINUOUSLY IMPROVE

The HR professional should be an advocate for and an active facilitator of the implementation of change and transition from the beginning to the end of the process. This chapter explores each of the implementing change steps and HR's role in this process. It also applies each step to a business case example where implementing change was selected as the HR value proposition to mitigate a critical business risk. The case is as follows:

A business is attempting to find ways to increase quality and reduce costs in order to compete effectively in their country. The business's executives believe that improving their procurement processes will be the fastest way to improve the quality of goods throughout the country and to lower the overall cost of purchases. Their strategy is to amalgamate their 12 separate purchasing departments across the country. They reason that centralized purchasing will reduce overall costs because they will be able to negotiate larger supplier contracts, and that they will be able to enhance the quality of the goods they purchase from a more selective list of national suppliers. The business currently has a small, centralized procurement office for about 10 percent of its purchases. The risk is how to implement centralized procurement for almost all of its purchases in an effective way so that the leaders and employees across the country will adopt the changes and so that turmoil will not be created among their suppliers during the implementation process. The executives agree that HR should take accountability for the HR value proposition of "implement change" to mitigate the business risks associated with centralized procurement. In this business, HR is highly credible in the area of implementing change, and they are viewed as a center of excellence with the organizational capability to provide expert advice to leaders on how to implement change.

This case will be referred to at the conclusion of the explanation of each step in the implementing change process. Throughout this case example, HR actively guided and worked with leaders to ensure that the change process was effective and efficient and that the change outcomes delivered the required results for the business.

Step 1: Urgency

In this step, leaders must understand and define the urgent and important business reason for the change. Employees often resist change if leaders decide to introduce change just for the sake of it and not for important and urgent business reasons. The more deeply embedded the current way of working, the more urgent and compelling the reasons need to be to motivate employees to participate in the change. Urgency is the "secret sauce" to a good implementing-change recipe. As leaders engage in implementing change, they often undervalue the importance of communicating the sense of urgency for the change. They need to communicate the urgency when the change team is put together, when they present the change concept, when they engage the stakeholders, and when they communicate the change to employees.

Leaders need to understand and internalize the urgency for the change even more than they need to understand what the new outcome of the change will look like and how it will operate.

Here is how Step I: Urgency, is applied to the centralized procurement case example:

The business executives believe that there is an urgent need to implement centralized procurement to improve the quality of goods purchased throughout the country and to lower the overall cost of purchases. The challenge is to ensure that these urgent and important reasons for the change are communicated and understood throughout the implementing change process. As a result, HR helps the executives document the urgency for the change in a project charter. This charter becomes part of the ongoing orientation and discussion with new leaders and employees as they proceed through each step of the implementing change process.

Step 2: Team

Once executives determine an urgent need for a change, the next step involves setting up a change team to champion the process. The team's change leader needs to be carefully selected. In fact, in one study,[2] selecting an effective change leader was the highest correlate of change success, which means that successful change projects usually have

---

2. Dr. Carol Beatty, Queen's University, Kingston, Ontario, Canada, conducted the research on more than 350 change initiatives and showed a correlation between change success and a skilled change champion. (Reported in www.networkedgov.ca/changechampion, Beatty, 2012).

excellent change leaders. As a result, the selection of the change leader should not be done without careful thought. Sometimes the leader of the department that is implementing the change is selected to lead a change; however, that person may not have the time or may not be motivated to implement the change effectively. HR should ensure that the right change leader is selected to lead the change initiative and that the leader is capable in that role.

The change leader's roles are as follows:

The Roles of Change Leaders

- *Develop and execute the change plans:* Change leaders develop, execute, and measure implementation plans in alignment with the business's overall strategy. At review meetings they recommend whether the change process should proceed or whether it should be terminated.
- *Build an effective change team:* Change leaders help the change team see the entire project and not just the specific areas over which the team will have responsibility. They also ensure alignment of team activities with the expected outcomes of the change.
- *Make things happen:* Change leaders must be able to make things happen and to push the project forward. They also need the personal drive and commitment to ensure that action will be taken on the decisions made by the change team.

Assisting the change leaders is an important role for HR professionals. Some of the ways they can contribute include the following:

- Identify the criteria for selecting and then recruiting the change leaders for a particular change process.
- Coach the change leaders throughout the process. Contribute knowledge of internal and external best practices about how change teams can function most effectively.

- Facilitate discussion among change leaders of different initiatives so they can share information and align their activities to the business's direction.
- Step in or find the resources that can help the change team start moving again if they become stuck and are unable to proceed. Guide the change leaders to follow the eight-step implementing change process through training, coaching, mentoring, and measuring how the change project is proceeding.

The change team members are expected to add value to the change project and to be committed to the idea the change represents. When change team members are assigned to a team but have no interest in that process, the results are often of lower quality. HR guides the change leader to keep the change team members focused and motivated. Also, throughout the implementing change process, they ensure that some continuity of change team members exists.

Many projects fail because the change leader and change team members are told that the project work is an "add-on" to their normal day jobs. Usually, excessive workload demands mean that the project will not work as effectively because people will not give it the time it deserves even if they want to be committed to it. The HR professional can advocate for the allocation of work time to a change project so that people experience work on the change team as part of their regular jobs.

HR should advocate for executive sponsors for major change projects. Here are some of the major roles of executive sponsors:

The Roles of Executive Sponsors

- Help ensure that the change occurs through their access and influence on the executive team.
- Help change leaders and the change team understand the urgent and important reasons for the change that the executives are concerned about.

- Work with the change leaders to identify cross-functional links between this change and others in the business.
- Provide the other executives with the necessary updates and discussion on the progress of the change and its anticipated impact on the business.
- Coach the change leaders on an as-required basis.
- Periodically measure and approve the progress of the change initiative at specific checkpoints (i.e., gate reviews).
- Ensure that the executive sponsor supports the change recommendations when they are presented to the executive team for approval.

When a change leader's performance is not adequate, the HR professional can help the executive sponsor determine the root causes of the poor performance. For example, the change leader may be ineffective because he or she is making inappropriate selections of individuals to assume specific roles in the implementing change process. When HR professionals contribute this kind of insight, they become part of the business's strategic thinking and are able to partner with the business leaders.

Here is how Step 2: Team, applied to the centralized procurement case example:

The logical choice for the change project team leader is the director in charge of the small, centralized purchasing office that currently exists. However, on two other occasions, this individual attempted to implement a similar kind of centralized purchasing and was unsuccessful. He is unenthusiastic about attempting to be a change leader for a third time. HR advises that if the current director of centralized purchasing becomes the change leader, the project will be at a high risk of failure.

The executives decide to choose one of the purchasing managers in a highly successful, high-quality purchasing office in one of the 12 offices. This individual has been talking about ways to enhance quality and reduce costs in purchasing, is highly motivated, and is well-respected among his peers. He selects team members from the other large purchasing offices and from several small purchasing offices. He also selects two major internal clients of purchasing offices so that the group will have diverse opinions in generating the most effective implementation plan. Quite astutely, he also invites the current centralized procurement director to join the team, but he declines, indicating that he is too busy. The chief financial officer is the executive sponsor responsible for supporting the project change leader. His role is to remove barriers that might get in the way and lead the process of executive team approvals as the project proceeds.

Step 3: Change Strategy

The first two steps of the change implementation process focus on urgency and the team. In this step, the change team defines what they believe is the concept that will resolve the urgent problem. They then can begin to plan the changes that will be needed in the organization and to identify how to assist people to embrace the envisioned changes.

The compelling reason for the change can be explained as a formula with three variables (Figure 10.2). The three variables are:

Figure 10.2: The Compelling Reason for the Change Formula

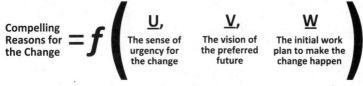

$$\text{Compelling Reasons for the Change} = f \left(\begin{array}{ccc} \underline{U,} & \underline{V,} & \underline{W} \\ \text{The sense of urgency for the change} & \text{The vision of the preferred future} & \text{The initial work plan to make the change happen} \end{array} \right)$$

This equation indicates that each of the three variables is essential for implementing change.

- *Urgency:* Change will not occur if people do not experience a sense of urgency for the change. The more imminent the urgency, the more intense the desire to achieve the vision of the change. If the change does not have urgency, motivating people to make the change occur will be a greater challenge. Under no circumstances should the urgency be fabricated and unreal. That kind of manipulation creates a loss of integrity in the process of implementing specific changes and in the role of leadership within the business.

- *Vision:* The "change vision" identifies the end state for a *specific* change initiative. The vision must be compelling to the team members and motivate people who are not on the team. When the vision is defined and communicated clearly, the change team can sense it, smell it, taste it, and see it clearly so that they know what they will have when the change is fully implemented. This level of clarity also helps the executive sponsor understand the change and will increase the likelihood that the concept will be adopted.

- *Work plan:* At this stage of the process, only the first steps of the work plan need to be clarified. The details of the entire plan cannot be known until further research and detailed planning has been undertaken. The initial work plan includes the following:
    - The initial actions in the implementation;
    - The metrics to assess progress and how the data will be collected and used;
    - The work plan to develop the detailed change plan.

Some change leaders are relieved that they have only the first steps to define. When this process is not followed, businesses often spend too much time up front on the whole plan. If the entire plan is done too early in the process, it can cause major delays and sometimes waste time in the process of implementing change.

Some implications of this U, V, and W equation (Urgency, Vision, and Work plan) are important to consider. Table 10.1 describes the consequences if any one of those three variables is missing.

At the conclusion of each phase in the change implementation process (indicated in Figure 10.1 by thicker lines) there are major checkpoints, referred to as "gate reviews." Gate reviews are specific milestone review points at which time executives or executive sponsors need to make a "go" or "no go" decision. Typically, most change projects have three gate reviews that occur at the completion of each of the phases of the implementing change process:

- *Phase I: Concept Adopt*—At the conclusion of Step 3, "Change Strategy," a gate review is held to decide whether to adopt the change concept or not.

Table 10.1: Consequences of Missing One of the Variables from the "Compelling Reason for the Change" Formula

Scenario	Consequence
The change initiative specifies the Urgency and the Work plan but not the Vision.	People have a desire to act without knowing where the business is going. They may go down the wrong path and make wrong decisions.
The change initiative specifies a Vision and the initial Work plan but does not clarify the sense of Urgency.	People may not be motivated to take action because there is no urgency to change.
The change initiative has a clearly defined Urgency and Vision to proceed but does not have an initial Work plan.	People may be frustrated because they won't know what to do first, although they may feel the desire to act and to begin the process of changing.

- *Phase II: Launch Ready*—At the conclusion of Step 5, "Detailed Planning," a gate review is held to decide whether the change project is launch ready or not.

- *Phase II: Implementation*—At the conclusion of Step 8, "Improve," a gate review is held to decide whether the project is completed, how it can be improved, and what can be learned from the project for the next change initiative.

Gate review points are chosen when the next step involves increased cost/investment of money and increased exposure to people. Steps 1–3 involve very little investment of money and require very few people to know about the project. Steps 4–5 require increased investment and more exposure to people. As a result, it is logical to have a "go or no go" decision point before Step 4. The same is the case at the end of Step 5. Steps 6–8 require the greatest investment and exposure to people. It is logical that prior to implementing the change project in Step 6, there would be a "go or no go" decision to confirm that the business should proceed with the project.

The gate reviews function as controls to ensure that the business analyzes the change implementation process carefully. The controls are not meant to slow down the process; rather, they are intended to increase the probability that the business will implement the change effectively. If the controls impede the process and get in the way of implementing the change, the business should reassess the controls to determine if they are a barrier to implementation. Also, gate reviews may be unnecessary for fairly simple changes that have lower implementation risks.

One advantage of gate reviews is that executives are removed from the change project in between these reviews unless the change leader requests otherwise. This creates a great deal of ownership for the change leader and change team. Also, when businesses use gate reviews properly to anchor the change process, the project has more precise definition, allowing for clearer follow-up measurements to determine the return on investment from the change. Also, the care in the development of the change increases the likelihood that the change will become part of the organization's ongoing way of doing business. The change is no longer viewed as a project; it becomes the new way for the business to operate.

HR contributes to this process during more complex changes by advising change leaders and their teams on how to prepare for the gate reviews and by reviewing their presentations to ensure they are prepared effectively.

Here is how Step 3: Change Strategy, and its gate review are applied to the centralized procurement case example:

The change team engages in a thorough process to gain insight into the issues associated with centralized purchasing and where it would enhance quality and reduce cost. After careful consideration they identify the change vision whereby 70 percent of all purchases will be centralized and 30 percent will still be conducted in the local offices. They also recommend having pre-approved national suppliers who will distribute all of the purchased goods from wherever they are purchased to the proper locations in a timely manner. The change leader and the executive sponsor review the recommendations and then proceed to an executive meeting where they engage the executives in a concept-adopt gate review. The change project is approved in concept and the change team is given the authority to proceed with engaging stakeholders and completing the detailed launch plans.

Step 4: Stakeholders

A common error in the process of implementing change is that stakeholders get involved too late in the process. Change teams should solicit stakeholder opinions in Step 4 immediately after the change concept is adopted. Here are five reasons to involve stakeholders in the process:

Five Reasons to Engage Key Stakeholders
1. To assess stakeholder support or resistance as a sample representative of a larger group.
2. To solicit new ideas that can help refine the change.
3. To gain insight about risk factors in the change.
4. To identify acceptable modifications to the implementing change process that would result in increased stakeholder support.
5. To engage the stakeholder to participate in the detailed planning of the change.

The guiding principle for selecting stakeholders is to interview as few as possible while still retrieving the maximum information about how the change will be accepted by various stakeholder groups. The goal is to ensure that the change project is not exposed to too many people before the change team really knows what it wants to recommend. HR should guide leaders in selecting the key stakeholders, understand the stakeholders' interests, and involve them in the process of defining the change. This step also helps stakeholders increase their understanding of the urgency, the vision, and the initial work plan for the change.

The stakeholder interviews should also reveal barriers and areas of resistance that will be important for the change team as it develops its detailed plans. Table 10.2 presents some examples of areas of potential stakeholder resistance.

Table 10.2: Areas of Potential Stakeholder Resistance

Barriers to Understanding	Barriers to Acceptance	Barriers to Action
• No strong sense of urgency • Ambiguity and uncertainty • Consequences of change are not understood • Lacking knowledge about what will change	• History of poorly managed change • Negative organizational climate • Top management support is lacking	• Skills or resources are lacking • Pace too fast, change too imminent, or timing is poor • No perceived rewards for the change

Once the data are collected from the stakeholders, they can be charted to see whether plans should be put in place to improve the stakeholder group's commitment to the change. Figure 10.3 presents the stakeholder chart that can be used for this purpose:

Figure 10.3: The Stakeholder Commitment to the Change Chart

Stakeholders	Understanding Their Sense of Urgency and Level of Understanding (H,M,L)	Acceptance Prior Experience and Support for Change (H,M,L)	Action Belief that the Change is Resourced Properly (H,M,L)	Impact Their Degree of Influence on Others (H,M,L)	Commitment to the Change Current → Required			
					Resistor	Neutral	Helper	Advocate
Example: Director	Poor	Low	Low	Medium		©→®		

The stakeholder commitment to the change chart identifies the following:

- The extent to which the barriers to understanding, acceptance, and action apply to each stakeholder;
- The impact and influence each stakeholder has on others;
- The current level of commitment of each stakeholder as a resistor, a neutral, a helper, or an advocate, and whether the stakeholder commitment level needs to improve to implement the change effectively.

After completing the chart, the change team develops its plan for how to improve the stakeholder's commitment to the change concept.

In many change projects, discussions with the stakeholders can be essential in helping the stakeholder to understand the urgency for the change and accept the change. There is no downside to discussions with stakeholders. The change leader loses nothing through the conversation. The HR professional should guide the change leaders to listen carefully and build their relationships with the stakeholders. Once change leaders understand stakeholders' interests, they can use that information to develop a detailed change plan.

Here is how Step 4: Stakeholders, is applied to the centralized procurement case example:

The team identifies a shortlist of stakeholders who would best represent the opinions of the large groups that will be affected by the changes. For example, the manager of purchasing in the office that is the greatest distance away from headquarters has strong opinions about specific suppliers in his local market. He believes they have been providing excellent quality products at low cost. He argues that these suppliers should be selected as national suppliers for all offices. The change team also interviews many other stakeholders, including a key stakeholder who represents the opinions of the smaller offices that will likely have to disband their procurement teams, the current director of the small, centralized purchasing office, and several key suppliers. The change team then completes the stakeholder analysis worksheet and identifies two stakeholder groups who need to be helpers but who will likely be resistant to the change. They develop a plan to enlist the support of those stakeholders and include it in their detailed change plan (see Step 5).

Step 5: Detailed Planning

This step focuses on defining in detail how the change will be implemented and on developing the necessary contingency plans in the event that the implementation does not proceed as envisioned. This step concludes with a gate review to determine if the business will launch the project.

Change leaders should collect the necessary data and measure progress to make detailed recommendations about how the change should proceed. They should also understand that not all changes require extensive research or a detailed gap analysis. A gap analysis measures the gap between the current state and the desired state. The change leader should have the wisdom to know whether the change vision will compel him or her to do a detailed gap analysis or whether a less formalized analysis of current reality will be acceptable. Here are two examples in which the change leader should question whether to conduct a detailed gap analysis:

- When the change that is envisioned requires a radical change from current reality, the leader must understand that the current reality and gap analysis will be less important.
- When a gap analysis can result in people becoming over-committed to defining the current reality. In this case, the gap analysis may block the creative process and inhibit the change team from focusing on developing the plans to implement the change.

For more complex change projects, it may be useful to engage in simulations or pilot studies to pre-test the changes before they are fully implemented. Pilots also increase the change team's confidence because they can point out with more certainty (at the gate review) that this change will likely produce the positive results they anticipate. The assumption is that a pilot study can be generalized to the real work environment, but this is not always the case. HR professionals should be aware of the traps that can occur in pilot projects, such as:

- *The pilot team is focused on the pilot and not the eventual implementation:* Sometimes the pilot project team can become so immersed in the success of the pilot that they find it difficult to pay attention to the more important issue of the broader implementation. The most important purpose of a pilot is to learn how the pilot results can be generalized to the full implementation. Debriefing the pilot project at the end is not sufficient. The pilot team needs to reflect on how to generalize what they are learning throughout the time they work on the pilot project.

- *Pilots often have team members who are more motivated than the general workforce:* The pilot project members frequently build intense relationships and have high commitment to making the pilot successful. Often, when a pilot is generalized to the larger work environment, the workforce does not have the same motivation and acceptance of the change. Specific strategies to motivate the entire workforce will be needed.

In some situations, a simulation of the change can achieve the same result as a pilot. A simulation is a "walk-through" of how the change will actually work in a simulated environment. Often a large training room is used to model how the change would proceed. Each of the steps of the change is talked through from beginning to end. The team anticipates contingencies and makes adjustments to the process. In contrast, pilot projects implement the change in a specific area within the business. If a simulation can test the change adequately, it is generally preferred; a simulation disrupts the business flow less than a pilot does and it reduces employees' exposure to the change before it is ready. Simulations can often be completed more quickly than pilots, and more aspects of the change can be controlled in the simulated environment.

As a result of the simulation and/or the pilot study and the analysis of how to implement the change, HR should encourage the change leader to identify specific quick wins that can be implemented immediately. These are easy-to-do, high-performance changes that can be done for minimal cost. Quick wins are valuable for a variety of reasons:

- If they can be done quickly and generate an immediate benefit, quick wins may avoid an elaborate implementation process and save time and cost.
- Quick wins have the benefit of helping executives understand that the change will actually work. A pilot study and analysis are theoretical for many executives. A quick win benefit will demonstrate that something can occur that will be beneficial to the business almost immediately.

- Quick wins provide ongoing motivation and momentum for the change team as they work on the initiative.
- Employees who will be affected by the change are often motivated by quick wins. They begin to believe that things really will change, and perhaps for the better.

While quick wins can motivate executives and the workforce, they can sometimes be so attractive to executives that they may want the entire change project to be implemented as one big quick win. HR professionals should advise change leaders about how to restrain the executives from having this response. They should also guide them to implement quick wins in the most effective way to maximize the acceptance of these changes and to use the quick wins as part of their communication strategy.

As the change leader and team plan the change implementation, they also need to consider their organizational design, roles, accountabilities, and communications approach to employees. HR professionals need to be experts in these areas (or have access to experts) in order to assist change leaders who may not have the necessary knowledge and skills. They coach the change leader on how to motivate people to explore and accept new directions and changes. Their professional knowledge can help remove people-related barriers and reduce resistance, ensuring that employees understand and will participate in implementing the change. HR professionals should also contribute to the communications approach that will be implemented after the gate review. They can also help design the training for all employees as described in Step 6 of the implementing change process.

HR also should guide the change leader to engage in a risk analysis of the change solution and the detailed plans. Figure 10.4 presents a useful approach to risk analysis.

The change team first lists all the potential risks associated with the change solution. They then plot the risks to identify whether the risks have a high likelihood of materializing and whether they will have damaging consequences if they do materialize. The risks in the

Figure 10.4: Risk Analysis Approach

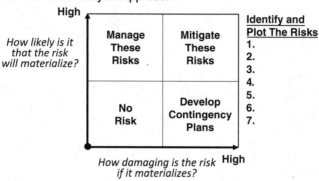

"Mitigate These Risks" box need mitigation strategies to minimize the impact of the risk or reduce the probability that the risk will occur. This chart should be presented along with the detailed change plan in the gate review at the conclusion of Step 5. Often, change teams present an alternate solution that is of a higher or lower risk than the recommended solution in order to offer the executives a choice for how to proceed with the change.

Launch-Ready Assessment

Figure 10.5 is the launch-ready assessment that can be used by a change team to assess its readiness to launch a change project, and it can be used by executives in the gate review at the conclusion of Step 5.

Step 5 culminates with the presentation at the gate review. At that review meeting, the executives determine whether the change will proceed or not or whether further work is needed. Astute change leaders need to know when a change initiative is not proceeding well and, if it is not, whether to recommend that it be abandoned or adapted. HR professionals can support change leaders in this role because they may have information about other changes in the business that could impact the change being considered. They may also identify early warning signals about potential employee or stakeholder resistance to the change that may be very useful for the change leaders.

Figure 10.5: The Launch-Ready Assessment

Launch-Ready Assessment

Change Element	Best Practice	Assessment Rating + ? -
Business Case for Change	The current state of the organization and urgency for change are clearly understood by all stakeholders.	
Preferred Future View	The preferred future view (end state) for the change initiative is consistently interpreted and shared by all.	
Leadership Capacity	The leaders values and behaviors are aligned with the business strategy. Leaders possess the skills to drive the change process to completion and accept the responsibility for doing so.	
Stakeholder Commitment	The necessary level of stakeholder commitment and engagement are in place.	
Communication	The infrastructure and plan is in place to build awareness of the change initiative and its objectives, communicate progress toward achievement of objectives, and encourage engagement with the change process and outcomes.	
Individual and Team Capacity	Actions have been taken to increase individuals' and teams' ability to accept and operate effectively in the new environment.	

Here is how Step 5: Detailed Planning, is applied to the centralized procurement case example:

The change team develops the detailed plan, which includes both business change and people transition recommendations. From the business change perspective, they describe how the centralized procurement office will purchase from anywhere in the world and that the purchaser can be working anywhere in the country. Also, the highest-quality, lowest-cost provider will be selected only if they can deliver to the entire national business in a timely fashion. They also develop the people transition plans. This includes: (1) hiring additional talent with experience in national procurement; (2) developing people they want to retain who formerly worked in procurement in the local offices; and (3) supporting people who will be asked to leave the organization. They also develop a strategy for communicating their change plan to all procurement employees, to all other leaders and employees in the business, and to affected suppliers to help them understand how the business will change its approach toward purchasing. After completing the detailed plan, the change leader and the executive sponsor meet to review the plans, and the sponsor orchestrates a gate review with the executive team. The executive team decides to support the project launch with some minor modifications, and they proceed to the implementation phase of the process.

Step 6: People

Many good changes fail because organizations do not give proper attention to Step 6: People. This step focuses on excellence in communication, training, and helping people adjust to change. HR professionals often have a particularly good understanding of this transition step and can contribute a great deal of value to the change leaders as they attempt to make change happen successfully.

Excellence in Communications

Throughout the change implementation process, communication is essential. However, it becomes particularly important at this step of the process. It is important to communicate regularly, clearly, and simply in a variety of ways. Most change leaders believe that if they explain the change to the workforce once, they will understand it and be willing to implement it. Unfortunately, in most situations this is not the case. People need to hear about the change several times and in different ways for them to really absorb what the change will be and to understand its implications for their own work. Effective communication during the implementation of change often includes the following:

- *Clearly communicate the urgency for the change:* One common mistake in communicating change is that the focus is often on *what* the change will be and not on *why* the change is needed. HR should guide change leaders to give equal time to explaining why the change is urgent and explaining the details of the change solution that will be implemented.

- *Multiple communications media are chosen to influence people to accept the change:* Employees learn through repetition, but they become irritated if leaders repeat themselves. The preferred approach is to repeat the message of the change but to do it in different ways so that it does not feel as if it was repeated. For example, employees could be told about the change, review written documentation about it, have discussion groups with other departments about the implications of the change for their areas, and hear about quick wins from the early implementation of the change. All of these methods are repeating the change story but in different ways so that it is not experienced as repetitious.

- *A specific time and a medium are identified for regular communication:* This technique is particularly useful for change implementation that will last over an extended period of time, such as moving to a new building or a drawn-out merger process. When people know that communication about the change will take place regularly, at a specific time, and through a specific medium (e.g., e-mail, town hall meetings, a blog, large-group voice mail), then they can adjust to the changes more effectively. It is important to retain a predictable time for the communication even if there are not many new developments to report.

- *Every action is linked to the desired and preferred future of the change:* This is another technique to help everyone understand why the change is being implemented. It also reinforces anticipated results. However, when actions occur that contradict the communications, people tend to believe the actions, and the credibility of the communications can therefore suffer.

- *Successes are identified and celebrated as they occur:* The positive aspects of successes motivate people to more readily accept the change. It is important to find ways to communicate the quick wins and celebrate achievements of milestones in the change implementation.

- *Manage expectations of the speed and quality with which the change will be implemented:* It is demotivating if change leaders promise more than they can deliver. They must be open and honest about the progress of the change initiative and the speed of implementation.

In the process of implementing change, HR professionals can help enhance communications. At a minimum, they can remind the change leaders of the importance of communicating the change. They can also assist the change leaders by guiding them to recognize the techniques of successful communication.

Focused Training to Prepare People for Change

When businesses introduce change, they often require training and development that will help employees be willing, ready, and able to accept the new ideas and put them to use. The premise is that enough time should be given for individuals to learn new things, to practice, to make mistakes, to receive coaching, and to gain confidence in the new way of working. People often perform less effectively immediately after a change is introduced. If they are expected to perform perfectly, they can become very resistant to the change, and the likelihood of effective implementation will be reduced.

HR professionals can help people assess their ability to succeed at the new behaviors required. People will need the opportunity to think about whether they have the competencies for the new kind of work. An understanding of the anticipated competencies will help people assess their own potential to perform this work. In addition, a variety of training and development initiatives delivered through electronic means or in groups can help employees accept and adapt to change. The following are three types of such initiatives:

- *Orientation sessions:* All managers and employees need to understand the change's urgency, the vision, the work plan, and its implications in order for them to commit to making it happen.
- *Basic skills training:* Employees will need basic skills training to know how to function within the changed environment. People need to learn about the change and understand how to access ongoing information as the change continually evolves.
- *More detailed training and coaching for the people who will be most affected by the change:* If the changes are in a specific area, the professionals in that area will need more intensive training and coaching to know how to respond to questions and how to implement the changes effectively. In addition, the people who are affected by the change will need to understand how they can access the new way of working and how it will change the way they work on an ongoing basis.

While the training should be done before people are asked to perform the new skills, people should also have opportunities to revisit the training after they begin working. Often, after people have the experiences of doing the new work, they have questions that would not have been anticipated when they were learning about the changes. Revisiting the material online and sharing these questions and answers after working in the changed environment for a period of time is a good way to reinforce and fine-tune the implementation of the new way of working.

Finally, HR professionals can consider conducting team-building activities both before and while the change is introduced. This focus on the change is an excellent way to help the team create an environment in which they can help each other work differently. Employees can also develop their team effectiveness as they plan to make the changes occur in the workplace.

Help People Adjust

Most changes, even if they are implemented effectively, require people to adjust. People sometimes have difficulty changing no matter how good the change is. In fact, quite ironically, sometimes the people who are most vocal about the need for change are the most resistant when that change is actually introduced.

A conscious effort needs to be made to help people adjust to a change. Some leaders assume that people have a personal responsibility to adjust to new situations. However, in planning for change, wise leaders know that they can create conditions in which it is easier for people to adjust. If they do this properly, they can also reduce the number of people who will be resistant. HR professionals should guide leaders to ensure that people adjust effectively.

The major areas of stress that typically occur in the process of change are due to the following:

- *The novelty and unpredictability of the situation:* For some employees, the novelty and unpredictability of the change can cause a great deal of stress. If they have never experienced this kind of change before or have no knowledge about the issue, they may not know how to respond to the change.

- *Ambiguity and uncertainty:* Ambiguity is a major stress for most people in general situations and especially during times of change. Often, the creators of the change are the only people who know the purpose of the change and its implications. Others who are affected by the change function are in a wait-and-see position. The ambiguity of the situation or the presence of conflicting information creates unnecessary stress. Typically, in the absence of clear information, people make up information. The rumor mill starts to work overtime and people paint the ambiguous change in the most negative way. The rumors escalate to the point that people panic about the changes without real information on which they can base their reactions.

- *Imminence and duration:* Changes that are going to occur immediately or that will last for an extended period often cause high levels of stress. Some leaders, in a spirit of candor, say things like, "If you believe things are tough now, wait until next year when things will be even tougher." Although they do not know if this is really true, they feel they are preparing people for the changes in the future. However, this statement actually backfires. The people hearing this feel that their stress will last for a much longer time, and this increases their anxiety and resistance to the change.

It is a leader's responsibility to help people adjust, and HR professionals should be skilled at guiding and coaching leaders in this role. The HR professional can also intervene where appropriate so that the adjustment process occurs effectively. Some strategies that can be used to overcome the three areas of stress include:

- *Develop understanding:* Many people do not truly understand why the change is occurring. The change may not make sense to them. They need to understand the longer-range picture of the preferred future so they can put it into context. People often create erroneous interpretations of an initiative if they do not understand and have discussions about what the change will achieve and how it will affect their work.
- *Provide information:* It is essential to provide information and to communicate readily. As described earlier in this section, people need to know what is happening. Communication should occur on a regular basis. Just knowing what will occur, even if it is not good news, eliminates some of the stress. As one leader once said, "The misery of not knowing is much worse than the misery of knowing."

- *Create a climate of social support:* Social support is perhaps the most effective way to reduce stress during change. People need to talk with others about the change. If someone is resistant, the challenge is to absorb the resistance by hearing it and not labeling it as bad. People need to understand that resistance is part of the normal process of change, especially when the change is of a difficult nature. The social support helps people explore options and consider how the change may actually work to their benefit.

- *Direct action:* Wise leaders know that in the process of change, they must give people something meaningful to do so they can be active as the change is being implemented. In one organization that was undergoing restructuring, the employees were asked to meet to discuss the new ideas and the implications for their work. Because they were engaged with meaningful work and joint problem solving, their anxiety about the change was reduced, and they took more ownership of the new way of working.

HR professionals can also help a change leader to be aware of the many other changes people in the business are facing. A change leader may think only of the changes he or she is trying to implement and not consider the multitude of changes that employees or managers are being asked to accept at the same time. The overload can cause problems and resistance, which HR professionals may be aware of because of their involvement with many different areas of the business. HR professionals can help to establish more realistic time frames and to stagger the changes so that they are implemented when they have the greatest likelihood of being accepted.

Here is how Step 6: People, is applied to the centralized procurement case example:

The change to centralized procurement does not just affect procurement—it affects everyone within the whole organization. In some offices, displacing just a few people can have a negative effect on many others. In this situation, all of the purchasing patterns that the offices have used need to change. The centralized procurement also has a significant impact on suppliers. Suppliers now need to bid for projects. Some will win, and many others will not receive the contracts they had in the past. Finally, some customers may have new parts in their products, and they may need to be brought into the discussion to understand the impact of the new list of suppliers on their products. As a result, the change leaders develop and communicate a broad communication plan in each of the 12 offices to enable employees to understand the urgency for this change, the end-state vision of centralized procurement (the 70/30 concept), and the implications for the employees. They also provide specialized training for procurement staff who will be transferring to new roles as a result of this change.

What they find is that a major challenge comes from the offices that have the most effective local procurement practices already. These offices are experiencing a reduction in quality and price because they previously had local suppliers who were better able to meet the needs of their local customers. By proceeding with national procurement, their local quality is lower and, in some cases, their costs are higher. These offices receive special attention during the transition. The people in these offices are highly skilled and they need to adapt to the national procurement centralization process. The change team develops targeted engagement approaches to keep these highly successful local offices involved in the change.

Perhaps the greatest challenge in the implementation of this project was the director of the centralized procurement office who was not selected as the project lead for implementing this change process. Although he had failed several times before in attempting to centralize procurement, he was not pleased that someone else was leading this initiative. Throughout the implementation, he attempted to challenge the change team on their plans, and ultimately he became such a barrier to the process that he was asked to leave the company. The manager who led the change project was asked to take over as the director of national procurement instead. Many saw this loss of key talent as a regrettable turn of events that perhaps could have been avoided had this individual agreed to be involved in the change team even if he was not going to be the change leader.

Step 7: Implement

The primary objective when instigating a change is to implement it so that it is not considered a change anymore—to move it from the status of a change to business as usual. The implemented initiative is successful when it is seen as the way that work is done and is not perceived to be an initiative anymore.

This step in implementing change is often more successful if it is done with certain principles in mind. These include:

- *Simplify the approach to fit the needs:* The implementation approach should be done in the simplest possible manner. The HR professional can help the change leader scale back the approach so that it achieves its objectives in the quickest and simplest way. It is important not to make the implementation process more complicated than it needs to be.
- *Expedite the approach as quickly as possible:* The launch of the new way of working should be done as fully and as quickly as possible. In this way, people will experience change at once rather than as a slow change over time. If it is clearly packaged and the implementation is done well, people will be more likely to respond to it positively. If a change takes too long to implement, it may be ignored or resisted.
- *Be tolerant of the need to modify the design:* Anticipate that in the process of implementation, modifications will be required. As with all plans, develop them clearly, but be prepared to adjust them once they are tested in real situations. It will be important to build the expectation that modifications and adjustments will occur to make sure the change is correct. The context will shape reality. Allow this to happen so that your design will be the most effective and the change will be implemented successfully.

Human resource professionals contribute to this step in a variety of ways, including:

- Redefining the people capabilities (such as performance measurement systems) to reflect the change in environment.
- Providing support for leadership and employee development.
- Modifying rewards and recognition systems to motivate people to participate in making the change occur successfully.
- Finding opportunities to communicate and celebrate successes in order to recognize accomplishments associated with implementing change.

Here is how Step 7: Implementation, is applied to the centralized procurement case example:

The project team finds specific quick wins that demonstrate progress with the change implementation. For example, one major quick win is that a supplier of office equipment is chosen and the cost for those products and services are subsequently reduced by over 30 percent. These savings are seen immediately as a benefit of centralized procurement. They also have some quick wins with the offices that are operating with lower-quality procurement and very high cost. The switch to centralized procurement shows immediate benefits for customers who appreciate the much better quality of products. In those local communities, customer retention and satisfaction improve significantly, which is of great benefit to the company. Over time the change becomes the new, normal way of doing business, and it generates most of the savings anticipated.

Step 8: Improve

There are three key aspects of this step: measurement, shared learning, and continuous improvement.

Measurement

Implementation does not conclude until the business realizes the value from the change as is evident through measuring its results. The implementing change process should have clearly defined measures with specific people accountable for the deliverables. When the process is functioning well, the business defines the measurement expectations as part of the "concept adopt" gate review in Step 3. Throughout the change, the business reviews the extent to which those metrics have been achieved. The end result of the change should be measurements that will not be a surprise to anyone. They should know how they are performing throughout the change implementation. The ultimate measure of success for most changes is that after the changes are implemented, people recognize the changes as the new way of operating on a regular basis.

Shared Learning

The lessons learned from the change process need to be shared, which allows the entire business to benefit from the change. It is a great loss for businesses if they lose their intellectual capital. The intelligence gained in a change process needs to be harnessed and reused for future benefit. The change implementation process culminates with an expectation that the learning and knowledge gained from this change process will be shared with others and will become part of the corporate memory. HR professionals have an important role to ensure that this shared learning takes place. Some ways they can achieve this include:

- *Ensure that change teams have a debriefing session at the conclusion of each implementing change project:* Someone should be there to document the discussion of what they learned so that it can become a part of the business's intellectual capital.
- *Publicize success stories that have been achieved through shared learning:* People then believe that the information they put into the system is actually being used, and they become motivated to continue providing information for the system.
- *Create a mentoring process in which people will be the custodians of shared learning for the business:* These people could be called upon when new changes are implemented to share their experiences and apply them to new challenges.

Continuous Improvement

Changes do not occur and then remain static. HR needs to guide the business's leaders to focus on continuous improvement with a readiness to modify the change to make it even more effective. Figure 10.6 presents a chart that is useful for debriefing shared learning and identifying areas for continuous improvement.

The measurement and sharing of learning often lead the change team to recognize that there are areas in which continuous improvement can still occur. At the conclusion of the implementing change process, the

Figure 10.6: Debrief Shared Learnings and Identify Continuous Improvement

Debrief Shared Learnings and Identify Continuous Improvement	
What worked:	What didn't work
What helped:	What hindered
Continuous improvement ideas:	

business makes clear recommendations for what is needed to continuously improve the change.

Businesses need to avoid the idea that once the change is implemented, they do not have to think about it anymore. This kind of approach can produce changes in which the benefits erode quickly. People regress to the old way of doing things and the change does not produce the anticipated results. HR professionals have a role in highlighting the importance of continuous improvement and developing recommendations to further evolve the change.

Finally, with the development of the continuous improvement recommendations, the executive sponsor holds a gate review meeting. At this review, he or she considers the extent to which the objectives of the change have been achieved, learns what has been gained from this process, and explores the opportunities for continuous improvement to further achieve the preferred future.

Here is how Step 8: Improve, is applied to the centralized procurement case example:

After the project is implemented, the change team, some of the key stakeholders of the process, and HR meet. In this meeting they update each other about what has been achieved up to this point. They identify that significant cost savings have been achieved and quality has improved overall. However, as with all projects, there are some areas that are not as effective as others, and they discuss those areas with full transparency.

The group looks at what worked and what did not work, as well as what helped and what hindered the process of implementing the change. They then develop recommendations for how to continuously improve this project and what can be learned for other similar projects. Of particular note, they believe they could have been more effective at engaging the highly successful local offices that are performing well in procurement to ensure that they became active participants in the change. They also identify that the gate review process was very helpful, the involvement of key stakeholders helped ensure that the change plan was as effective as possible, and the communications approach to all employees yielded tremendous benefits. They also acknowledge that HR's guidance throughout the process was essential for the success of the change project. The group generates a summary report and presents it to the executive in the final gate review to declare that the project, at that point, is completed. The change team is congratulated and officially disbanded. The accountability for continuing the implementation of the change is transferred to the new director of centralized procurement, and it becomes part of the ongoing work of that particular department.

CONCLUSION

The HR value proposition of implementing change is a very important organizational capability. HR professionals need to be highly skilled in this area so they can take the lead on implementing change and advise leaders on how to implement change effectively. HR also has to be willing to take the medicine it applies to other parts of the business and use the implementing change process themselves. HR professionals will lose credibility if they are unable to implement their own changes successfully. In addition, HR professionals' experience in initiating changes in their own areas will benefit them in assisting other business areas. As a result of its role in the implementing change process, HR is able to build its credibility and become a very important strategic asset for leaders and for the business.

SUMMARY

- Businesses are undergoing constant change in order to survive and thrive. Too often, though, they focus only on planning the change and not on implementing it. HR has a critical role to play as the process experts on implementing change. They need to establish themselves as a credible source for providing guidance on the most effective way to implement change in order to achieve the desired business outcomes. HR professionals also need to be the resident experts who can advise leaders as they implement change.

- When HR chooses the HR value proposition of implementing change, it can mitigate a major risk associated with business strategies not being implemented effectively.

- Change and transition represent distinctly different parts of the implementing change process: (1) change refers to the business steps required when planning and implementing change; and (2) transition refers to the human steps that are important in change.

- The eight steps in the implementing change process define the leaders' and HR's roles in helping the change occur successfully. The eight steps are:

  - Step 1: Urgency: Leaders must define the urgent and important business reason for the change.

  - Step 2: Team: Once an urgent need for a change is determined, the next step involves choosing a change leader and setting up a change team to champion the process.

  - Step 3: Change Strategy: The change team defines what they believe is the concept that will resolve the urgent problem. They then begin to plan the changes that will be needed in the organization and identify how to assist employees to embrace the envisioned changes.

- Step 4: Stakeholders: Change teams should solicit stakeholder opinions immediately after the change concept is adopted. The stakeholder interviews may uncover barriers, areas of resistance, and new ideas that will be important for the change team as it develops its detailed plans.
- Step 5: Detailed Planning: The change team defines how the change will be implemented and develops the necessary contingency plans in the event that the implementation does not proceed as envisioned.
- Step 6: People: The change team ensures excellence in communication, training, and helping people adjust to the change. They also engage in overcoming resistance to change.
- Step 7: Implement: HR and the change team ensure that the change is implemented so that it is not considered a change anymore—moving it from the status of a "change" to "business as usual."
- Step 8: Improve: There are three key aspects of this step: measurement, shared learning, and continuous improvement. The process concludes with an executive gate review to debrief shared learning and identify areas for continuous improvement.

• The HR value proposition of change implementation is a very important organizational capablity. HR professionals need to take the lead on change implementation and advise leaders on how to implement change effectively. HR also has to be willing to take the medicine it applies to other parts of the business and use the implementing change process themselves.

CHAPTER ELEVEN

MAKING LEADERSHIP-DRIVEN HR HAPPEN

At the conclusion of a very dynamic, meaningful, and fun executive session on leadership-driven HR, the senior HR professionals were asked: "What are the barriers to implementing these approaches?" They worked in small groups to identify the barriers they would encounter. The lists from the small groups were long, but they had some common themes. They then analyzed each of the barriers and brainstormed what could be done to overcome them. By the end of the discussion, they summarized all of the great ideas into one word: "FOCUS." They determined that they must "focus, focus, focus" in order to make leadership-driven HR happen.

One of the key messages in *Leadership-Driven HR* is that HR needs to focus on its priorities and to lighten up other work that is of a lower priority. The best example of focus is the emphasis on the HR value proposition. Often, HR professionals can identify many HR value propositions. The problem is that if HR takes on too many key priorities, they will likely do none of them well. The alternate approach is to pick the top-priority HR value proposition that mitigates a critical business risk. At the same time, HR needs to be diligent and lighten up its role in other areas to make room for its priority work. In other words, HR will succeed only if it achieves a clear focus on its priorities and a reduced role in other lower-priority areas.

A major barrier to the implementation of leadership-driven HR is that too often HR professionals are included in executive discussions "after the fact" rather than working as an indispensable part of the development of business strategy. Some HR professionals complain that they are "not at the table," which means they are not involved as business partners with the executives who make the big decisions. This exclusion from the strategic discussions with executive leaders frustrates many HR professionals because they believe that if they are not part of the business strategy, they will not be able to understand the major business risks and discover the best ways to mitigate these risks effectively.

This issue is so important to senior HR professionals that they often use it as a criterion for whether they should pursue a senior HR position or not. HR's position can easily be seen in the organizational structure. Organizational charts showing that the most senior HR person reports to the president often signals that HR is essential to the business strategy. Even mid-level HR professionals look to the senior levels of the structure for this indication of HR's role in the organization. If HR reports to the president, it probably is essential to the business, and if it does not, then HR is more likely used for transactional and administrative functions.

So why is it that HR is *not* at the executive table in some businesses? There are three possible reasons:

1. *HR is not an area of essential risk for the business:* For example, some organizations are more product-distribution oriented, and people and organizational capability issues may be less crucial to their success.
2. *The president does not see HR's value:* The president may have had negative experiences with senior HR professionals in the past and thus chooses to limit HR's role in strategy. This approach can be very problematic, especially when there are business risks associated with people and organizational capabilities.
3. *The HR professionals have not demonstrated the capacity to be at the executive table:* For example, if the senior HR professional contributes only from an HR perspective and not from a business perspective, he or she may not be as useful at the executive table; therefore, the president may choose not to have that role present for strategy discussions.

Reason #1 is not a primary concern if HR truly is not essential for the business. In that case, it may be appropriate that HR should not be at the executive table. There are many professionals in organizations who would like to hear what executives discuss so they can act upon the executive issues effectively. However, only the people who are essential to the creation of the strategy are included because their voices need to be part of the generation of the ideas (not just the implementation of the ideas).

The primary concerns are with reasons #2 and #3. In both of these situations, HR should be part of the executive team because HR needs to contribute to generative discussions on business issues. However, in reason #2, HR is shunted to the side because the president has a bias against it. In reason #3, HR is not living up to the level of performance that the executive leaders require, so HR is not included in the executive discussions.

For HR to convince the president that it should be at the table and for HR to demonstrate that it has the capability to contribute ideas, HR needs to have a relentless focus on business priorities. It needs to clearly define its HR value proposition and how it will deliver value for the business with a clear line of sight to the external customer. By demonstrating that kind of focus, HR will be invited to engage in executive conversations and will be able to do the following:

- Contribute meaningfully to business strategy and drive value for the business.
- Develop effective ways for HR issues to be incorporated within the business strategy.
- Develop clear communication plans to ensure that all business leaders understand the business and HR focus.
- Be more effective at implementing the leadership-driven HR approaches.

We use the mnemonic of "FOCUS" to help HR professionals focus on what they need to do to overcome the barriers to effective implementation of leadership-driven HR. The letters in FOCUS stand for the following:

Implement Leadership-Driven HR with FOCUS
F: Forward thinking
O: Outside-in
C: Co-create
U: Up-to-date
S: Synergies within HR

Let's take a look at the five areas of FOCUS. Each area gives examples of barriers to implementing leadership-driven HR and then presents the activities or attitudes that are important in order for HR to overcome the barriers and deliver value for the business.

F: FORWARD THINKING

Examples of Barriers to Making Leadership-Driven HR Happen

Here are five examples of barriers that HR professionals could identify that would benefit from HR having a "Forward-thinking" approach:

- HR is too reactive—firefighting versus being proactive and strategic.
- HR is being pulled into the "weeds" and therefore is not able to get to the forward-thinking strategy.
- The rest of the business has not caught on and is not pulling HR forward.
- Leadership won't let HR "in" at the strategic level.
- Leadership has traditional views of HR and perceives that there is no need for HR strategy.

Using "Forward Thinking" to Overcome These Barriers

For HR professionals to be part of the executive conversations, they must have a forward-thinking mindset. They should demonstrate excellence in sensing what might occur even before it happens. They need to be effective at weaving together patterns from the business, the customers, the leadership, and the employees to understand what is likely to occur and then develop contingencies for it.

Unfortunately, many HR professionals resort to long lists of projects as the way to describe what they are doing. While the lists may identify important work, they are often unfocused, overwhelming, and misunderstood. The alternative approach is for HR professionals to document their forward-thinking viewpoints in a succinct way so that they are highly focused, easily communicated, and clearly understood.

One effective method that HR can use to demonstrate its forward-thinking approach is to summarize the HR direction in an HR strategy "one-pager." Figure 11.1 shows an example of an HR strategy one-pager for a hi-tech business:

Figure 11.1: An Example of an HR Strategy One-Pager

Business Vision and Strategic Imperatives		
HR Value Proposition: Build Leadership Capacity		**HR Metrics:** ROI of Human Capital

People Capabilities	Organizational Capabilities	Partnerships with Leadership
1. Meet talent needs through integrated recruitment, development, and performance management	4. Build and reinforce a culture of innovation	7. Partner in business strategy implementation within each division
2. Build capacity of leaders to be leaders of innovation and engage and align employees and teams	5. Deliver HR value for the business technology transformation to enhance external customer service	8. Ensure coordinated HR service delivery (within HR) to achieve effective business partnerships
3. Implement succession management process	6. Develop the HR professionals' capacity to implement change	9. Implement the HR 'cloud' technology to maximize employee self-service

10. HR strategic deliverables are built on excellence in foundational HR services

The HR strategy one-pager summarizes HR's forward-thinking view. It should show the direct link between the HR value proposition and the overall business strategy.

The text at the top of Figure 11.1, "Business Vision and Strategic Imperatives," should be expanded to specify the actual business vision and the business's priority strategic imperatives. In the example one-pager, the HR value proposition, "Build Leadership Capacity," was chosen to mitigate a critical business risk to one of the business's strategic imperatives. The metric, "ROI of Human Capital," is the way for HR to prove its value to the business. The one-pager also should identify the priority people and organizational capabilities that HR will deliver to meet the specific needs of the business and its customers.

Let's look at the example one-pager to get an idea of the parts of the document and how they relate to one another.

- *People capabilities:* HR deliverables 1–3 identify that HR will meet the business's talent needs through recruitment, development, or perform-ance management, whichever fits the needs best. The one-pager also indicates that this organization needs to build leadership capacity by developing leaders of innovation. Also, this organization needs a succession management process to build its future leadership capacity.
- *Organizational capabilities:* HR deliverables 4–6 identify that HR will build a culture of innovation to make it easier for leaders to become leaders of innovation. HR will also work on a special project with the business leaders to implement the technology transformation in order to serve external customers better. Finally, the one-pager includes an expectation that HR will develop its own talent in implementing change so that it can add more value for the business as it continually evolves.
- *Partnerships with leadership:* HR deliverables 7–9 identify how HR will work with the business leaders. This includes that HR will be partners with the leadership in each division in the implementation of their various strategies and HR's commitment to work within the HR department in a coordinated and seamless way as they partner with business leaders. Also, HR will implement "cloud" technology for its transactional and information services so that leaders and employees can be self-reliant with many foundational HR services.

Deliverable 10, "HR strategic deliverables are built on excellence in foundational HR services," indicates that HR has other ongoing work—this includes areas such as payroll, benefits, pension administration, compensation, and employee relations. HR should engage in a careful review of this foundational work to ensure that it does not distract HR professionals from focusing on and achieving the first nine strategic deliverables.

For most HR departments, the one-pager is an essential method of explaining HR's forward-thinking view to business leaders and how this view will deliver value for the business. When HR develops a clear strategy one-pager, they will have a better chance of overcoming the barriers associated with the perception of HR as "firefighters" who are not engaging in forward thinking.

In addition, HR can enhance its credibility in this area by forecasting contingencies that may occur and planning how they would respond to those contingencies. During any given year, issues and challenges may emerge that will divert HR's attention from its forward-thinking strategy. The business might engage in a new initiative; there might be a business downturn that could require changes in the workforce; or there might be labor or employee issues that require an unusual amount of HR attention beyond what was originally planned. Figure 11.2 shows the same HR strategy one-pager but with some areas faded. These are the areas that HR would lighten up in the event that HR needed to divert 30 to 40 percent of its attention to another major challenge during the year.

Figure 11.2 shows that HR will delete, delay, distribute, or diminish its focus on certain major deliverables (deliverables 3, 6, and 9) as well as on its measurement of the ROI of human capital as part of its contingency plan. When HR professionals show they are ready to refocus their efforts as events unfold, they are further demonstrating that they are forward-thinking and planning for all contingencies. When they take this view, it's also clear to them and to the HR team that some priorities have to be lightened up in the event that the contingency plan has to be activated. In one organization, a senior HR professional was very disturbed that his project deliverable could be put on hold if the contingency plan had to go into effect. However, after some discussion, it actually helped him and the HR team to know what the business's highest priorities were. When a major crisis did occur during the year,

Figure 11.2: What HR Will Lighten Up as a Contingency Plan

Business Vision and Strategic Imperatives		
HR Value Proposition: **Build Leadership Capacity**		**HR Metrics:** **ROI of Human Capital**

People Capabilities	Organizational Capabilities	Partnerships with Leadership
1. Meet talent needs through integrated recruitment, development, and performance management	4. Build and reinforce a culture of innovation	7. Partner in business strategy implementation within each division
2. Build capacity of leaders to be leaders of innovation and engage and align employees and teams	5. Deliver HR value for the business technology transformation to enhance external customer service	8. Ensure coordinated HR service delivery (within HR) to achieve effective business partnerships
3. Implement succession management process	6. Develop the HR professionals' capacity to implement change	9. Implement the HR 'cloud' technology to maximize employee self-service

10. HR strategic deliverables are built on excellence in foundational HR services

the HR team was ready to activate their contingency plan because they were forward-thinking.

When HR is forward-thinking and can describe its HR value proposition and priority deliverables on a strategy one-pager and on a contingency plan, the executive leaders will recognize that HR has the credibility to contribute to strategic discussions. HR can also demonstrate its value to leaders for each of the business areas by applying the same strategy one-pager approach in order to help the business leaders develop their own strategy one-pagers.

O: OUTSIDE-IN

Examples of Barriers to Making Leadership-Driven HR Happen

Here are five examples of barriers that HR professionals could identify that would benefit from HR having an "Outside-in" approach:

- HR lacks a line of sight to the external customer.
- The organization views HR's role as internal support.
- HR is too busy to listen and has too much transactional work.

- HR has too much focus on getting jobs done.
- HR doesn't have enough time or resources.

Using an Outside-In Approach to Overcome These Barriers

Two key expectations of leadership-driven HR are that HR has a clear line of sight to the external customer and that HR needs to take an outside-in approach to their work[1]. Some HR professionals argue that they are unable to know what the external customer believes, and as a result, they only focus on delivering value within the organization. Although most HR professionals believe it is important for HR to know what the external customer needs and wants, they struggle with the implementation of that approach.

Nevertheless, HR needs to be relentless in taking an outside-in approach, rather than an inside-out approach. As described in Chapter Two, the outside-in approach means that HR understands what the customer and the business leaders require in order to determine HR's focus in supporting the business strategy. The outside-in approach also becomes a very important filter to enable HR to select the most valuable HR priorities.

For example, all of the HR priority deliverables identified on the HR strategy one-pager (in Figure 11.1) should have a clear description of how they contribute value to the external customer. If HR professionals cannot define how they deliver value to the external customer, then they should question why they are priority deliverables.

Here are some examples of how HR leaders have overcome the barrier of not having a clear line of sight to external customers:

- *Visit customers regularly:* One HR leader encouraged the entire executive team to commit to spending one day a month with external customers. This HR leader also spent time with external customers, working with sales reps, and visiting customers' homes for a full day each month. That one day a month kept him connected and engaged

---

1. See Dave Ulrich, John Younger, Wayne Brockbank and Mike Ulrich in "HR from the Outside In" that presents their research on the six competencies for the future work of HR. New York, McGraw-Hill Companies (2012).

with the ultimate customer. It also taught him a great deal about some of the challenges employees faced when they visited customers. The HR leader also encouraged his HR employees to find a way to meet external customers in order to understand what they were thinking and, ultimately, what the implications would be for the HR people capabilities and organizational capabilities.

- *Maintain a close connection to marketing:* HR should work closely with the market researchers in the marketing department. Researchers collect data about what customers believe on a regular basis. They know what delights and dissatisfies customers. HR should study that customer information to identify its implications for determining if and how people and organizational capabilities need strengthening. In fact, it is often more important for HR to study the marketing information before it studies the employee engagement data. The market research information may lead HR to consider new ways to deliver value for the business, and it may help focus HR's attention on specific problematic business areas that could help HR to better interpret their employee engagement data.

- *Attend business meetings:* HR professionals must get out of their offices and attend departmental meetings with their business leaders. One HR professional regularly attended meetings and sales events with the sales management team to hear the issues they were discussing and to learn what was important to customers. This information was very useful in creating a line of sight to what customers required. It also helped HR to understand the implications for its priorities in people and organizational capabilities.

Another way for HR to demonstrate an outside-in approach is to emphasize a focus on outcomes rather than on process. When HR focuses on processes, the emphasis is on what HR needs to do and how they can ensure that those processes are delivered at a very high level of effectiveness. However, HR professionals are often concerned that they are not able to achieve meaningful outcomes on a regular basis. This frustration becomes demotivating for HR and simultaneously reduces HR's overall credibility to deliver value for the business.

When HR focuses on outcomes, it starts in the reverse—with what the customer or the business needs from HR and how HR will deliver that outcome, or in other words, from the outside in. HR needs to augment the outside-in approach with the following:

- *Projectize:* Reconceptualize processes so that they become a series of projects. "Projectize" means to build in start points and end points for work. Every area of ongoing work should have milestones to mark when it begins and when it has achieved a meaningful outcome.
- *Measurement:* Measure and track outcomes to show that HR is delivering a return on investment and then document the outcomes that HR has successfully achieved.
- *Communications:* Focus on communicating what HR plans to deliver to the business. Often businesses have communications departments that are put in one place with expertise in external and internal communications. However, the communications department is HR's marketing arm for all people and organizational capabilities, so HR must develop expertise in this area or else form very close alliances with the communications specialists. HR should be able to provide insight on internal communications from the outside in. This includes being socially perceptive of what will motivate employees, what will likely be perceived poorly, and how to interact with employees so that important messages will be heard and understood.

C: CO-CREATE

Examples of Barriers to Making Leadership-Driven HR Happen

Here are five examples of barriers that HR professionals could identify that would benefit from HR having a "Co-create" approach:

- HR lacks a connection to the organization's business areas.
- HR fails to link the HR strategic priorities to organizational requirements.

- The business has a top-down attitude and long-standing senior directors.
- There is a perceived threat to functional leaders' space.
- Leaders resist doing more themselves.

Using a Co-Create Approach to Overcome These Barriers

It's important to understand the levels of relationships that HR can have with business leaders so that HR can understand the value of Level 4 relationships in overcoming barriers to leadership-driven HR.

Figure 11.3 shows the four levels of relationships that HR can have with business leaders.

Figure 11.3: Four Levels of Relationships that HR Has with Business Leaders

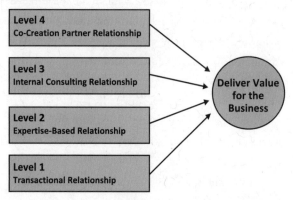

Level 1, "Transactional Relationships," can be a barrier for HR's ability to deliver work of greater value. HR professionals are sometimes inundated with transactional requests from business leaders that take up a great deal of their time. As a result, they do not have the time to work closely with business leaders. Some transactions are necessary for HR to do and some are simply requests for HR to do clerical work that business leaders do not want to do themselves.

Level 2, "Expertise-Based Relationships," reflects the many areas where HR has unique technical expertise—providing solutions, expert advice, or technical coaching. Although HR will always retain some work at levels 1 and 2, it needs to find ways to elevate its value to business leaders and increase its interactive work to levels 3 and 4.

Level 3, "Internal Consulting Relationship," focuses on assessing needs and facilitating a method of dealing with an issue. It begins after the business leader identifies a problem or opportunity and then seeks support from HR. An example of this level of relationship is when an HR professional is asked to help out with a team that is not working well together. The HR professional needs to understand, assess, and design an intervention to respond to the challenge in order to meet the business leader's needs. When HR is functioning in an internal consulting relationship, HR is supporting business leaders after the fact, or *after* the problems arise.

Level 4, "Co-Creation Partner Relationship," focuses on how HR professionals gain insight into issues and propose solutions even *before* the problems arise. They are part of the creation of the strategy and plan. They demonstrate foresight to identify potential issues with people and organizational capabilities even before they occur. When HR professionals co-create with business leaders, they are functioning as business partners. Essentially, an HR business partner is an advanced level of a consulting relationship. All HR business partners need to have a well-developed competence in internal consulting; however, most HR professionals who are engaged in internal consulting are not working as HR co-creation partners.

Some distinctions between an HR co-creation partnering relationship (level 4) and an internal consulting relationship (level 3) include the following:

- HR co-creation business partners are invited into conversations with business leaders even before there is a problem. The HR business partners are part of the senior management's strategic planning and thinking meetings. On the other hand, most HR professionals—when they act only as internal consultants—are invited into meetings and conversations after the strategy has been set and only when a problem of some kind has occurred.

- The focus of HR co-creation partner conversations is on how to give the business competitive/comparative advantage, or at least achieve competitive/comparative parity. These conversations often extend beyond the people and organizational capabilities typically reserved for HR professionals. In contrast, an HR internal consultant often comments only on the people and organizational aspects of business issues.
- The HR co-creation partner relationship is characterized by a situation in which the business leader wants to see and support the HR professional as much as the HR professional wants to see and support the business leader. They are partners in the true sense of the word. On the other hand, as internal consultants, HR professionals often want to see and support the business leader more than the business leader wants to see and support HR.

When HR professionals co-create plans and strategies with business leaders, they need to focus on delivering outcomes that enhance the business's overall performance. The three variables that are most useful in assessing the quality of the co-created outcomes are as follows:

- *Wise recommendations:* These are recommendations that reflect the right thing to do for the business in anticipation of issues that may arise. The direction chosen should be the simplest possible recommendation for the anticipated need so that it can be easily communicated and also repeated with relative ease. It also should be measurable so it can demonstrate the added value it provides.
- *Educates and empowers:* The process of co-creating should be educational for business leaders so that when that situation or a similar one arises, they will have a better chance of being able to respond to it independently.
- *Enhances the relationship between the HR professional and the business leader:* The quality of the relationship between the HR professional and the business leader is important. A positive co-creation partner relationship will mean that the business leader will seek out the

HR professional the next time he or she anticipates an issue; and the business leader will also be more likely to be receptive to the HR professional's insights and observations.

Sometimes business leaders are not motivated or are even resistant to co-creating plans and strategies with HR professionals. Wherever possible, HR professionals need to pre-empt the process and develop co-creation partner relationships with business leaders on a regular basis. This may be more easily said than done. If leaders are resistant to this idea, HR should find the leaders that are more open to it and start where there is a readiness to develop co-creation partnerships. By building a repertoire of successes with various leaders, HR will develop credibility with other business leaders who will then see the value of co-creation partnerships with HR.

However, even with the best intentions, HR professionals may encounter resistance. One HR professional referred to the process of winning over a resistant business leader as "two steps forward and one step back." There are many bumps in the road to relationship building. Some business leaders may regress by resorting to power too quickly and telling HR what to do. Others regress in more subtle ways. Some may manipulate overtly or subtly, and others may avoid discussing the important issues. Some tactics that may be helpful for HR in overcoming resistance and influencing business leaders are as follows:

- *Engage in influence activities before the need arises:* In most situations, HR professionals do not have the authority to demand that business leaders work with them. Rather, HR professionals must achieve results through influence without authority. When business leaders have hierarchical power, they can exert their authority at the moment of need to ensure that others follow their directions. Some HR professionals make the error of believing that they too can influence a business leader at the moment of need even when they do not have authority. Unfortunately, influencing without authority at the moment of need can result in resistance from the business leader.

To succeed, HR professionals must begin influencing "pre-need" to build relationships with the business leaders and increase the likelihood that they will collaborate with HR. These influencing tactics include the following:

- Build and maintain a broad network of internal and external contacts, including key decision makers and organizational influencers.
- Demonstrate a sincere desire to be personally connected with the business leader, showing interest in the business leader's direction, cross-functional alignment, and team engagement.
- Always represent business and HR decisions, directions, and interests above personal priorities.
- Seek out and skillfully incorporate diverse perspectives and offer to engage in dialogue on issues in anticipation of future needs.
- Encourage business leaders to take personal ownership of your insights so that they can represent those ideas confidently.

After engaging in these kinds of pre-need influencing tactics, the HR professional will have a better chance of becoming a co-creation partner with the business leader even before the real needs arise.

- *Communicate in the language of the business leader:* HR professionals sometimes communicate with business leaders using HR jargon that the leaders do not understand or relate to, which can result in resistance. The preferred approach is for HR professionals to adjust their communication style to speak in the language of the business leader. This means that if the business leader thinks in political, financial, or personal gains terms, structure your influence approach in their language style to maximize understanding. Talk in terms of financial benefits to the business leaders who are only concerned about the bottom line; talk in terms of political success to the business leaders who are only concerned about promotion or enhancing their current position. Another influence tactic is to attend conferences or learning events with business leaders and engage them in conversation about the topics presented that are of interest to them. Also, HR professionals should communicate during low-stress times for business leaders. For example, find out when they are more willing to listen to people. Sometimes it is over breakfast; sometimes it is later in the day; in any case, communicate when they are most open in order to maximize receptivity.

- *See yourself as a colleague and not as a subordinate:* Some HR professionals are nervous around business leaders and show it in the manner in which they approach them and speak to them. This behavior can cause the business leader to resist collaboration with HR as a co-creation partner. Instead, HR professionals need to visualize themselves as the business leader's equal. HR professionals should consider how they would talk with business leaders if they were the business leaders' equal. Would the HR professionals change their tone, ask more direct questions, or provide more of their insights about what to do?

- *Know when it's time to move on as the HR partner of the business leader:* HR professionals and business leaders should have periodic discussions about how they work together. This will provide an opportunity for HR professionals to reflect on the extent to which they are contributing value for the business and allow them to offer coaching to the business leaders as required. One perceptive HR professional in a manufacturing business realized that she had to move on to another business area in the company when she found that she was planning changes in an area of the organization that she had already changed a few years earlier. She realized it was time for someone else to contribute fresh ideas to add value to that business leader. She moved to another business area in the company, and the transfer worked exceptionally well. It is important that HR professionals know when to move on in order to continue being successful in their co-creation partner relationships with business leaders. Business leaders need fresh ideas on an ongoing basis. A periodic change in HR professionals may be the way that fresh ideas and viewpoints can be sustained.

U: UP-TO-DATE

Examples of Barriers to Making Leadership-Driven HR Happen

Here are five examples of barriers that HR professionals could identify that would benefit from HR having an "Up-to-date" approach:

- The HR mindset and behaviors are entrenched in how work was done in the past.
- HR professionals ask, "What's in it for me?"
- The organization has a static culture and there is resistance to change.
- There is a lack of transparency about HR developmental needs.
- HR has "shoemaker's children" syndrome—it develops others but not itself.

Using an Up-to-Date Approach to Overcome These Barriers

HR is professionalizing its field of expertise at the same time that businesses are rapidly changing. HR professionals often struggle to keep up with the evolution of their businesses and to understand the emerging issues that are causing these changes. In addition, HR professionals frequently do not invest time in their own professional development to learn how to expand their repertoire of people and organizational capabilities and deliver value for the business. Often, HR professionals refer to themselves as "shoemaker's children," alluding to the image of expert shoemakers who build and repair shoes for others while their children go barefoot.

HR professionals must invest in "HR for HR." They must stay up-to-date with the developments in the business and with their own HR profession. If HR does not have credibility as a profession that understands the business and knows the latest approaches within HR, then there will be little chance to deliver value for the business. For example, the HR strategy one-pager (see Figure 11.1) includes an HR priority deliverable (#6) to "develop the HR professionals' capacity to implement change." This priority deliverable is an example of how HR professionals are expected to keep up-to-date on the latest approaches so they can deliver even greater value for the business.

Figure 11.4 shows the areas where HR must be up-to-date. Let's explore each area of Figure 11.4 separately:

Figure 11.4: Areas Where HR Must Be Up-to-Date

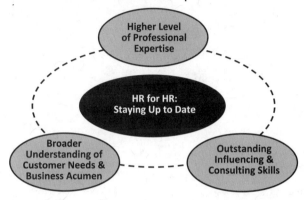

- *Higher level of professional expertise:* HR professionals need to be up-to-date on the latest developments in people and organizational capabilities. In particular, HR professionals need to invest time and energy into learning how to deliver the organizational capabilities, which is an area that many HR professionals are less familiar with. They need to be very knowledgeable, forceful, and articulate with business leaders about the process of culture transformation, organizational restructuring, change implementation, business alignment, and ROI of human capital. If HR professionals have done their homework, worked diligently on their own development, and established co-creation partner relationships with business leaders, they will have an audience for their insights.
- *Broader understanding of customer needs and business acumen:* HR professionals need to hear the voice of the external customer as described in the outside-in section. They need to find ways to know continually what the customer interests are and how both they and their business partners can meet those interests. Also, HR needs to have a good understanding of the flow of work. This is the core business

acumen that HR professionals must acquire. When they know the flow of work, they will have greater credibility to build co-creation partner relationships with business leaders in areas that require organizational capabilities (as described in Chapter Six).

- *Outstanding influencing and consulting skills:*[2] HR professionals need to excel at influencing and consulting in order to become co-creation partners with business leaders. The essence of consulting skills is to gain insight into a business leader's issues and to discover possible solutions. To achieve that outcome, HR professionals need to be very interested in and perceptive about the market as well as the competitive analysis of the business leader's part of the business. With knowledge of the leader's business, HR professionals are able to ask business leaders astute questions and intrigue them on the spot. HR professionals listen intently to the business leader to deeply understand issues, discover the question that needs to be answered, and then ensure that the solution resolves the question exceptionally well.

When HR professionals are up-to-date in their professional expertise, in their understanding of customer needs and business acumen, and in their influencing and consulting skills, they will have a greater ability to overcome the barriers to leadership-driven HR and deliver value for the business.

S: SYNERGIES WITHIN HR

Examples of Barriers to Making Leadership-Driven HR Happen

Here are five examples of barriers that HR professionals could identify that would benefit from a "Synergies within HR" approach:

- Different parts of HR lack opportunities to share ideas with one another.

---

2. For a more detailed description of the internal consulting process, see David S. Weiss, *High Performance HR: Leveraging Human Resources for Competitive Advantage* (Toronto: John Wiley & Sons, 2000), 102–112.

- HR partners and subject matter experts do not see the need for HR's internal alignment.
- HR lacks commitment, discipline, and structure.
- The belief that "I can do it better by myself" is prevalent in HR.
- HR professionals are resistant to collaborate and too often are nay-sayers.

Using Synergies within HR to Overcome These Barriers

HR needs to be the model of organizational excellence in order to have the credibility to co-create and add value for the business. This means that HR professionals must function well internally as a team and work synergistically within HR. By doing this, HR becomes greater than the sum of its parts. All HR professionals do the work in their areas of expertise, but they also know how to contribute to others' areas of expertise and create something greater. HR professionals must work together in alignment with external customer requirements and with the business strategy direction. They all use the HR strategy one-pager to guide what they do. They are all highly engaged and give their discretionary efforts to the business and to the HR department. HR's brand is very strong within these businesses as an essential part of the success of the business and as a model of how to run a department.

For example, the HR strategy one-pager (see Figure 11.1) includes an HR priority deliverable (#8) to "ensure coordinated HR service delivery (within HR) to achieve effective business partnerships." This priority deliverable is an example of how HR professionals are expected to achieve synergies within HR so they can deliver value for the business. However, in too many situations, HR professionals do not work in synergy with each other. This may be due to unclear HR direction, which makes alignment difficult; challenging interpersonal or inter-professional conflicts; or general neglect to consider synergies within HR as important.

One way that HR professionals can build synergy is by investing time in openly sharing ideas with each other about what they know about the business and HR. The HR professionals' combined knowledge of the business is always greater than any one HR professional's knowledge and, in many cases, is a good starting point to build synergy within HR. HR professionals should consciously make time to discuss how the business is evolving and share that information with each other. They should also bring various business leaders into HR meetings to understand business challenges and their implications for HR. HR then becomes its own internal laboratory of knowledge-sharing that allows HR professionals to build synergy by understanding the business collectively.

In a similar way, HR professionals should use the knowledge that external consultants gain when they are engaged to support the business. Often, HR professionals bring in external consultants but do not spend sufficient time gaining insights about what the external consultants have learned about the business. When external consultants provide service to an organization, HR professionals should have access to the knowledge and insights that the consultants gained. Then HR can use this information to deliver ongoing value for the business.

HR also needs to build synergies and excellent communications within the HR department. This is especially important in organizations that have structured HR as a matrix of HR subject-matter experts (SME) and HR business partners. These organizations are usually larger and can hire HR specialists who excel in specific subject-matter areas, such as recruitment, compensation, training and development, and total rewards. The HR subject-matter experts are usually assigned an area of expertise that they deliver for the entire business. They also hire HR business partners who work with specific business leaders to co-create solutions to meet their localized business requirements and to implement the work of the HR SMEs locally.

Although conceptually this model makes a great deal of sense for larger organizations, HR needs to work diligently to ensure that the HR subject-matter experts and HR business partners work in synergy with each other. If they do not, the entire model could fail. Essentially, the challenge is that the HR business partners are set up to respond to the needs of their local business leaders while the HR SMEs are set up to respond to the needs of the total business. These two groups of HR professionals do not always have the same perspective, which produces an

HR business that does not work in synergy and is not internally aligned. In some cases HR becomes fragmented. In addition, sometimes the HR SMEs and HR business partners find themselves in a triangular relationship between each other and the business leaders. Sometimes business leaders give the HR business partners the responsibility for specific work, and at other times they give responsibilities directly to the HR SMEs. This can lead to a lack of synergy within HR if the HR SMEs and HR business partners do not clarify their roles and collaborate well together.

HR executives should consider the following approaches to building synergy between the HR business partners and HR SMEs:

- *Include HR business partners and HR SMEs on the HR leadership team:* Through their dialogues with one another, the HR business partners and HR SMEs will make explicit attempts to develop mutual accountabilities and share learning with each other.
- *Create the expectation that each HR business partner should be a project leader on at least one organization-wide project:* The logic here is twofold. First, an organizational expert is used for a challenging assignment. Second, it forces the HR business partner to focus on a business-wide project to balance out his or her focus on the local business needs of specific departments.
- *Create the expectation that each of the HR SMEs should be an HR business partner for one of the business areas:* For example, in one organization the HR SME for compensation was also the HR business partner for the legal department. A dual role forces the HR SMEs to think about the local impact of their organization-wide initiatives.

In addition, the HR business partners and HR SMEs should enhance the synergy between themselves by working more collaboratively with each other. Here are some recommendations:

- The HR business partners should share any relevant developments involving business leaders with the HR SMEs and should work with the HR SMEs to meet the business leaders' needs. At the same time, the SMEs should give early warning signals to the HR business partners about upcoming changes in people and organizational capabilities and associated cost issues.

- HR business partners should have a general working knowledge of all the people and organizational processes developed by the HR SMEs and operate in accordance with these processes. At the same time, the HR SMEs should have a working knowledge of the HR business partners' areas of expertise and business priorities.
- The HR SMEs should keep the HR business partners informed of business leaders' requests when they receive them directly. They then should collaborate with the HR business partners to gain insight into and discover solutions for the business leaders' issues.
- HR business partners should take responsibility for marketing and communicating the work of HR SMEs to the business leaders and support the development and implementation of their work.

The need for synergies within HR is also necessary among the HR subject matter experts themselves. The HR SMEs should have a general knowledge of the other areas of HR subject-matter expertise, develop cross-expertise solutions, consolidate metrics to assess overall performance, and coordinate communications. In a similar manner, the HR business partners should engage in knowledge-sharing with the other HR business partners so that services to several business leaders can be achieved at high quality and low cost without sacrificing service and timeliness. Essentially, to achieve synergies within HR, all the professionals in HR have to work collaboratively and share information and knowledge with each other.

HR should also expand its view of synergies within HR to include three additional areas of work that may not be structured within HR. These are:

- *Payroll, labor relations, sales training, communications:* HR should ensure that it works in synergy with payroll (if it is in the finance department), with labor relations (if labor relations is a separate department), with sales training (if it is in the sales department), and communications (if it is in its own department).

- *Areas tangential to HR:* HR should ensure that it works in synergy with other areas that are tangential to HR such as legal, finance, and information technology. At a minimum these groups should coordinate when they deploy new programs so that they do not overwhelm the business with new requests at the same time.

- *External vendors:* HR needs to ensure that it works in synergy with external vendors who are delivering ongoing HR work as outsourced service providers and external consultants.

CONCLUSION

The journey for leadership-driven HR is not over—rather HR will need to continually adjust, learn, and transform over the next decade and beyond. Businesses are rapidly changing in ways that will have significant implications for how HR delivers value for the business. Business leaders are also changing. With the retirement of many leaders and new entrants into the leadership role, HR will be challenged to guide the new leaders as they take on more complex responsibilities. In addition, HR itself will continue to go through rapid change as businesses attempt to find ways to save costs, utilize technology, and get economies of scale from the transactional services HR delivers. HR will need to focus on higher-value work within the business and on finding ways to lighten up other transactional work. As new technologies are developed, HR will be affected directly—both in deploying the technologies and in addressing associated issues related to security and compliance. There are many implications of this rapid, continual evolution of the human resources field and the expectations of human resources professionals.

HR professionals must be forward-thinking and up-to-date on issues so that they can shape the future rather than always being in a reactive mode. They need to see the changes that might affect HR even before the executives see the problems emerging. Rather than retaining HR's former approach, HR should take the initiative to make leadership-driven HR happen and create a new way of delivering value for the business even before being asked to change. In this way, HR will be more in control of the changes that occur rather than having the changes pushed upon them.

In addition, universities and HR continuing education need to significantly shift what they teach about HR to the kinds of topics described in *Leadership-Driven HR*. These educational institutions are too often focused on a human resources model that emphasizes policies and specific practices that now are delivered in radically different ways. The universities should be think tanks that are two steps ahead of HR, just as HR tries to be one step ahead of their business leaders. The challenges for the educational institutions are great and will continue to be a significant area of development over the next decade. For example, some universities are investing in master's and doctorate-level degrees in HR. By creating these higher-level educational programs, the universities will have the opportunity to build the HR curriculum from scratch, which will ensure that they will be up-to-date and potentially leading edge. Some universities expect that professors in HR continue to work for clients in consulting capacities so that they can stay abreast of what is occurring in businesses and have exposure to the innovative ideas that are being developed and practiced by HR professionals in those businesses. The professors are then able to include the knowledge, fresh insights, and examples they have gleaned from their on-site experiences in what they teach to prospective HR professionals.

Governments also need to recognize the transformation that is occurring within human resources and the strategic value that HR can provide for public, not-for-profit, and private sector organizations. They need to invest in developing highly skilled HR talent to take on strategic HR roles. Governments can also introduce incentives to motivate businesses, educational institutions, and consultants to engage in research on the new dynamics in the workplace that will optimize performance and effectiveness. They can also encourage various non-profit organizations to collaborate and share services so that they can better manage the costs associated with HR transactional services.

HR is experiencing an exciting time of dramatic change that will affect public and private sector businesses, customers, citizens, and the HR profession. HR needs to embrace this new reality rather than attempting to hang on to the way it was in the past. The past is gone. HR needs to look forward to the new reality and shape its own future so that it can deliver value for the business. *Leadership-Driven HR* is a road map that will help HR to drive value for the business, guide HR to deliver value through leaders, and ensure that HR is driven to lead.

Let me close with a story:

A student comes to a master with a bird cupped inside his hands. He asks the master, "Is the bird in my hands alive or dead?" The master knows that if he says the bird is dead, the student will open his hands and the bird will fly away. And if the master says, "The bird is alive," the student will close his hands and crush the bird. After a moment's reflection, the master says, "Whether the bird is alive or dead is in your hands."

Whether HR is alive, will thrive, or just survive, is in HR's hands. It's time to thrive.

SUMMARY

- One of the major messages in this book is that HR needs to focus on key priorities and to lighten up other work that is of a lower priority. The best example of this focus is the emphasis on the HR value proposition. At the same time as it focuses on this proposition, HR needs to be diligent and lighten up its role in other areas to make room for the top-priority work. The letters of the word "FOCUS" are used in this chapter to frame five recommendations for HR to overcome barriers and implement leadership-driven HR.

- F – Forward thinking: HR must have a forward-thinking mindset. HR professionals need to demonstrate excellence in sensing what might occur even before it happens. They need to be effective at weaving together patterns from the business, the customer, and the employees in order to understand what is likely to occur and then develop contingencies even before the problems arise.

- O – Outside-in: Two key expectations of *Leadership-Driven HR* is that HR has a clear line of sight to the external customer and that HR needs to take an "outside-in" perspective for their work. HR needs to hear the voice of the external customer and focus on process outcomes that will bring the outside-in approach to life.

- C – Co-create: When HR professionals co-create plans and strategies with business leaders, they need to focus on delivering outcomes that enhance the business's overall performance. When HR professionals have co-creation partner relationships with business leaders, they are functioning at the strategic business partner level.

- U – Up-to-date: HR is professionalizing its field of expertise at the same time that businesses are rapidly changing. HR professionals need to keep up with how the business is evolving and with the emerging issues that are causing these changes. In addition, HR professionals need to invest time into their own development to learn how to expand their repertoire of people capabilities and organizational capabilities to deliver value for the business.

- S—Synergies within HR: HR needs to be a model of organizational excellence in order to have the credibility to co-create and add value to the business. This means that HR professionals must function well internally as a team and work synergistically within HR. They also need to work together in alignment with external customer requirements and with the business strategy direction.

- HR is experiencing an exciting time of dramatic change that will affect public and private sector businesses, customers, citizens, and the HR profession. HR needs to embrace this new reality rather than attempting to hang on to the way it was in the past. The past is gone. HR needs to be looking forward to the new reality and shape its own future so that it can deliver value for the business. *Leadership-Driven HR* is a road map that will help HR to drive value for the business, guide HR to deliver value to leaders, and ensure that HR is driven to lead.

Index

Page numbers in italics indicate figures.